REAL WORDS:
LANGUAGE AND SYSTEM IN HEGEL

JEFFREY REID

Real Words

Language and System in Hegel

UNIVERSITY OF TORONTO PRESS
Toronto Buffalo London

© University of Toronto Press Incorporated 2007
Toronto Buffalo London
Printed in Canada

ISBN 13: 978-0-8020-9172-7
ISBN 10: 0-8020-9172-5

Printed on acid-free paper

Toronto Studies in Philosophy
Editors: Donald Ainslie and Amy Mullin

Library and Archives Canada Cataloguing in Publication

Reid, Jeffrey
Real words : language and system in Hegel / Jeffrey Reid.

(Toronto studies in philosophy)
Includes bibliographical references and index.
ISBN 13: 978-0-8020-9172-7
ISBN 10: 0-8020-9172-5

1. Hegel, Georg Wilhelm Friedrich, 1770–1831.   2. Language and
languages – Philosophy.   I. Title.   II. Series.

B2949.L5R43 2007   121'.68092   C2006-904769-3

This book was published with the support of a University of Ottawa,
Faculty of Arts publications grant.

University of Toronto Press acknowledges the financial assistance to
its publishing program of the Canada Council for the Arts and the
Ontario Arts Council.

University of Toronto Press acknowledges the financial support for
its publishing activities of the Government of Canada through the
Book Publishing Industry Development Program (BPIDP).

041608-p8

To my loved ones

Contents

viii Contents

Acknowledgments

I wish to thank my *maîtres à penser* at the Université de Paris IV–Sorbonne: Jean-François Marquet and the late Henri Birault.

An earlier, somewhat different version of 'The Objective Discourse of Science' appears in *Hegel and Language*, edited by Jere Paul O'Neill Surber, (Albany: SUNY Press, 2006). 'The Ontological Grasp of Judgment' originally appeared in *Dialogue* 45, 1 (2006). 'Why Hegel Didn't Join the 'Kant-Klub': Reason and Speculative Discourse' is a revised and translated version of an article in *Archives de philosophie* 66, 2 (2003). 'The Fiery Crucible, Yorick's Skull and Leprosy in the Sky: The Language of Nature' is a slightly revised and extended version of an article in *Idealistic Studies* 34, 1 (2004). 'The State University: The University of Berlin and Its Founding Contradictions' originally appeared in *Owl of Minerva* 32, 1 (2000). 'Hegel's Critique of Solger: The Problem of Scientific Communication' is a revised and translated version of an article in *Archives de philosophie* 60, 2 (1997). 'On Schleiermacher and Postmodernity' originally appeared in *Clio* 32, 4 (2003).

Introduction

This book comprises a series of essays. I do not use the term 'essay' lightly. It refers to a certain non-fictional literary form, one that should be compact, coherent, self-sufficient, and evocative. The essays here assembled under one cover are meant to have this monadic quality. They are self-contained, free-standing pieces with individual perspectives that open onto something unique: the question of Georg Wilhelm Friedrich Hegel and language. The units of this book are therefore not to be taken as chapters, in the ordinary sense. They are not meant to form the premises of an argument leading to a conclusion. Rather, they are to be seen as 'ideas pointing towards something central,' as Friedrich Schlegel describes the aim of his philosophical fragments.

Consequently, the reader may begin and, of course, stop anywhere; nevertheless, there is an order to the series. The first three essays deal mainly with the theoretical dimensions of systematic (or scientific) language in Hegel; the next three deal with concrete expressions of that language, with some of the actual content of the system; and the last three examine Hegel's thoughts on some linguistic expressions that he views as non- and even anti-systematic. The tripartite nature of this series is, I think, purely accidental.

Given this book's structure, the addition of a summarizing conclusion would be largely cosmetic. Rather, I have closed with another opening, a path for future consideration that these essays, taken together, seem to invite us to take.

The subject of this book is, as noted, Hegel and language. I have been thinking and writing about this for the past ten years because I believe that Hegel has a very particular grasp of the relation between language and objectivity, one that teaches something new about the way we look at the relation between ourselves and the world. Hegel's notion of language, as it obtains within his system of philosophy, rejects the idea of truth as an accurate reflection between words and what they represent. In fact, as I argue in the first essay, Hegel's notion of scientific language (i.e., the language of his system) implies a type of discourse that itself is true objectivity. In other words, Hegel invites us to see scientific *logos* as real, actual, and true, where there is no distance between signifier and signified, where the word is the effective thing, the real embodiment of thought.

This means that the words of Hegel's system are meant to be objective in the sense that they 'take place' in the world, and true in that they are not the arbitrary constructions of the individual philosopher. Such objective truth is possible only if we look beyond the formal point of view and take the content of language into consideration. For the systematic philosopher that Hegel is, the objective truth of the whole must depend on that of its contents. The ultimate discourse of Hegel's system can only be considered to be objectively true if the discourses making up its contents possess their own objectivity and truth. To see this, we have to take the actual contents of Hegel's science into account, as expressed in his completed system: *The Encyclopedia of Philosophical Sciences*. By doing this, it becomes clear that the true and objective content of the system is linguistic in nature; the stuff of the system is language understood as the real embodiment of thought.

Thus, the objective content of Hegel's Philosophy of Objective Spirit (also that of his *Philosophy of Right*) is the real language of the contract, laws, and constitutions. The actual content of the *Encyclopedia*'s Philosophy of Nature is the writings of the natural scientists of his day, which Hegel had read and incorporated. The effective content of Hegel's Philosophy of History is not events observed but the written accounts of historians. Similarly, Hegel's Philosophy of Religion is actually the philosophy of theological writings and doctrines, and the real content of his Philosophy of Art is the 'language' of art and its history. Most importantly, the very real objectivity of the system's contents, the fact these contents actually 'take place,' guarantees the true objectivity of (Hegelian) science as a whole, meaning that it takes place in the world. Of course, the conception of science as real language means it must itself be actual. The effective objectivity of scientific language makes it the existing discourse of the university, and thus scientific language participates in the ethical life of the State.

The first essay of this book, 'The Objective Discourse of Science,' deals specifically with the notion of language that I have just been presenting, how it is implied by the inherent scientific demands of Hegel's system. We discover a type of scientific language that is objectively true not because it *reflects*, however accurately, a disengaged reality, but rather because it *is* the objective middle term between being and thought. In this way, it becomes possible to see how the objects of Hegelian science are meant to be taken as its content, and how, within this context, the syllogism should be understood as the grammatical extension of predication or judgment.

Essay 2, 'The Ontological Grasp of Judgment,' seeks out the source of Hegel's scientific language in Johann Christian Friedrich Hölderlin and Johann Gottlieb Fichte. Within Hegel's system, judgment (*Urteilen*) is thought's original dividing from identity into difference. At the same time, judgment is an act of predication where 'subject' must be understood in both a grammatical and psychical sense. Thus, judgment expresses a language act or proposition (*Satz*) that is a self-positing, out of the concept's initial identity, into the difference of existence. Having looked at the grammatical aspects of this ontological positing, the essay presents an example where the psychical notion of this self-positing obtains: in Hegel's theory of embryonic development and his diagnosis of Novalis's morbid state of sentimentality.

The third essay, 'Why Hegel Didn't Join the 'Kant-Klub,' is a re-evaluation of Hegel's early take on Immanuel Kant. Hegel's non-participation in the Kantian reading group at the Tübingen Seminary, where he studied with his friends Hölderlin and Friedrich Wilhelm Joseph von Schelling, can be explained as the rejection of the critical, unilateral discourse of understanding (*Verstand*), in favour of the dialectical discourse of reason (*Vernunft*), discovered in Kant's first *Critique*. In Hegel's first writings on Kant, we witness an awakening sense that the language of philosophical truth must go beyond the principle of non-contradiction. Philosophical truth can only articulate itself in the speculative language of reason, a language that is capable of expressing both identity and difference, which later develops into the language of philosophical science.

The next three essays deal with some of the actual contents that make up the system, as expressed in the *Encyclopedia of Philosophical Sciences*, showing how these contents should be grasped as objective discourse and how this discourse, as philosophical science, is embodied within the State, through education.

Essay 4, 'The Fiery Crucible, Yorick's Skull, and Leprosy in the Sky,' seeks to show how the chaotic contingency of nature forms a true content of the system, through the discourses of the positive natural sciences. This entails looking at the Philosophy of Nature and discovering to what extent it may claim to incorporate natural Otherness or contingency and how it does so. The problematic relationship between thought and nature is a dynamic one, mediated by the activity of positive scientific knowing, articulated in the writings of natural science, and taken up within the systematic project of knowing all of nature. This openness to positive science for its discursive content allows us to think of Hegel's system as open to the future. A 'Concluding Unscientific Postscriptum' examines the explosive 'letting go' of Nature out of the Idea, in light of Big Bang cosmology.

Whereas the preceding essay asks how the chaotic contingency of nature can become the content of philosophical science, Essay 5, 'Presenting the Past,' poses the same question regarding human history: how does it become objectively true discourse? The essay examines the epistemology of Hegel's historiography and how the writing of history is related to what he means by the famous (and often misunderstood) expression 'Reason in History.' Briefly, if Reason refers to human self-recognition in Otherness, then this process can only happen through our recognition of ourselves in the past, through a process where 'the past' becomes 'our past.' This can only take place through the incorporation of past historical texts into a current philosophical reflection.

The sixth essay examines the objective embodiment of scientific discourse in its systematic totality: the State university. For Hegel, the university remains a corporation where the objective content of philosophical science actually takes place or is taught in the faculties of medicine, law, theology, and philosophy. Hegel's *Encyclopedia* becomes not only the teaching manual for classes in philosophy, but the linguistic embodiment of the State university itself. Furthermore, the central position of this organism within the body of the State ensures the worldly participation of the discursive content of science. The objectivity of scientific discourse itself, in its ultimate form, participates in the life of the State through university teaching.

The final three essays examine cases of unscientific language that, consequently, engender worlds other than the one in which systematic science takes place.

The essay entitled, 'Music and Monosyllables: The Language of Pleasure and Necessity,' presents a language that articulates a very unscientific or subscientific form of consciousness that we find in the *Phenomenology of Spirit*: the erotic pleasure-seeker. Here, we discover how the punctual nature of this way of knowing the world, through the metronomic aspect of individual satisfactions, necessarily iterates itself in monosyllables, in staccato utterances that engender an atomistic reality. The essay examines how the actual musical notes of the stone statue at the end of Mozart's opera *Don Giovanni* may be the best linguistic expression of the erotic pleasure-seeker's destiny.

Essays 8 and 9 look at Hegel's critique of two of his contemporaries at the University of Berlin: K.W.F. Solger and Friedrich Daniel Ernst Schleiermacher. Both critiques can be understood in terms of Hegel's notions of scientific discourse and objectivity. Solger's philosophical failure stems from the fact that the arbitrary forms of expression (e.g., the dialogue, essays) which he applies to speculative or dialectical content actually contradict this content. Solger recognizes an absolute speculative truth that is indistinguishable from Hegel's: the Idea-God negating itself to become its Other. However, Solger fails to see that the only form of expression that is adequate to truth is one that is no more than the systematic presentation of objective content, content that is already there in the substantial linguistic expressions to be found in art, religion, law, natural science, history, etc., and is therefore not arbitrary. As well, the fragmented forms of Solger's discourses actually create a world defined as the public, which is opposed to the world in which (Hegelian) Science takes place.

'On Schleiermacher and Postmodernity' examines how the theologian is symptomatic of a reality that is both inimical and contemporary to Hegel's science. The essay concludes with considerations of how the world engendered by discourses foreign to Hegel's science may actually be the world that we live in, as postmoderns living in a world that neither reflects the values of the Enlightenment nor the aspirations of Romanticism but one that has become a monstrous hybrid of both.

The concluding 'Last Words,' while recapitulating the themes developed throughout this book, invites us to reflect on how the world we live in is formed by the real words we use and how this consideration engages us ethically.

Three of the essays here are slightly revised versions of articles published earlier in academic journals. As well, I have translated and made available to the English reader two essays that previously appeared in French in *Archives de philosophie*. Two other essays have been substantially expanded from their original form to include previously unexplored dimensions, and finally, two are new, and I hope significant, contributions to the question of language and system in Hegel. My goal has been to assemble for the reader, under one cover and in one language, the fruits of my research and reflections on this question.

REAL WORDS

1 The Objective Discourse of Science

The question of language goes right to the core of Hegel's notion of systematic science, of truth that actually takes place in the embrace between thought and being. If a language of science is one meant to convey objective truth, then Hegel's singular take on Science must imply a special grasp of both its language and objectivity. What sort of discourse can claim to express objective truth within an idea of science that sees itself as the systematic articulation of existing knowledge? To answer this question we must guard against importing epistemological and linguistic notions foreign to the Hegelian idea of objective truth, and we must also avoid importing notions of objectivity and discourse that are alien to Hegel's idea of Science.

Failure to comprehensively understand the nature of Hegelian scientific language has allowed to go unchallenged a widespread misunderstanding regarding the nature of Hegelian objectivity. This misunderstanding can be bluntly summarized as follows: the world itself operates dialectically, obeying an inherently dialectical logic. Many who know something of Hegel will probably find nothing objectionable in this statement. In fact, it appears readily verifiable with regard to that part of worldly objectivity that Hegel deals with on the Spirit side of his philosophy, for example, the rise of consciousness and intersubjective relations. Indeed, spirit, as human activity, can easily be said to reflect thought or 'mind,' which, as the *Logics* tell us, is inherently dialectical. And it is this objectivity or 'second nature'[1] that most commentators are interested in. When the natural world itself is brought into consideration, however, there is some embarrassment. It is indeed hard to verify, for example, that cosmological phenomena and chemical reactions operate along strictly dialectical lines. Hegel's Philosophy of Nature, therefore, tends to be taken less seriously, or ignored.[2] However, even when the inherently dialectical nature of Hegelian objectivity is ascribed solely to the Spirit side of his philosophy, crucial (Kierkegaardian, Marxian) questions arise concerning the coherency of the entire philosophical endeavour. If objectivity itself operates dialectically, what is the status of the philosopher subject (i.e., Hegel)? Or, more precisely, what is the status of Hegel's scientific discourse? From whence does this discourse derive its own objectivity and truth? It should be obvious to readers of Hegel that his scientific discourse cannot claim to simply *represent* or *reflect* objectivity, and garner its own truthfulness and objectivity from the exactness of this representation.[3]

Such a view could not help but fall within what Hegel refers to as (Kantian) subjective idealism. That is, the representation, whether faithful or not, would never be more than mere appearance (*Schein*), the reflection of Hegel's own self-certainty; the supposed Truth, stemming from personal observations, would, in fact, reflect nothing other than subjective certitude.[4] In other words, this view contradicts Hegel's explicit rejection of scientific truth that is based purely on confirmed observation (perception) of empirical, experimental data, and we find it reiterated in all his major works and in a good many of his minor ones.[5] This does not mean that Hegel entirely discounts empirical science. For example, as I will show, there is a place, or a level, for the representations of the natural sciences within the body of systematic (philosophical, Hegelian) science. However, as we will see, this level of representation only achieves objective truth through a particular notion of discourse that is essential to this science.

Hegel's repudiation of sense perception as an adequate ground for systematic, objective truth must be understood in linguistic terms; sense certainty goes hand in hand with the notion of referential language, with the idea that language refers to, reflects, or denotes an objectivity that is real but somehow removed from the language itself. According to this view, truth and objectivity are entirely based on the exactness of the reflection, on the faithfulness of how 'sentence-tokens'[6] signify Reality. Although many commentators understand Hegel's critique of sense perception and its corresponding referential language,[7] they seem unable to break away from the idea of Hegel-empiricist, the lucid and profound observer of the world around him. I believe this is because they have been unable to grasp the true nature of Hegel's scientific language as non-referential, where there is no distance between signifier and signified, and where the objectivity of language is not the impoverished objectivity of 'sentence-tokens.'

In dealing with the question of how Hegel sees the truth of his discourse as objective, therefore, I want to show that his claim to scientific truth implies a particular grasp of objectivity that is different from the one summarized above, and a particular notion of language that is not referential and that is constitutive of Hegelian objectivity. More explicitly, I will argue that the Hegelian idea of Science supposes a discourse that is not only objectively true but is also, itself, true objectivity.

The use of the term 'objectivity' in the preceding paragraphs may cause some consternation. This is because we are accustomed to using the term in two distinct acceptations: (1) in the sense of non-subjective, non-arbitrary truth; (2) in the sense of a concrete reality existing outside the subject. By saying that, for Hegel, science is a discourse that is 'not only objectively true but is also, itself, true objectivity,' I am purposely conflating the two acceptations. For Hegel, scientific objectivity is non-subjective, non-arbitrary truth existing as a concrete reality. I am also saying that this reality is discourse, scientific discourse itself.

It is also important to emphasize a point that may, at first, appear redundant but is crucial. Scientific discourse, for Hegel, is exclusively that discourse which deals with the objects of science. This clearly implies that there are objects that are not addressed by science, that is, there is a non-scientific objectivity, and there are also discourses that are non-scientific. However, if we are to take Hegel's scientific claims seriously, as I am doing, then we must respect this often ignored distinction. Not all objectivity is scientific. Not all discourse is scientific. The discourse of science does not deal with all objectivity.

Initially, the issue is how scientific discourse can be objectively true, that is, how it can relate to its objects, for example, to such worldly manifestations as the State, History, Art, Religion, and Nature without merely reflecting them.[8] According to my argument, these manifestations must somehow be embodied in true scientific discourse as its true, objective content.

This idea of *content* that is also the *object* of science is important to grasp. Hegelian science does not study its objects in a detached analytical way, in order to draw conclusions about them and test these conclusions against empirical data. Hegelian science claims to hold within itself, as content, the objects of its discourse. Or, science is no more than the ultimate articulation of its objects/contents. Hegel expresses the richness of this content by using the term *Gehalt*, rather than *Inhalt*. To use a vulgar example, the former term might apply in stating, 'milk is content-rich in vitamins and calcium,' while the latter might describe the contents of a suitcase. As *Gehalt*, content should be seen as essential to what it makes up.

There is no mystery about what the *Gehalt*-objects of science are; they can be found in the table of contents of the *Encyclopedia of Philosophical Sciences*. This content, like scientific truth itself, is *essentially* text, that is, not the inherently meaningless natural occurrences of disengaged objectivity, but meaningful discourse. In other words, I am arguing that scientific discourse derives its truth and objectivity from its contents, which are themselves grasped as true and objective discourse. To understand the objectivity and truth of scientific discourse (and its contents), I am therefore proposing a certain linguistic notion that I believe is found in Hegel: language that does not simply reflect what is otherwise 'real,' language that does not *refer* to its object, but rather language that actually *is* its object (and content) and is, therefore, objective and true. The word is truly the thing, but not in the sense of *das Ding*, a common, indeterminate, natural object in a sea of contingency, but rather in the sense of *die Sache*, a more meaningful, content-rich existence. How is this content-rich language possible?

Whether we question a modern-day theoretical physicist or an eighteenth-century empiricist, his or her definition of objective truth in science will involve the adequation of thought and being, of concepts and experience. For example, a subjective theory (thought) takes on objective truth when it can be adequated to reality (being). The adequation of thought and being also lies at the heart of the Hegelian scientific endeavour.

According to the notion of Hegelian scientific objectivity that I am proposing, the adequation of thought and being is *realized* in language, in a language that can, therefore, be grasped as truth and 'objectivity,' in both senses of the word, namely, language that is not based on subjective representation and language that is itself a real object or thing (*Sache*)[9] that is both thought and being. This language occurs in several different contexts, and each of these expressions forms specific, objective content for Science. The total content of Science, thus, appears as the true and objective discourses of natural science, subjective and objective spirit, art, and religion. This is another way of saying that the Hegelian project, consisting of finding true objectivity in the meeting between (natural) being and the dialectical or negating activity of thought takes place, on the highest scientific or systematic level, in the articulation itself of the *Encyclopedia*. The first part of the work, 'The Science of Logic' (thought) and the second, the 'Philosophy of Nature' (being) find their truth in the third part, the 'Philosophy of Spirit,' whose last word is precisely 'Philosophy,' that is, philosophical discourse itself.

True Content: The 'Name' and the 'Word'

A brief passage from the *Encylopedia*'s 'Philosophy of Spirit' helps us understand more precisely the linguistic notion that we are dealing with, namely, a language that is to be taken as true objectivity, as the realization of thought and being. Here, scientific language is presented as the objective result of a meeting between representing intelligence (thought) and the mere linguistic sign, or 'name,' as Hegel puts it (being):

> The being [*Seiende*], as name [*Name*], needs an other [*eines Anderen*], meaning from the representing [*vorstellenden*] intelligence, in order to be the thing [*Sache*], true objectivity.[10]

This reference describes scientific discourse at its most formal level, in the context of subjective spirit, where content is supplied by representing intelligence, by understanding.[11] The 'name' or sign that is to be inhabited by representational content should be understood as an arbitrary, empty, naturally formed being,[12] open to any 'meaning,' just as a certain given name can apply indiscriminately to any individual person. The name, as a singular, naturally formed thing (*Ding*) must, indeed, be understood as simply found-there by representing intelligence. Here, we are operating at the level of sense-certainty as it is expressed in the *Encyclopedia*, where denomination can never reach beyond the singular appellation of individual objects, where every object has its name and only its name, which, like the object referred to, is simply found there readymade, without having been 'worked up by intelligence.'[13] What Hegel means by 'name' is the senseless externality of the mere meaningless and arbitrary 'sign,'[14] a being simply found-there and as yet divorced from any signification; the term 'word' denotes what Hegel sometimes calls the 'representational name,' that is, the formerly senseless 'sign' that is now filled, by intelligence, with the content of representation. In other words, a 'name' is not yet a 'word.'

This distinction between 'name' and 'word' can be borne out to some degree by Hegel's statement, in *Encyclopedia* §463, that 'names as such' are 'senseless words.' This, indeed, seems to imply that (significant) words are something other than empty, contingent, naturally formed names.[15] Words, or 'representational names' are richer in content (*Gehalt*) than are the empty 'names as such' with which we began. Intelligence has supplied the latter with representational content, and the result is in the order of 'true objectivity,' what Hegel is calling *die Sache*, as opposed to *das Ding*.

The point I am making is that 'the thing (*Sache*), true objectivity' is still language. It is simply a language that has greater truth and objectivity than the mere empty signs with which we began, because now the form of language has taken on content.

It is also crucial to understand that in the passage from 'name' to 'word,' we move through two orders of objectivity, from nature to 'second nature,' from natural, contingent, impoverished objectivity to the 'true objectivity' of the scientific word. Although this level of objectivity and truth is still relative, in that its content is still representational and, therefore, still somewhat subjective, it is nonetheless higher than the arbitrary objectivity of the natural world, which can itself be seen as nothing more than an infinite number of meaningless 'signs' that are only *potentially* significant. Far from being truly objective, this world of immediate sense-certainty reflects, in fact, the most radical form of subjectivity. Sense-certainty is a form of *self*-certainty.[16]

Even at the level of discourse that we are currently dealing with in the paragraphs of the *Encyclopedia* under discussion, namely, representational discourse *within* the scientific system, representing intelligence fills the mere 'name' to form a significant *word* that should be taken as itself incarnating a certain degree of both objectivity and truth. This scientifically meaningful word is what Hegel is calling 'the thing (*die Sache*), true objectivity.'[17] Within the *Encyclopedia* system, the representations expressed in the words of science should, then, be taken as more than purely natural or purely subjective and arbitrary; they are determined scientific representations that arise, for example, within the natural sciences, and which must be subsequently incorporated into the overall system of science. In other words, the representations expressed in the words of science must themselves become part of the total content of philosophical science. In the 'Philosophy of Nature' this language obtains in the numerous examples that Hegel cites from the natural sciences of his day, for example, in his lengthy exegeses of Franz Anton Mesmer's findings, or his espousal of Goethe's colour theory. For the natural, empirical sciences to become part of the system, their own discourse must be seen as already content-ful and objectively true, although still representational.[18] The above-defined 'word' enables us to understand how this is possible. Representing intelligence penetrates nature, as it invests itself in the completely natural names (empty signs) found already there, to produce meaningful words. In fact, that is all representing intelligence can appropriately carry out. Now, however, within Hegelian science, the subsequent pronouncements of representing intelligence can be taken as objectively true, where objectivity and truth are no longer based on the reflection between (natural) 'objectivity,' on one hand, and language, on the other.[19]

Although in the context of theoretical intelligence, where the discussion on the 'name' arises, we are not yet dealing with systematic philosophical discourse as such, Hegel is telling us that representational discourse, as it arises *within the system*, already possesses a certain degree of true objectivity and objective truth. As the realized result of thought (representing intelligence) and being (the 'name'), it is truer and more objective than either, or rather, it combines the hard, natural reality of the name with the abstract essentiality of thought to form something that is truly objective and essential.

Thus, the scientifically significant word appears as the 'middle term'[20] between thought and being. It is a particular being that is at the same time thought, or vice versa.

Scientific Grammar: From Predication to Syllogism

The expression 'middle term' introduces my contention that an analysis of the act of predication or judgment alone is not sufficient to grasp Hegel's concept of scientifically objective discourse; to do so, one must look beyond the proposition, to the syllogism, and consider it as a grammatical extension of the act of predication. Failure to do so leads one to concentrate on the relationship between language and thought rather than on the more fundamental relation between being and thought. Failing to grasp language as the objective middle term embodying the two extremes, leaves language external to both thought and being. As such, language can do no more than reflect either thought or being, but never actually *be* them. It is only by actually *being* thought and being that language can be considered to be scientifically objective.

In the Preface to the *Phenomenology*, Hegel deals with the question of how the subject-predicate form can be grasped as dialectical, in terms of what he refers to as the 'speculative sentence.'[21] In this context, the grammatical subject is to be understood as consciousness losing itself in its predicate that, in turn, 'recoils' back onto the subject in search of a ground. The grammatical subject can, thus, be seen as an empty name that is receiving content from its predicate, or as conscious thought determining itself through predication. In both cases, the issue is 'the dialectical structure of the proposition' and how the speculative sentence 'reflects the fact that, for Hegel, consciousness itself is essentially a dialectical activity.'[22] This seems to show that considering the act of predication in terms of its 'dialectical activity' can do no more than provide us with a reflection, where language can provide only an (arbitrary) analogy of thought.

Furthermore, if we consider philosophical language to be no more than an accurate reflection of thought, truth comes to depend entirely on the external, and arbitrary judgments of a judicious Hegelian philosopher or an equally subjective 'we'. This can sometimes lead to readings where truth in Hegel is viewed as the result of public judgment or a linguistic community of shared reference, à la Wittgenstein.[23] According to my argument, the objective truth of scientific discourse in Hegel depends on neither the insightfulness of individual readers/listeners nor on general public consensus.[24] Scientific discourse does, indeed, become actual (or *wirklich*). However, it is important to understand that the worldly actuality of scientific discourse is the result of its objectivity, and not the opposite.

Objective truth remains extremely problematical when a reflective distance is maintained between the language of science and thought, when the relation between the two is merely analogous. In Hegel, this problem arises when scientific discourse is examined *only* in terms of the predicative sentence, even when this is understood speculatively or dialectically.

Commentators concentrating on the *Phenomenology of Spirit* as the main area of research in their investigations into Hegel's philosophy of language are necessarily confined to examining the dialectical workings of the predicative statement. Scientific truth, thus, is construed as the accurate reflection or adequation between this language (dialectical) and thought (dialectical). This reinforces the misunderstanding I invoked earlier: for commentators to discover truth in the relationship between language and the *world*, the latter must also be seen as *inherently* dialectical.

In fact, the scientific inadequacies of the propositional act of predication are revealed through Hegel's later writings on judgment, particularly as they appear in the *Greater Logic*.[25] More specifically, if scientific discourse does, indeed, imply a notion of objective truth dependent on meaningful content (*Gehalt*), then the predicative (judgment) form seems inadequate precisely in terms of its inability to hold any content beyond that which is subjectively representational. It seems an argument might be made that Hegel's evaluation of the predicative form, or the form of judgment, undergoes a depreciation over time. From his dialectical or speculative investigations into the copula,[26] which led to his analysis of the speculative sentence in the Preface of the *Phenomenology*, Hegel comes to see the syllogism as a more appropriate grammatical form in which to grasp scientific expression.[27]

This is borne out by the fact that much of the *Phenomenology*'s 'speculative sentence' analysis is taken up again in the *Greater Logic*, although in a context where judgment (predication) appears as the transitional moment between the concept, as an original, immediate, that is, still unmediated whole, and the fully developed syllogism that articulates moments of the universal, the particular, and the singular. In fact, Hegel understands judgment 'etymologically' as *Ur-teilen*, the original dividing necessary for the concept to be able to re-unite itself, but now syllogistically mediated. Thus, 'judgment is the dividing of the concept by itself.'[28]

Defining predication in terms of division leaves little room for content, and in the *Greater Logic* Hegel deals specifically with this problem. Real content can neither be held in the subject nor the predicate, which are related in a purely arbitrary, and, in fact, subjective fashion.[29] 'The subject can find itself taken, with regard to the predicate, as the singular with regard to the universal, or again as the particular with regard to the universal, or as the singular with regard to the particular.'[30] Consequently, subject and predicate are once again taken as no more than 'names,' empty markers or, continues Hegel in the same passage, 'something undetermined that must still obtain its determination.' Hegel's speculative solution in the *Greater Logic* is to maintain that this determination takes place in neither the subject nor the predicate but in the copula, which must become the 'filled and determined unity of the subject and the predicate, as their concept.'[31] When the copula is understood in this way, as an existing unity underlying both subject and predicate, the judgment 'passes into'[32] the syllogism.

I am insisting on this passage between judgment (predication) and syllogism in order to reinforce my argument about the nature of scientific discourse in Hegel, as language that must be grasped as objective, true, and content-ful (i.e., 'filled and determined'), as discourse that must be understood as the existing 'middle term' between thought and being, or between subject and predicate. It is this same 'middle term' that I invoked above as the significant word in scientific discourse, which Hegel refers to as 'the thing [*die Sache*]' or 'true objectivity.'[33] Hegel's analysis of the syllogism should be understood as the 'elenchus' of his grammatical analysis of the predicative form. The syllogism expresses the true destiny of the copula, as a mediating, content-ful middle term that determines the two extremes (subject and predicate) in such a way that the whole proposition becomes an objective concept. This is what Hegel means when, referring to the syllogism of necessity, he writes, 'In that this syllogism determines the extremes of the concept precisely as totalities, the syllogism has attained ... its truth, and has thus passed from subjectivity into objectivity.'[34]

Considering the syllogism as the conceptual development of predication allows us to grasp the systematic (scientific) implications of Hegelian language, as presented in that system called the *Encyclopedia*, and to see how Hegel's notion of objectively true discourse implies a language capable of embodying meaningful content (*Gehalt*). A discussion of Hegel's notion of scientific language, therefore, requires an analysis that goes beyond the formal linguistic dimension. This emphasis on content rather than form runs generally counter to how linguistic analysis is understood today. I want to look at a specific instance of how Hegelian scientific discourse can be said to hold objective content.

The Real Words of Objective Spirit

The specific content of Hegelian science that I want to look at is private property, that is, the first element of what appears as Objective Spirit or the State in the *Encyclopedia*. In dealing with this issue (*Sache*), I am obviously not attempting to exhaust it as a question but merely trying to show how it can be seen to form the objective content of scientific language, content that renders scientific language itself objective, without this objectivity depending on truth defined as the external adequation between signified and signifier. Property, like any other content of science, must then be conceived as a language that is the objective mid-

dle term between being and thought. 'Property' is particularly reveal-
ing in this light because its objectivity, whether we refer to a house, a
field, or a horse, strikes us as completely natural and 'objective'. In fact,
it is precisely because of this natural, immediate aspect that the thing
(*Ding*) of property cannot as such become part of scientific discourse.
The natural thing has not been mediated (or negated) by thought. We
have to see how the discourse of property is more objective than property itself, understood as a simple, natural thing (*Ding*).

Concerning property, Hegel's insight is that it is not truly objective
until it passes from one individual will to another. The meaning of this
'passing' is neither in the subjective affirmation of possession, in
declaring in a purely predicative way that 'this is mine,' nor in the simple 'names' or linguistic signs that immediately represent or reflect this
bit of earth, the house, and so on. These signs are as natural and
impoverished as the things (*Dinge*) they reflect. The scientific meaning
of property, its true objectivity, the fact that it can become a thing in the
sense of *Sache*, is only manifest when it is transferred (sold and bought)
from one will to another. This meaning manifests itself[35] in the language of the contract. Hegel writes: 'The interiority of the will that sur-
renders the property and of the will that receives it is in the realm of
representation, and the word is, in this realm, act and thing [*Sache*].'[36]
The contract must be grasped as a language having an objective existence, both 'substantial'[37] and true. This truth is the following: the
essence of property is to pass from one will to another; this essence is
manifested in the real words of the contract. Thus, we grasp concretely
the meaning of the Hegelian idea that essence (*das Wesen*) can be
thought of as being that has been (*gewesen*).[38] Only insofar as the
purely natural being disappears (is negated or mediated) in the passage from one will to another can essence emerge. However, rather
than dissipating in a 'formless tumult of church bells or the warm ris-
ing of vapors,'[39] the essence of property is objectified in contractual
language, understood as the middle term of a syllogism whose two
extremes are natural being and thought (here, in the form of will).

We can understand how the written, consensual contract is a more
truly objective representation of property and possession than my simple predication of something as 'mine.'[40] When property changes
hands, it does so on paper and in writing. Its possession only thereby
becomes something objective, 'substantial,' and of 'value.'[41] It is this
objectivity that enables property to be recognized by the persons
involved as well as by others, and thereby to effectively participate in

the social space of *Sittlichkeit*.[42] I believe the same point of view can be said to apply to other fundamentally linguistic expressions of content within objective spirit: laws, constitutions,[43] and even world history.[44]

It is important to understand what I am arguing here. I am not saying that objective spirit is nothing but text. I am saying that objective spirit must already be objectively true language for it to be part of scientific discourse. Or, from another point of view, for scientific discourse to be objectively true and truly objective, its content must also be objectively true and truly objective. The content of science (which is itself discourse) is language understood as itself content-ful, that is, as the existing middle term between being and thought. So, if Hegel's science is to incorporate such objective expressions as private property, justice, the State, and world history, these expressions must be grasped as text that is, at least to a certain degree, objectively true / truly objective; philosophical science does not observe natural events, it reads texts.[45] These are considered truer and more objective than what we might be tempted to call the immediate 'real' world, which for Hegel is merely natural and undetermined and, therefore, less real than the world as penetrated (determined) by thought and manifest in meaningful language.

Objective spirit forms one of the main contents of science. I believe the other objects and/or contents of the *Encyclopedia* should also be seen as objective discourse: the Philosophy of Nature,[46] the contents of Subjective Spirit, Art,[47] Religion,[48] and of course, Science itself. In fact, Science is nothing more than the systematic, speculative articulation of its contents, of its objects, namely, the discourses I have mentioned. Science *thinks* the objective truth (or the true objectivity) of its own contents and knows itself to be true and objective. This knowledge is the existing discourse of science, that is, *logos*.

The Actuality of Science

The idea of true objectivity as essentially linguistic may seem rather bloodless and two-dimensional in that it appears to reduce worldly richness to the words on a page. However, such an objection is based on a notion of language other than the one I have been presenting as Hegel's.

Hegel never denies the world's richness, and we know he enjoyed an enviable social life beyond the sphere of academe. But we must distinguish between scientific objectivity and the world in general.

Science deals solely with scientific objects. We are not talking about Krug's pen[49] or any other arbitrary, singular, natural object. Scientific objects are the contents of science. Their names can be found in the *Encyclopedia*'s table of contents. They are true and objective discourse.

As objective, they also exist in the world. The objectivity of the contract means that it can be read and recognized by individual wills within the State as *Sittlichkeit*. Similarly, the laws of the City and the constitution itself are *lived* by the citizens, whether litigiously or not. On another level, 'international public law'[50] determines, to some extent, the reciprocal activity of States between themselves (i.e., the constitutions, laws, institutions, etc.), and world history is read as the discourse of the discourses of history. In the same way, the linguistic expressions of art and religion *participate* in the life of the City. Once more, however, it is important to recall that it is not because these discourses participate in the world that they are objective, but rather the contrary: it is because these discourses are objective and true that they must manifest themselves as actual (*wirklich*).

What about the actuality of philosophical discourse as such, that is, of the *Encyclopedia* and the other Hegelian writings? Beyond any worldly participation of its contents, what actuality might scientific *logos* itself have within the City? A plausible response may be found by simply recalling that Hegel spent almost his entire adult life teaching and that almost all of his texts were conceived as teaching manuals used within the State's education system. So, perhaps, we can say that the actuality of scientific discourse itself, as objectively true *logos*, can be found in its pedagogical application.

Ironic Discourse and the Vereitelung of True Objectivity

At the beginning of this essay, I argued against a particular conception of Hegelian objectivity, that of the 'world' progressing through its history, determined by dialectical laws or logic, to an apotheosis of absolute truth. This is a misconception, first, because Hegelian philosophy is not concerned with all objectivity, with 'all things' as Protagoras may have meant the expression, but with *scientific* objectivity, that is, with objectivity worthy of being the object (content) of scientific discourse and, therefore, capable of sustaining meaningful truth. We are not talking about any indiscriminate objectivity of contingent things.

Scientific objectivity is, for Hegel, necessarily linked to a particular idea of scientific discourse, to content-ful language, understood syllogistically as the middle term between being and thought. Non-scientific objectivity has its own language or, rather, *is* its own language. As I wrote above, Hegel's personal involvement in Berlin's teeming world of letters, popular theatre, and journalism shows how far he was from refusing or denigrating such worldly things. However, one must be careful to distinguish this realm from that of science and to 'direct one's activity and work solely on that area which is worthy of them.'[51] Above all, when the language of non-scientific objectivity is directed *against* science, against the organic, content-rich discourse of speculative philosophy, its opposition constitutes a threat with necessarily objective repercussions.

This is what Hegel means by irony: 'the self-conscious evacuation [*Vereitelung*] of what is objective.'[52] The 'evacuation,' depreciation, or 'rendering vain' (all of which translate the German word *Vereitelung*) of objectivity has to be understood linguistically, a fact made clear by the rest of the cited passage, taken from Hegel's *Review of Solger's Posthumous Writings and Correspondence*, where Hegel deals with Friedrich Schlegel. Here, irony is first defined grammatically, in terms of what Hegel refers to as the language of judging. This type of critical language is defined elsewhere as an act of predication that 'tears apart [*auseinanderreisst*] the different abstract determinations immediately united in the concrete singularity of the object, and separates them from the object.'[53]

The evacuation that ironic discourse operates on the discourse of true objectivity, on language as the objective middle term between thought and being, sunders the holistic reality of the scientific word. The language of ironic judging is prejudicial to Science because it separates significant content from the words themselves. These become arbitrary reflections, subjective representations or signifiers with no objective significance. The grammatical subject is once again reduced to the status of an empty sign, a sort of name that can predicate anything.

Referring again to the passage from the *Review* of Solger's work, we can see why Hegel writes, 'judging is a decidedly negative tendency against objectivity' and why 'such judgments do not take contents into account, but rather vacuous representations that reject the thing [*Sache*] of religions and philosophies.'[54] The 'thing of religions and philosophies' is precisely what constitutes the true content of Science, the doctrines that form the existing middle terms of Science in its syllogistic deployment. In ripping apart these expressions and reducing them to signs, on the one hand, and pure essence, on the other, ironical discourse injures Science and the objectivity it implies, or *is*, as objectively true discourse.

Within the conceptual movement that animates Hegel's system, the divisive force of judgment is the necessary first moment of division (*Ur-teilen* = original-dividing), without which there can be no mediation and reconciliation. However, fixed at the level of ironical discourse, judgment constitutes a divisive force that works as a fixation or a blockage within the organic whole, fragmenting true objectivity into an infinite number of individual things (*Dinge*), simple signs presenting themselves for subjective determination. The language of irony engenders a world radically opposed to the one embodied by the real words of Hegelian Science.

2 The Ontological Grasp of Judgment

All good Hegelians know that the true relation the philosopher discovers between identity and difference must not be expressed as a disjunctive statement, forcing a Kierkegaardian decision between the two terms. Neither is their relation a static one. Although what Hegel calls speculative thought can be represented and understood through such handy mantras as 'the identity of identity and difference,' the real relationship between identity and difference is one of movement, specifically, the epic movement of the concept. Indeed, the Hegelian concept recounts the journey from an initial position of immediate, inchoate identity, through the unsettling, conflicted experience of difference, then back home, where the trials are remembered and celebrated as formative of an enriched, mediated identity. This essay deals with the first crucial move in this process, the moment of 'setting out' Hegel refers to as judgment, or *Urteil*. As if by happy coincidence, the German word itself expresses this 'original dividing' (*Ur-teilen*) of the concept,[1] that allows it to move from its initial, nuclear identity to its moment of self-differentiation. Without the first step of judgment's original dividing, the movement of the concept cannot take place and the speculative or systematic articulation of identity and difference that characterizes Hegel's notion of science, is impossible.

The question of judgment in the Hegelian articulation of identity and difference gains even deeper resonance when we reflect that 'Urteil' also refers to the fundamental linguistic act of predication, according to a tradition in grammar and logic that is easily identified in Aristotle and Kant before reappearing in Hegel. This means that for our speculative philosopher, the original dividing that engenders conceptual movement and makes truth, or the identity of identity and difference, possible is also a linguistic form, the form of the predicative proposition.[2] So the question of identity and difference, through judgment, is inescapably related to language.

This might lead us to conclude that, for Hegel, the first movement of speculative thought is *reflected* in language or that there is some degree of correspondence between forms of thought and forms of language, leading us to observe that certain forms of thought can be adequately expressed or reflected in language. However, it seems to me Hegel goes much further. He also asks us to accept that the movement of the concept is not purely formal or 'logical,' as the term is generally understood, but rather *onto*-logical, in that it involves existence or being. In other words, according to Hegel's logic, the original division or the first move from identity to difference, articulated as an act of predication, must also be taken as a move to determinate being, a move to existence, as expressed, *at first* only abstractly, in the copula 'is.'[3] If this is the case, if judgment's act of predication is a logical move into being, then the truth of this movement is not merely its correspondence to the formal articulations of thought. Judgment must be more than a linguistic *representation* of the logical; it must be ontological.

To recapitulate, in Hegel's notion of judgment, we have thought's original dividing from identity into difference, which also must be a move into existence, articulated in the linguistic form of predication in the proposition. I want to look at how this is possible, and I want to do so by retracing the path of my own investigation into the origins of Hegel's ontological idea of judgment.

Jere Paul Surber, in his article 'Hegel's Speculative Sentence,' put into words something that I had come to believe implicitly or accept without looking into further. Surber points out that Hegel, when referring to the logical form of *judgment*, that is, predicative propositions within a scientific context, asks us to accept the term 'subject' in both a grammatical sense, and as an expression of consciousness, of the self.[4]

Hegel's strange claim, as articulated by Surber, struck a chord of recognition because I had recently been confronted with the notion in two separate areas of inquiry. One area is directly related to why I had been reading Surber's insightful article in the first place: the question of scientific discourse in Hegel. I want to briefly summarize this first inquiry and then do the same with the second, where the question of 'judgment' appears in a completely different context: how Hegel explains the early development of the individual mind. I hope that revisiting my own encounters with the Hegelian idea of judgment will illustrate why Surber's assertion resonated in me and how I have come to understand the apparently audacious Hegelian claim that the subject of a scientific proposition must also be grasped as a self. This understanding should then shed light on the ontological nature of Hegel's notion of judgment and its crucial role in identity and difference.

When I first read Surber's article, I had been working on a piece about Hegel's idea of objective truth and how this could be captured in scientific language. The problem, as I saw it, was how Hegel's notion of systematic science could claim objective truth when the discourse making up that system does not rely on a type of truth that depends on the adequate correspondence or reflection between language and empirically observed 'reality.' In other words, for the discourse of Hegelian science to be objectively true, it must itself claim to be true objectivity and not simply the accurate reflection of detached reality.[5]

To summarize this intuition in still another way, scientific language in Hegel must somehow be the existing middle term of being and thought, and not simply the representation of one or the other. This sort of representation, for Hegel, is always tainted with the hues of subjective idealism. Objective scientific language must somehow do more than represent truth, it must *be* truth as objectively there. It must be the *actual* mediation of being and thought, and not just the formal adequation between the two. This implies a type of discourse in which the sign is not separate from the signified, in which the word is the thing, a being that is also a thought.[6]

Such a discourse is therefore necessarily ontological. It is thought that is really objective or existing and true. To put flesh on these theoretical bones, we can find examples of this type of discourse in the contents of the system itself. This is because the various contents of the *Encyclopedia of Philosophical Sciences* should be grasped as objectively true discourse, in the sense I have just been presenting. Religion is a content of Science in that religious doctrine is language that is the true, existing middle term between thought and being. Art is a content of Science insofar as it is considered existing, objective, true discourse. The same applies to the State, in that laws and constitutions are the objectively true content of science, and history, as the object or content of science, is essentially historiography.

In this way, the discourse of science itself, that is, the *Encyclopedia*, can be seen as the discourse whose actual content is true, objective, existing discourse. Science is true and objective because its content is so.

Within such a system of science, language is necessarily ontological. It is *logos*, understood as the existing middle term between being and thought.[7] This emphasis on the 'middle term' also reveals the inadequacy of the form of judgment, of simple predication, when it comes to embracing real content, and it explains why Hegel's logic comes to put forward the syllogism as the most appropriate form of scientific discourse.[8] Whereas the bilateral form of judgment (A is B) seems to leave little room for intermediary content, the syllogism holds a middle term, the space of the particular, even essential content of science, as we can already find in Aristotelian logic.[9]

Regardless of the syllogistic form science, as a system, takes on (Universal, Particular, Singular), we still must, even as Hegelian philosophers, express the speculative truth that forms the system in the common language of predication, in judgments or propositions. The question is how to grasp this grammatical form, within the context of science, in an ontological way, as discourse that is both thought and being. This leads us back to the original remark of Surber's, which refers to the passage on philosophical language in the Preface to the *Phenomenology*. Hegel asks us to accept 'subject' simultaneously in both a grammatical and psychical sense. The grammatical subject of the proposition is also the 'self' of the proposition. How is this possible? Does Hegel rely on the convenient homonym *Subjekt* as sophistic equivocation, in order to advance what appears to be a highly tendentious notion of language?

I now want to briefly look at the second area of investigation where I was confronted with Hegel's ontological notion of judgment.

Whereas the first encounter with the homonymous nature of 'subject,' in the context of judgment, arose from an enquiry into the logic of the predicative proposition and led to the area of subjective consciousness, the second encounter ran in the opposite direction. It began with the question of subjective consciousness, and more specifically with its actual development within the human individual. I had been working on Hegel's theory of mental illness, as it is related to his diagnosis of the early Romantic poet Novalis, who had suffered and eventually died of a condition Hegel qualifies as *Gemüt*.[10] The word is generally translated as 'soul' or 'heart' and as such can be taken as simply describing the overly sentimental bent of the romantic mind. I wanted to show, however, that Hegel uses the word as a technical term describing a very specific mental illness, within the framework of a sophisticated theory of psychopathology.

Hegel's theory of *Gemüt* is found in the Philosophy of Spirit section of the *Encyclopedia*,[11] where the philosopher explains the genesis of the individual conscious mind (Subjective Spirit), from the first articulations of the natural soul (*Seele*), in the section entitled 'Anthropology,' through the elaboration of the conscious individual, in 'Psychology.' In parentheses, it is remarkable that Hegel uncovers what he considers to be the normal psychic structure of the individual mind through the analysis of a psychopathological condition, in the same way modern, Freudian psychoanalysis arrives at a description of normal mental structures through the study of mental illness. Of course, in both cases, the relation between pathological states and normal psychological structures is reciprocal. The illness helps us understand what is normal and what is normal helps us understand the nature of illness.

This is the context in which Hegel presents the normal development of the individual psyche. It is the possibility of pathological regression[12] that allows us to grasp what constitutes a healthy development. In order to show this, he goes back to the very beginnings of the individual, as the fetus within the womb.

Initially, the fetus exists within the mother as an undetermined entity, a pure potentiality. Here, the mother acts as the soul of the fetus, its entelechy or realization, to use an Aristotelian analogy. Actually, Hegel uses the term 'genius'[13] to describe the mother's initial relation to the fetus within. That the mother is the genius of the fetus means that the mother determines its destiny.[14] This determination is brought about by what Hegel calls *judgment*, a relationship that is not 'real' but 'magical'[15] and where the mother's nature must be understood in terms of a grammatical subject determining its predicate. The mother's natural soul is 'in this judgment, subject in general, her object is her substance, which is at the same time her predicate.'[16] In other words, the mother is 'subject' in both the grammatical and psychical acceptations of the term. In the normal relation between the mother and the fetus, we witness 'the psychical judgment of the substance, in which the feminine nature can, in itself, break itself in two ...'[17]

Through this act of judgment, this original dividing, the mother passes on to the fetus the natural qualities of the individual, or its soul, that is, the talents, predispositions, and natural determinations that will later be developed, or not, through education and the rise to individual consciousness and understanding. According to Hegel's 'genetics' the mother passes on to the baby all that is natural. The child's development will be a progressive freeing from the determination of the maternal-natural, at first through habituation, where the child begins to determine and appropriate 'his' nature through the self-mastery of his body, in order to fashion a second nature in the form of learned habits.[18] The father's role in the child's formation seems confined to making possible the child's schooling and entry into civil society and the rational world of the State.[19]

It is important to understand the dialectical nature of judgment, in the anthropological context. As the child becomes conscious and rational, it is precisely its conscious understanding that now takes on the role of the determining 'genius,' the role that was originally that of the mother/subject determining her fetus.[20] In other words, it is now conscious understanding that determines the inner soul (passed on from the mother) through judgment. Now, conscious understanding is the subject that determines, as its predicate, the natural soul of the individual, its talents and predispositions but also the bottomless well of memories and representations that make up its 'subconscious' mind.[21]

This is where the possibility of mental illness arises. A regression may occur where the determining genius, the subject of judgment, slips from conscious understanding and reverts to the unconscious soul of the individual. Indeed, Hegel's theory of mental illness displays a pattern similar to that of Freud's oedipal complex, in that the determining genius rejects the father and falls once again into the hands of what was originally the mother, the unconscious, natural soul.

The concept of judgment as ontological is clearly central to this theory of the psyche and its attendant pathology, and I also hope to have given some indication of how *Urteilen* is fundamental to the ontological nature of objective discourse, as the existing copula between being and thought. Immersed as I was in these two areas of inquiry, it is easy to see why Surber's statement about the homonymous nature of 'subject' in the Hegelian idea of judgment struck a chord of recognition within me that awoke me, one might say, from my dogmatic slumber. I began wondering how Hegel came up with the idea, where it came from, and what might justify it.

As often occurs in such circumstances, whether through some unconscious memory or pure serendipity, I just 'happened' to be leafing through a book I hadn't looked at in a long time, when I came across the answer to at least part of my questioning. I had been rereading Jacques Rivelaygue's brilliant *Leçons de métaphysique allemande*[22] and quite fortuitously came across his commentary on a short text by

Hölderlin entitled 'Judgment and Being' (*Urteil und Sein*), within a chapter on Hegel's early development. In Rivelaygue, I found the following sentence: 'The move from a subject-predicate relation (of judgment) to a subject-object relation happens because Hölderlin is thinking within a Fichtean framework, where the two relations are identical; in the first principle (I = I, I am I) the subject and the predicate correspond to the I-subject and the I-object.'[23] In other words, in Fichte's foundational principle, *Ich bin Ich*, we have an act of predication that is identical to the relation between the self-positing subject and itself as posited object.

Perhaps we can say that Hegel, through Hölderlin, was inspired by Fichte's principle in coming to his own understanding about judgment as ontological. According to the Fichtean paradigm, the proposition 'I am I' is immediately ontological, in that the proposition (*Satz*) is understood as a self-positing (*sich setzen*) into existence. Indeed this is the point of Hölderlin's short text,[24] to show that, as we find stated in its first paragraph, 'being is judgment,' and as such cannot be expressed as a statement of identity. Being involves difference or rather, self-differentiation.

In the Hölderlin text, we can therefore see that the judgment form, exemplified by 'Ich bin Ich,' expresses the self-positing of the subject, through the copula 'am,' into objective existence, into being. This self-positing must also be understood as a self-differentiating, grasped as the original dividing or separating of the identical self into otherness. Indeed, it is Hölderlin who first uses the etymological device of writing 'Ur-theilung' to express judgment as this original division, a device that clearly impressed Hegel. It is only through this original dividing that identity can differentiate itself and recognize itself in its otherness, or, as Hölderlin writes, where 'I recognize myself as myself in the opposite.'[25] Further, Hölderlin sees that it is only through this self-othering that the 'I' can be what it is, a subject.

To put this another way, Hölderlin sees that Fichte's foundational principle, I = I, cannot express an identity without contradicting itself. This is because, for the 'I' to be an 'I' it must be a self-conscious subject, and for it to be self-conscious it must be able to take itself as the *object* of its reflection. If we say the formula expresses a pure identity, then we negate the meaning of the term 'I' because we negate any possibility of making oneself the object of one's reflection, which is a necessary condition for consciousness and selfhood. So, although Fichte does not himself recognize it, I = I *actually* expresses the *difference* in identity through a proposition that is an original dividing (judgment), and it does so because the subject of the proposition is a self-positing self that posits itself as an object.[26]

Jacques Rivelaygue betrays his Heideggerian inspiration when he interprets judgment's interplay between identity and difference as a 'tension,' rather than as a self-differentiation. This enables him to attribute to Hölderlin a Heideggerian notion of 'being' involving the unreconciled contradiction or Heraclitean tension between the opposites of identity and difference, which might also be expressed as the tension in being's veiling-unveiling. However, it seems to me that the 'being' Hölderlin is referring to has more in common with what we later find in Hegel, where being only differentiates itself from nothing through determinative propositions, that is, through judgments that predicate a subject through the copula. This is why the *Science of Logic* introduces *pure* being, in itself,[27] in a written phrase that is *not* a judgment nor a proposition, where the subject (being) does not posit itself, and where there is no copula: 'Being, pure being, without any further determination.' Such unpredicated being can be 'nothing more nor less than nothingness.'[28] In fact, it is *identical* to nothingness. For being to *be*, it must differentiate itself from this identity, because, as Hölderlin puts it, contradicting the absolute pretensions of Fichte's foundational principle, 'identity is not absolute being.'[29] Being involves difference.

For being to really be, for existence to come into being, the concept 'in itself' must come out of its identity into difference, through an original division that is judgment. This notion of judgment is ontological: 'being is judgment' and is nothing without it. Or, to say it another way, without judgment there can be no subject-object difference and therefore, no predicated determination and no actual being.

If Hegel's inspiration for his ontological grasp of judgment was indeed Hölderlin's text and its Fichtean framework, then perhaps, I reasoned, there might be some direct reference to it or trace of it in Hegel's writings or letters, particularly since the text was apparently penned in 1795,[30] a period when both philosophers were very much in contact, although Hegel was still in Berne and Hölderlin had not yet left Jena for Frankfurt, where the two would be together in 1797. I believe such a trace can be found in a letter to Hegel from 26 January 1795, where Hölderlin shares his preoccupation with Fichte's *Wissenschaftslehre*, and particularly with the problem of identity and difference, implicit in any notion of an Absolute I, which Hölderlin identifies with Spinoza's substance.[31] In fact, Hölderlin's letter summarizes the same points he makes in his text 'Judgment and Being,' stating explicitly that identity without difference cannot include being because it is, in fact, nothing.

> [Fichte's] absolute I (= Spinoza's substance) contains all reality; it is everything and outside it there is nothing. For this absolute I there is therefore no object, for otherwise all reality would not be in it; but a consciousness without object is inconceivable, and if I am myself that object, I am as such limited ... and am not absolute. Therefore, in this absolute I, no consciousness is conceivable; as absolute I, I have no consciousness and to the extent that I have no consciousness, I am (for myself) nothing; therefore the absolute I is (for me) equivalent to Nothingness.

As an indication of the influence of these ideas on Hegel's contemporary thought, we might refer to his manuscript fragment that begins with the words, '*Glauben ist die Art* ...' (Faith is the way ...) dated in early 1798. This text is barely understandable without reference to Hölderlin's text, 'Judgment and Being.'[32]

So it seems fair to accept that Hegel derived his notion of judgment as ontological from Hölderlin. Besides the dialectical heartbeat, already apparent in the self-differentiation Hölderlin ascribes to being, and which Hegel will later transplant into his idea of the concept, it is the Fichtean tone of the whole inquiry that is at the core of the matter, in spite of the fact that, for the former Tübingen schoolmates, Fichte does not recognize the difference at the heart of his own principle of identity. Nonetheless, both Hölderlin and Hegel are inspired by the statement of Fichte's first principle in their grasp of judgment as an act of predication where the subject of the sentence is a self-positing self, where *der Satz* (proposition) is a *Setzen* (positing). What else do these origins tell us about Hegel's ontological grasp of judgment?

To answer this, I believe we must take seriously the 'absolute' claims that are apparent in both Fichte's discovery of 'Ich bin Ich' as the foundation of science and Hölderlin's reading of Fichte, where what is at stake is explicitly the 'absolute I,' containing, as does Spinoza's substance, 'all reality.'[33] In other words, the context in which Hegel himself discovers the ontological nature of judgment is not that of individual consciousness or Kant's transcendental subject, but the context of the absolute subject. It is in this context that the original division of judgment is at once an act of predication and an act of creation, where the original identity differentiates itself into being. Further, again referring back to Fichte's *Wissenschaftslehre*, this positing is the foundation of systematic science. I think these elements are easily discernible in Hegel's own notion of *Wissenschaft*, which relies on an absolute subject,[34] also known as the Idea, that 'freely lets itself go,'[35] out of its absolute identity or 'uniqueness'[36] to become the difference of nature and then reunites with itself through the process of spirit. Thus, in Hegel, the primordial and foundational judgment, the first act of self-differentiation, occurs in the *logos*[37] of the Idea, in the proposition 'Ich bin Ich,' not grasped as the expression of Fichtean identity but rather, as Hölderlin saw, as the positing of worldly difference through the copula. Identity and difference can now be recapitulated and reconciled in the syllogistic structure of Hegel's *Encyclopedia of Philosophical Sciences*.[38]

If it is indeed the *logos* of the Idea that provides the source for Hegel's ontological notion of judgment and if this *logos* is recapitulated in the discourse of systematic, objective *Wissenschaft*, then it is within the framework of this system that propositions or judgments should be seen in this light, as 'speculative propositions,'[39] where the subject posits itself in its predicate as both identical and different. It is within this systematic framework that Hegel's notion of judgment can claim to make sense.[40] This means that the contents of Science, or the contents of the system as manifest in the *Encyclopedia*, can be seen as ontological discourse, as language that *is* both identity and difference or thought and being, *even though these contents are expressed in the common propositions or sentences (Sätze) of predication*. It also means that the still-inchoate expressions of mind or spirit, as we saw with reference to the dialectic of identity and difference between mother-child, can be articulated *as* acts of predication.

Because it is ontological, we can say that the systematic discourse of Science is objective, that it is not subjective in the arbitrary sense, which is why Hegel takes pains to distinguish the judgments and propositions of Science, that is, scientific discourse, from the arbitrary personal or 'subjective' form of judgment, where it is the individual subject who determines the predication, rather than, ultimately, the absolute subjectivity of the Idea. In fact, the arbitrary, personal form of judgment can take the form of barbarous irony, which Hegel describes as a form of vanity that attacks and attempts to sunder the beautiful, Athenian unity of Science, evacuating, or rendering vain (*vereiteln*) its content.[41] It is striking that in portraying this vain personal judging Hegel has recourse to Fichte's founding principle of identity. Here, however, where the two personal pronouns face each other as images in a mirror, where my propositions are mere iterations of myself, Fichte's principle is truly employed to express identity, solipsistic self-identity devoid of real, worldly difference.[42] As the subject of my personal judgments, I speak only in order to see *myself* reflected in my discourse, and nothing more.

It is this ambiguity or instability of the judgment form, its immediate or unmediated expression of both identity and difference, which ultimately means it is deficient and must be superseded in the syllogism, where both identity and difference are at home (*bei sich*) in the mediated middle term, which is the content-full, objective language of systematic Science.

3 Why Hegel Didn't Join the 'Kant-Klub': Reason and Speculative Discourse

In 1790, at the Tübingen *Stift,* a reading group was formed to study and discuss Kant's works. The best minds of the college took part in the group, including Hegel's friends Schelling and Hölderlin, but Hegel himself did not join in.[1]

Commentators who refer to this lack of participation in the 'Kant-Klub' generally see it as confirming something they already know: at this time, Hegel was not very interested in Kantian philosophy, because the theoretical content of Kant's three *Critiques*, and particularly the first, did not correspond to Hegel's own interests, which were principally politico-religious or pedagogical, as attested to by his passion for Rousseau.[2] In fact, this idea that the young Hegel was not interested in the *Critique of Critical Reason* is based principally on a brief testimonial found in the letter of a former classmate, Christian Leutwein, written some forty years after their time at the *Stift.*[3]

H.S. Harris, who does not subscribe to the lack of interest thesis, puts forward a more material explanation for Hegel's not participating in the Kant-Klub: one of the participants was J.F. Maerklin, who had been promoted to a scholarly rank above Hegel's at the *Stift* (Maerklin was a former classmate of Hegel's from Stuttgart, where Hegel had been at the top of the class)[4] and Hegel resented the fact. This hypothesis is not very satisfying, however. On one hand, both Leutwein's and Schwegler's recollections refer to Hegel's desire to hide his disappointment, something he could easily have done within the Kantian reading group. Above all, this explanation does nothing to advance enquiry into the *formation* of Hegel's early thoughts on Kant.

The relation between Hegel and the Kant-Klub tells us something about how Hegel's thoughts on Kant developed in the period between

1787, where we find the first traces of reflection on the Königsberg philosopher, and 1802, when *Faith and Knowledge* is published, the first substantial Hegelian text on Kant. Indeed, the question of the relation between Hegel and the Kantian group at the *Stift* is all the more pertinent since this gestational period includes but few references to Kant.

However, this paucity of references is not indicative of a lack of Hegelian interest in Kantian philosophy as it is expressed in the first *Critique*. On the contrary, the first references to Kant, in the extracts that Hegel copied out, from primary and secondary sources, shows that not only was Hegel interested in the *Critique* but he had already appropriated certain elements that would prove essential to the development of his own philosophy.

Consequently, retracing the sources of Hegelian thought on Kant will serve to refute the idea that Hegel did not participate in the Kantian circle due to a lack of interest for critical philosophy. Further, more strikingly, the first trace references to Kant in Hegelian thought illustrate that the non-participation in the Kant-Klub is entirely consistent with the ideas Hegel had already developed regarding the *Critique of Pure Reason*. These ideas on Kant, which will express themselves fully at Jena in *Faith and Knowledge*, are already in development in 1788 at Tübingen. Hegel's relation to the Kant-Klub can only be understood within this development.

I want to show that the ideas Hegel had already formed on Kant were at odds with the tone of the Kantian group and particularly with the interpretation of the first *Critique* put forward by the guiding spirit of the group, *der Kantianer enragé*[5] Immanuel Carl Diez, in his polemical reaction against the professor of theology, Gottlob Christian Storr. In other words, the interpretation of Diez, who led the group and who was radically opposed to Storr, was sufficient to keep Hegel away from the Kantian circle, because that interpretation was already fundamentally opposed to Hegel's. The problem, however, is that if we set Hegel against Diez, it seems we should at the same time side Hegel with Storr, which commentators are rightly loath to do. Indeed, the general feeling is that Hegel, teaming up with his friends Schelling and Hölderlin, were in full revolt against the orthodox theology of Professor Storr and, above all, against the use he made of the Kantian *Critique* in support of his theology.[6] However, in making Hegel a rebel, like his friends Schelling and Hölderlin, it is hard to understand why Hegel would not have joined Diez's circle. Hence recourse to the explanations I mentioned above: either Hegel was not really interested in Kant or he kept away from the circle for purely personal and arbitrary reasons.

In fact, there is no need to turn to these explanations, of which the first is manifestly false[7] and the second hardly convincing, if it can be shown that Hegel had no taste for Diez's radical interpretation of the *Critique of Pure Reason* and did not entirely repudiate the interpretation favoured by Storr.[8] To show this, however, it is first necessary to look at how Hegel himself understood the *Critique of Pure Reason*, in 1790, at the time of the Kant-Klub. We will see that this understanding implies a certain Hegelian idea of language, indeed of *logos* (language as thought), and that it is this idea that prevented him from adhering to Diez's interpretation against that of Storr. It was consequently this early Hegelian idea of *logos* that prevented him from participating in the Tübingen Kant-Klub.

Rosenkranz, in his Hegel 'Ur-biography,' claims without hesitation that Hegel read the *Critique of Pure Reason* while in his second year at the Stift, in 1789.[9] This claim is most likely based on the handwritten and dated extracts from the *Critique* that Rosenkranz apparently had access to but which no longer exist. The missing extracts hypothesis is all the more credible since Hegel chose to take the private, elective course, given by J.F. Flatt, Storr's assistant, entitled 'Empirical Psychology and the Kantian *Critique*,' in the summer of 1789. That Hegel took this course has been established by Johannes Hoffmeister and confirmed some thirty years later by Dieter Henrich, through study of another Hegelian manuscript, this one dated 1794, to which Hoffmeister gave the rather grandiose title of *Materien zu einer Philosophie des subjektiven Geistes*, but which mainly consists of a kind of catalogue of psychological terms. Henrich confirms that the central portion of the 1794 manuscript corresponds perfectly to the content of the notebook of another student who took Flatt's 1789 course. Consequently, Hegel seems to have taken the Kant course and incorporated its content, from his own class notes, into the 1794 manuscript on human psychology.[10]

Hoffmeister's remarkable analysis of the central portion of the manuscript on psychology further establishes that its content represents a compilation taken not only from the *Critique of Pure Reason* itself, but also from secondary literature, such as works by Iacob Friedrich Abel, Johann Schultz, and Karl Leonhard Reinhold. Interestingly, it was Flatt who seems to have put together this compilation while preparing his 1789 course, which Hegel followed, faithfully taking and conserving the notes he would later refer to in writing his 1794 catalogue of psychological terms.

It seems therefore incontestable that Hegel was interested in the first

Critique from 1789, to the extent that he copied out extracts from it and chose to take and pay for a course that dealt with its subject matter. I will return to the 1794 manuscript, whose centre is drawn from 1789 material, the year when Hegel began to study Kant's work. However, I first want to present indications that Hegel familiarized himself, at least to a certain degree, with the *Critique of Pure Reason* from the moment its second edition was published, in 1787. Besides the historical interest this might have, showing that Hegel was interested in the first *Critique* two years before the generally accepted date, more importantly, these traces or indications reveal the notion of language that I mentioned above, namely the idea of a *logos* opposed to the one that can be attributed to Diez, the leader of the Kant-Klub.

In 1787, when Hegel was still at the Stuttgart Gymnasium (he was seventeen years old), he copied out long extracts[11] from a book on psychology by Christian Garve, entitled *Prüfung der Fähigkeiten* (Examination of the Faculties), which had been published in 1769. Within these extracts is a passage on the reasoning faculty, where Hegel has modified the original text so as to make a distinction that Garve does not make. Hoffmeister discovered that Hegel introduces a technical term, *Verstand* (understanding), which he substitutes in a particular context where Garve had used the term *Vernunft* (reason), in order to subsequently define the two concepts. Although the distinction Hegel makes in opposing 'understanding' to 'reason' does not adopt the Kantian idea of reason as it is presented in the first *Critique* (Hegel defines reason as the faculty to make abstractions from singular instances, in order to create general concepts),[12] by referring to the *Verstand* as a judgment-producing faculty, Hegel is clearly inspired by its Kantian definition. Further, just as Kant presents the activity of judgment (*das Urteilen*) as an essentially linguistic act, namely the propositional act of predication between subject and predicate, it is in the linguistic context of judgment that Hegel substitutes the term *Verstand* for what Garve had presented as *Vernunft*. Thus, in Hegel's manuscript extract, the understanding becomes the power to 'determine the signification of words' and to use a word as 'a sign'[13] in order to represent a general idea. In other words, by substituting the term *Verstand* for the term *Vernunft* in the passage copied from Garve, Hegel seems to take up the idea that Kant expresses in the first section of 'The Analytic of Concepts':[14] the understanding is 'a faculty of judging' where judgment is an act of predication attributing meaning to words, initially taken as signs. Hegel will never abandon this notion of the understanding as directly associated with a certain type of discourse, although this type of discourse will come to be opposed to another form, namely the discourse of speculative reason. However, in 1787 this notion has not yet developed. In fact, the idea of a discourse specific to reason will only begin to appear on the Hegelian horizon in the text I mentioned above, the 1794 manuscript on psychology. For those interested in exploring the enormous Kantian heritage in Hegel, it is interesting that the discourse of speculative reason, the defining element of Hegelian language in all its specificity, can also be seen (as is the discourse of the judging understanding) as arising out of Hegel's reading of Kant. However, while the judging discourse of the understanding is drawn from the Kantian *Verstand*, the discourse of speculative reason will be inspired by the Kantian notion of reason in its dialectical activity.

As I said above, the *centre* of the 1794 text on psychology (the entire text is about twenty pages in *Dokumente zu Hegels Entwicklung*) comes from Flatt's course on Kant, which Hegel took in 1789. The last part of the manuscript, however, which interests us here, cannot be drawn from the same source. The reason is simply that this part of the text contains explicit references to the *Critique of the Faculty of Judgment*, which was only published in 1790.

As well, the tone and content of the last section of the manuscript is different from what precedes it. It seems rather like a personal summary of the 'main themes and forms of these two *Critiques*'[15] (the first and third), which Hegel appended to his hybrid manuscript. Indeed, this last part of the manuscript seems like a personal reflection on the theoretical side of Kant. It is even possible that these pages were drawn from a lost essay that Hegel wrote in 1790 for his Magisterium, entitled 'On the Judgment of Common Human Understanding, Concerning the Objectivity and Subjectivity of Representations,' a subject that is clearly Kantian in its theme, written in the same year the Kant-Klub was meeting.[16]

The part of the manuscript that is of interest here is divided into three main sections: A. *Verstand*; B. *Reflectierende Urteilskraft*; C. *Vernunft*, with a subsection to C, *Kosmologie*.[17]

Under *Verstand*, Hegel summarizes some of the results of his reading of the *Critique of Pure Reason*: 'The forms of thought are not sensible intuitions but categories, concepts within the nature of the understanding, hence a priori – and there are as many original concepts as there are types of judgments.'[18] The operation of the understanding, as a faculty of determinant judgment, consists in subsuming (*subsumieren*) objects under general concepts.

Under 'Reflective Judgment,' Hegel presents, in two paragraphs, with references to the *Critique of the Faculty of Judgment*, the idea of judgments that proceed from the particular to the general or the universal, while alluding to the purposiveness of natural objects and art.

At the beginning of the final section, which deals with reason, although the title is missing, Hegel writes, 'Reason is the faculty to conclude' (*schliessen*) or rather, we should say, 'to syllogize,' since he continues with, '*schliesst unmittelbar, oder mittelbar. Obersatz, Untersatz, Schlusssatz* (major, minor, conclusion).'[19] To put this differently, reason proceeds syllogistically. From a universal premise, from an unconditioned presupposition that cannot be proven, it seeks knowledge of the particular. As opposed to the understanding and its categories, the syllogism of reason does not depend on sensible intuitions but only on concepts and judgments. The source of these concepts, writes Hegel, is ideas that, by their unproven nature are 'problematical concepts.'[20] The two unconditioned ideas Hegel refers to are those from the *Critique of Pure Reason*, that is, the unconditioned ideas that give rise to the paralogisms and antinomies of the 'Transcendental Dialectic.' Hegel deals with both under the title of '*Kosmologie.*'

It is clear that the Hegelian conception of reason has undergone a Kantian transformation since the 1787 text (copied, for the most part, from Garve's text), where reason was simply defined as a capacity of abstraction. Here, in the manuscript on psychology, reason is distinguished from the (Kantian) understanding primarily by the fact it does not deal with sensible intuitions. The lack of empirical grounding leads to the dialectical articulations of reason's paralogisms and antinomies. The transcendental nature of reason's dialectic in the first *Critique* also inspires Hegel to give a logical turn to the faculty of reason. This is reflected in the syllogistic form he uses to explain the status of ideas, which are at first reduced to the level of unproved, unconditioned premises. This logical turn helps place reason in the same context in which Hegel had already situated the judgment-producing understanding. To summarize, the understanding judges and thereby expresses itself in simple predicative propositions, while reason concludes through syllogisms, which incorporate the understanding's predicative statements as propositions (major, minor, conclusion). This distinction between judgment and syllogism is fundamental to all future Hegelian logic and hence, we can say, to his ontology. It is the onto-logical dimension of reason's discourse, as distinct from the discourse of the understanding, which will allow us to grasp Hegel's attitude toward Diez and Storr and therefore to the Kant-Klub of Tübingen.

We must not get ahead of ourselves, however. Let us continue our discussion of the early manuscript, which precedes by many years any genuine ontological theory of the syllogism as found later in the *Greater Logic* and the *Encyclopedia Logic*. In the manuscript on psychology (1794), it is when Hegel addresses the dialectical antinomies inherent in metaphysical reasoning on cosmology that the discourse of reason appears, as opposed to that of the understanding.

The discourse of reason, as presented in the manuscript, is simply, as Hegel claims on two occasions, a discourse where one proposition and its opposite (*Satz und sein Gegensatz*) can both be true.[21] In other words, the discourse of 'speculative reason'[22] is not governed by the principle of contradiction. We may just as well affirm that the universe is unlimited as affirm it is limited; we can just as easily claim it is governed by necessity as claim it is governed by free will, and so on. While the understanding is limited to judgments that affirm A = A (a thing is what it is), reason, in its dialectical antinomies, affirms that a thing both is and is not what it is (A = A and A = B).

This distinction between two modes of discourse, outlined in the manuscript on psychology and clearly inspired by a reflection on the Kantian antinomies, is taken up again and further developed several years later, in 1800, in Hegel's first published article, his 'Difference between the Systems of Fichte and Schelling' or *Differenzschrift*.

In this text, we find an explicit, formal presentation of the difference between the judgment proposition of the understanding (*Verstand*) and the propositions of speculative reason (*Vernunft*). While the understanding can only express identity, as given in the formula A = A, we find that 'the highest [formal] expression of *reason* ... expresses the antinomy [where] A = B and A = A ...,'[23] on condition that each of these formulae of reason expresses both the identity and the difference between subject and object. In other terms, reason articulates the identity of identity and difference or absolute identity. Reason expresses the fact that the grammatical subject is both identical to and different from the object.[24] However, it is important to understand that where the expression of reason is concerned, as the identity of identity and difference, we are no longer dealing with formal grammatical logic. Indeed, the ontological aspect of reason's discourse, mentioned above, is already apparent in this first Hegelian publication, since Hegel links the antinomic proposition to 'sufficient reason.'[25] Following Leibniz, we know that sufficient reason expresses raison d'être, whereas the purely logical proposition of the understanding, the principle of non-contradiction or identity, remains on the level of possibility.

The ontological dimension of reason's speculative proposition is rendered still more concrete in *Faith and Knowledge* (1802), the first Hegelian text containing a coherent, sustained reaction to the *Critique of Pure Reason*. Here, we find a comprehensive expression of what I am claiming to have found, in embryonic form, in Hegel's first manuscripts, namely the discourse of reason and its ontological dimension, as opposed to the formal propositions of predicative judgment, products of the understanding.

We have seen how the first articulations of the discourse of reason are developed from a reflection on Kant's dialectical antinomies. Now, in *Faith and Knowledge*, Hegel rediscovers the discourse of speculative reason in the stated project of the first *Critique* itself: the investigation into the possibility of a priori synthetic judgments. The interpretation or appropriation of Kant's project provides Hegel with a way of looking at and using propositional language such that it becomes capable of expressing the onto-logical identity of identity and difference. Such language therefore becomes adequate to his idea of speculative reason. This is why, writes Hegel, what the Kantian question, 'How are a priori synthetic judgments possible?' actually expresses is the 'true idea of reason.'[26] 'This problem expresses nothing else,' Hegel continues, 'than the idea that in synthetic judgment the subject and the predicate, the former being the particular and the latter being the universal, the former being in the form of being and the latter in the form of thought – than the idea that this heterogeneity is at the same time a priori, i.e., absolutely identical. The possibility of such a position is simply reason, which is nothing other than this identity of heterogeneous terms.'[27]

In other words, a priori synthetic judgment is an act of predication that supposes, or rather recognizes, the pre-existing or a priori identity between subject and object, two terms that will then differentiate themselves through the propositional form of judgment. Thus, reason is the identity that is immanent in the difference between particular and universal, and a fortiori (and this is fundamental to grasping Hegel's notion of speculative discourse) between being and thought. Briefly put, in the discourse of speculative reason we find an expression of the truth: the differentiated unity of being and thought.[28]

Hegel clearly interprets what Kant means by 'a priori synthetic judgment' in his own way. The term 'judgment' is reduced to its grammatical form; a priori is taken as that which is already there; and 'synthetic' is related to 'the synthetic unity of apperception,'[29] which becomes, for Hegel, 'an original synthetic unity, i.e., a unity that must not be understood as the product of opposed terms but as the truly necessary, absolute, original identity of two opposed terms.'[30] As well, by grounding its synthesizing ability in the Kantian synthetic unity of apperception, the speculative proposition of reason may also find there the original identity of 'the subjective and the objective.'[31]

The original identity of reason 'does not present itself in the judgment,'[32] that is, in the predicative or propositional form itself, but, writes Hegel in 1802, in a 'Mittlebegriff' that is the 'Schluss' or in the syllogism.[33] We have seen that already in the text on psychology Hegel associated reason with the syllogistic form, in order to distinguish it from the predicative form of the *Verstand*. However, in grammatical terms, or in terms of the predicative form of judgment between subject and object, the original unity or identity can only be presented in the copula *is*.[34] The judgment form tends to hide the speculative nature of the copula, while reason demands that we grasp the copula as it really *is*. To put this another way, reason is the existing discourse of the original unity of identity and difference. Reason goes beyond the logical form of judgment in order to express the being in the copula *is*. The verb of reason is thus ontological.

I will push this idea even further to show how it is fundamental to my argument about the Kant-Klub. To the extent the original unity of reason, represented in the copula, expresses the *being* of absolute identity, or the being of the identity of identity and difference (or the identity of the particular and the universal or the *existing* identity of being and thought, of object and subject), the original unity is ultimately the affirmation of divine existence. As Alexis Philonenko puts it, the supreme speculative proposition must thus be 'God is an existing being.'[35] Consequently, the verb of reason or the verb of absolute identity in Hegel tends to be not only ontological but onto-theo-logical. We have seen how this idea develops out of notions that Hegel appropriates from the *Critique of Pure Reason*, through the antinomies of reason and the idea of a priori synthetic judgment.

I am not claiming that Hegel had already developed a theory of the proposition of speculative reason in 1790, when he remained removed from the *Stift*'s Kant group. However, it is clear that at this time he had already made the distinction between two types of discourse: the discourse of the understanding, which is founded on and expresses the principle of non-contradiction in the formal act of predication, and a discourse of reason that goes beyond the simple predicative judgment of identity in order to express and embody the inherent difference of being.

At Tübingen, the theologian G.C. Storr used the *Critique of Pure Reason* to prove the truth and authority of the Revelation. Indeed, if the understanding is incapable of grasping the thing-in-itself, of knowing the truths of the soul, the world and God, then these truths could only have been transmitted by Revelation and miracles. Thus, the doctrine of the Trinity and the Bible necessarily constitute acts of Divine Revelation. Furthermore, according to Storr, the Revelation is immediately beyond the reach of any attacks from Enlightenment (*Aufklärung*) reason in its attempts to analyze such revelatory acts as the life of Jesus, the Resurrection, the Trinity, and the Word, reducing them to just so many historical facts. Kant had indeed shown that the understanding could not reach such truths.[36]

It is easy to see why Storr is associated with the defense of orthodox Christianity and why his adversary, Immanuel Carl Diez, the *Kantianer enragé* and the leader of the *Stift*'s Kant-Klub, is often characterized as a kind of liberator in the struggle against dogmatic authority. It is true that Diez used Kant's first *Critique* in a way that was diametrically opposed to Storr's use of the same work. According to Diez, since Kant had shown that the only knowledge possible is that which passes through the forms of sensible intuition, space and time, and then through the categories of understanding, Storr's 'Revelation' was impossible. The disciples could have had no knowledge of Jesus and His life beyond the empirically historical realm. The theologian's task is thus to study the Bible's historical facts, to recognize in it what is conformed to reason and to deconstruct its symbolic content.[37]

My conclusion is therefore the hypothesis that, for Hegel, Diez's project was confined to the element of understanding (*Verstand*). In holding exclusively to empirical truth and finding nothing more in Kant's dialectic of reason than the proof of reason's inability to attain the truth, Diez rejected any possibility of dialectical or speculative reason in the Hegelian sense (the seeds of which were already sewn in 1790). As well, by refusing to recognize as meaningful the dialectical activity of reason, Diez's discourse could not get beyond the form of judgment inherent in the *Verstand*, namely non-contradictory, predicative statements in the form A = A. Moreover, and crucially for Hegel, Diez's judgments were aimed at the doctrines of Christianity, which already represented an embodiment of the discourse of speculative reason, namely *logos* as Divine Revelation, whose highest expression is 'God is an existing being.' Such a discourse is distinct from the language of the understanding and its notion that words are mere linguistic signs, mere predicates that may or may not be attributed to a given subject.

On the other hand, by presenting the Bible as Divine Revelation, Storr presupposed the possibility of a speculative discourse in the Hegelian sense, that is, a discourse that goes beyond the understanding, free from the principle of non-contradiction and therefore onto-theo-logical. Briefly, for Hegel, a discourse that expresses the idea of the Trinity, the idea that One Person is at the same time Three, is already a discourse of speculative reason.

According to my hypothesis, Hegel did not join the Kant-Klub because the language holding sway there seemed opposed to any possibility of a discourse expressing the identity of identity and difference, that is, a discourse of *absolute* identity, where the Idea-God pronounces itself as being in the world.[38]

One final word. In stressing what he seems to have rejected in Diez, I do not mean to push Hegel into Storr's arms. It is clear that Hegel never espoused the kind of orthodox dogmatism that sees the truth of Revelation as the exclusive realm of faith. Hegel's project, as he had already expressed it at an early age, consists of 'discovering the just mean, where the truth is found,'[39] by overcoming unilateral oppositions. Thus, where religion is concerned, it is a matter of preserving the real gains of understanding's knowledge, the most important of which is freedom from dogmatic church authority, without sacrificing the content of faith. Such a project can only take place in the *logos* of philosophical science, in the substantial discourse of speculative reason.

4 The Fiery Crucible, Yorick's Skull, and Leprosy in the Sky: The Language of Nature (With a Concluding Unscientific Postscriptum)

The strange images in the title of this essay are Hegel's own. They occur in three different contexts where each is used to portray, or represent, truth that can and must also be expressed in the systematic, speculative discourse of Science.[1] I believe that these textual references, taken together, help us understand, in a new way, one of the most persistently troubling aspects of Hegel's philosophy: the systematic relationship between thought and nature.[2] Rather than attempting to contribute to this debate by referring primarily or indeed exclusively to the conceptual articulations of the *Encyclopedia Logic* and the *Greater Logic*, reinterpreting Hegel's richly speculative language in a 'definitive' fashion, I want to approach the problem from a different angle, both by beginning with the ideas in their imaged, intuitive presentation and by referring to texts that have never been taken together, as I am doing, to form an argument.

Each of the three textual references and its image raise a conceptual issue. It is the investigation into these issues that determines the course of inquiry of this essay. This can be articulated in several ways. On one hand I am inquiring into how Hegel's Philosophy of Nature is meant to work within his system of science as embodied in the *Encyclopedia of Philosophical Sciences*. However, on a more radical level, my inquiry deals with the problem of natural otherness itself: how does a comprehensive system of thought incorporate or comprehend the deep difference of nature?[3] The answer to both inquiries is the same. We arrive at it by lingering before the three pictures I am presenting and following the conceptual issues that derive from each of them: (1) How 'other' is natural otherness? (2) How does natural otherness become part of the system? (3) What form does natural otherness take within the system?

These three questions, with their corresponding images, are the three main headings of this essay. Thus 'the leprosy in the sky,' the 'fiery crucible,' and 'Yorrick's skull' represent the lineaments of my argument.

The Gleaming Leprosy in the Sky, or How 'Other' Is Natural Otherness?

The poet Heinrich Heine describes in his memoirs how he, as a young man, met Hegel at a dinner party in Berlin. Following a satisfying repast, and before retiring to the whist tables, the two great figures of German letters found themselves beside each other, looking out the window at the starry nineteenth-century sky. Heine, enthusing about the stars, called them the abode of the blessed, to which Hegel grumbled: 'the stars are only a gleaming leprosy in the sky.'[4]

This remark of Hegel's always pleased me: it bespeaks his refusal to be edifying. However, it also illustrates a challenge to those of us who study him: what does Hegel make of the chaotic contingency of nature or, to put it another way, what are we to make of Hegel's philosophy of nature? This crucial part of the system, which appears at the crossroads between the Logic and the Philosophy of Spirit in his *Encyclopedia of Philosophical Sciences*, has generally been seen as an embarrassment to those who believe Hegel is an important thinker.[5] True, against today's notion of science as theoretical[6] and experimental, it is hard not to be perplexed when we read Hegel's *Naturphilosophie*. Here, it seems we are meant to believe that nature itself runs along dialectical lines or that the laws of nature are dialectical rather than causal, mathematical, or statistical.[7] At first glance, it would appear that natural phenomena are meant to follow the same logic that we find in the *Logics* themselves and throughout the Hegelian system. In other words, it is hard to take seriously a philosopher who explains the solar system as obeying the dialectical beat of In-itself (e.g., the sun), For-itself (e.g., the moon), For-another (e.g., the comets) and the In-and-for-itself (e.g., the earth).

We might call the view identifying nature and logic the *processional* way of understanding Hegel's philosophy of nature. According to this view, nature itself appears as a blind process that follows an inexorable, orderly logic of development. Hegel's *philosophy* of nature is supposedly the accurate reflection of this process. William Maker has called this common interpretation of the philosophy of nature absolute or metaphysical idealism: Hegel is perceived as reducing everything to the articulations of thought.[8] The processional interpretation is particularly well represented in contemporary French thought, through those thinkers, both Hegelian and anti-Hegelian, who either studied with or were inspired by Jean Hyppolite's anti-anthropological view of dialectical progression, both in history and in nature.[9] Thus, Marxist thinkers are able to view Hegel as the upside-down, idealist image of materialist dialectics. For both scientific materialists and processional idealists, the movement of reality follows dialectical logic, whether it is reality that determines the logic or vice versa. Of course an absolute idealism is very hard to distinguish from an absolute materialism, and consequently when Engels writes: 'the dialectical laws are really laws of development of nature and therefore are valid also for theoretical natural science,' he could easily be expressing the point of view William Maker attributes to the absolute idealists.[10]

Indeed, most of the literature on Hegel's philosophy of nature seeks to understand how he relates nature to thought.[11] The processional view perceives them as being immediately interpenetrated, leaving no room for natural difference between them.[12]

The processional view, however, is self-contradictory in terms of Hegel's own conception of systematic science, since it seems to imply his system is the arbitrary construction of a philosopher who observes the natural progression from outside it and records his impressions in a Philosophy of Nature.[13] Hegel denies the constructivist view of 'his' system in too many places to mention. However, this is what the processional view ultimately implies: our philosopher must simply be the one who happened to be perceptive enough to observe, from an external position, that everything in nature runs along dialectical lines and who was able to write a philosophical system describing this process. The Philosophy of Nature and its integration into the *Encyclopedia* would thus depend entirely upon the observations of the philosopher who recounted them, who thus becomes the only thing holding the system together. Kierkegaard, an ex-Hegelian in good standing, was right in noticing the absurdity of the processional view, although it was the only one he knew, in that the supposedly objective system of science becomes an arbitrary, subjective artifice that supposedly reflects the inherent logic of nature itself. In fact, the objectivity of the philosophy of nature lies elsewhere than in the reliability of Hegel's account. It lies in the actual *content* of the philosophy, which is drawn from the work of the natural sciences of the day. It is true Hegel wrote the philosophy of nature, but in doing so, he referred to what he felt were the pertinent texts of his time. I will return to this later.

As well, how can we possibly reconcile this idea of the wise philosopher who observes the laws of logic reflected everywhere in nature, with the man who, looking out on the night sky, into the very heart of nature, sees only 'a gleaming leprosy in the sky'? How can a philosopher who is supposed to believe that nature runs on the same inexorable laws as those governing logic, look out on the heart of nature itself and see only chaos, contingency, a pox on the sky? The processional view attributed to Hegel's philosophy of nature encounters an insurmountable dilemma when faced with the bad infinity of natural contingency: for the philosophy of nature to be an accurate reflection of nature's processional logic, it must ignore or leave out natural contingency,[14] but in doing so, it can no longer be an objective account of nature. Clearly then, the philosophy of nature must be something other than Hegel's faithful account of nature's immanent logic.[15]

Most importantly, Hegel's reported description of the heavenly vaults as a 'leprosy in the sky' does more than simply evoke the theoretical problem of contingency, a problem he deals with in the *Greater Logic*.[16] Hegel's epigram displays a real revulsion to nature itself, to its overpowering, chaotic, undisciplined presence, to its refusal to be ordered, to its swarming lawlessness, to its tendency to slide into bad infinity.[17] In other words, Hegel's epigram seems to reveal a radical, pressing 'otherness' in nature itself that cannot simply be left out of his *philosophy* of nature, as if such an account could proceed, diligently following an immanent logic, regardless of nature's most persistent, contradictory quality. Understanding Hegel's philosophy of nature therefore seems to imply coming to grips with this otherness of nature, with the 'gleaming leprosy in the sky.'

The rich diversity of answers to this question can perhaps best be grasped according to the degree of otherness the commentators recognize between nature and thought in Hegel, ranging from a strictly processional view, where nature and logic are assimilated, to a view like Maker's, which recognizes the absolute otherness of nature in order to guarantee the reciprocal autonomy of reason.[18] Regardless of these differences of degree, however, their lines of interpretation tend to encounter the same problems with regard to Hegel's systemic claims. These are the same difficulties that arise in the systematic articulations of Spinoza and Fichte: how can the substance really act on itself as another, or how can the I = I really incorporate a not-I? I believe this is because interpreters of Hegel tend to see any relation between thought and natural contingency as static, rather than recognizing the dynamic, actual character of their mediation.

The Fiery Crucible or How Does Natural Otherness Become Part of the System?

Twenty-odd years before his Berlin dinner with Heine, some time between 1803 and 1806, when Hegel was at Jena in his first university post, he wrote a strange, feverish, almost poetic passage in a personal journal. The fragments of this journal – or the *Wastebook* aphorisms (*Aphorismen aus Hegels Wastebook*), as they are sometimes called – are important for several reasons. They reflect Hegel's *personal* thoughts and inquiries at a time when he is struggling to develop his own system, a struggle of false starts and aborted attempts that would eventually produce the *Phenomenology of Spirit*, published in 1807. As well, the Jena fragments show how our philosopher's thought is growing apart from that of his friend and colleague, Schelling. This is particularly true with regard to their visions of nature and its philosophy.[19]

One journal entry is of particular importance, I believe, for anyone interested in the question of Hegel's philosophy of nature. The passage is highly metaphorical, or as Hegel would say, intuitive. In fact, it represents a succinct mythological account that portrays the entire system in terms of what might be called a cosmogony. Hegel himself describes the passage as a 'myth,' which he borrows from Jakob Böhme and qualifies as 'barbarous.' However, it is important to stress that this does not discount it; it simply means the portrayal is representational, creating a picture for the intuition rather than involving a scientific development.[20] In this way, Hegel's myth is representational in the way that revealed religion presents us with a picture-thinking version of speculative truth, through the idea of the Trinity, for example, or the idea of the fall.

The mythical account in Hegel's Jena aphorism begins with the creation of nature. This moment is expressed as a loss of 'punctuality,' where God, as the absolute singular, 'lets itself go' in order to become nature. Rather than seeing that his creation is good, however, God is 'enraged' by his dispersal, by this otherness he has become as (*als*) natural contingency. 'In becoming nature,' begins Hegel, 'God bestows himself in the glorious, silent orbits and forms, and becoming aware of this expansion and his lost punctuality, is enraged by it.'[21] It is this rage and the resulting violence visited on the 'expansion' that will enable us to understand how Hegel incorporates the otherness of nature into the system of science. First, however, I want to look at the 'lost punctuality' Hegel uses to describe the transition from God to nature. This is crucial, because what Hegel is really talking about here is the passage between logic and nature. In other words, the divine expansion into natural dispersal is the representation of the passage that occurs between the *Encyclopedia Logic* and the Philosophy of Nature, where, in more conceptual terms, the Absolute Idea, as a pure in-itself, as pure thought or pure undifferentiated concept, 'lets itself go' to become the complete otherness of nature. This 'letting itself go' (*frei entlassen*) is the expression we find at the end of the *Encyclopedia Logic*, where Hegel describes the self-othering of the Idea into nature.[22] The movement is reiterated at the beginning of the philosophy of nature in the form of a question and answer. '[Since] God is absolutely self-sufficient, that which has no need, how does he thus come to decide to become something absolutely Other? In fact, the Godly Idea is just this: to decide to posit this Other outside of itself and to take it back again, in order to be subjectivity and spirit.'[23] I am tempted to say that my essay is no more than an explication of this remark.

The expression *frei entlassen* has received a certain amount of scholarly attention, probably because its esoteric flavor seems to hold the key to the problem of natural otherness, by providing an origin: how 'other' can nature be when it is the self-othering of the Idea?[24] One solution might be to grasp the 'letting go of otherness' in the same way one self lets go of or frees the other self in the dialectic of recognition in the *Phenomenology of Spirit*, a solution proposed by Hermann Braun.[25] However, this interpretation seems problematical, in that it reduces the scandalous otherness of natural contingency, the leprosy in the sky, to the status of another self, one who must, in turn, recognize 'me,' evacuating the tension between nature and thought in a kind of dialectical 'happy ending.' As well, Braun's interpretation loses the 'punctuality' of the Idea, as expressed in our aphorism, or the Idea's 'absolute uniqueness,' as expressed at the end of the *Greater Logic*, by presupposing the existence of another self, whom I 'let go.'[26]

Dieter Wandschneider observes that while Hegel reiterates in numerous places the *frei entlassen* of the Idea into nature, he never explains why this occurs.[27] Wandschneider attempts to supply an answer by concentrating on freedom, in much the same way we find in Richard Dien Winfield's interpretation of the philosophy of nature, where the independence of thought is guaranteed by its lack of natural

determination. As is the case in Winfield, Wandschneider's interpretation sacrifices the ontological status of nature qua nature to ensure the
self-determinacy of thought.[28]

For Wandschneider, the Absolute lets itself go as nature because, as
the dialectical and self-grounding ideal, it must differentiate itself from
something that is not-ideal, not-absolute, from which it is free. Thus,
'with the Ideal, there must also be a Not-Ideal.'[29] This means that
nature is defined in purely negative terms, solely as the Not-Idea that
the Idea needs in order to determine itself as the Absolute. As dependent upon what it is not, namely the Idea, Nature loses the *Selbstän-
digkeit* (independence) Hegel explicitly assigns to it,[30] its *difference* as
'the sphere where contingency and external determinability maintain
their right,'[31] where the heavenly vaults are a 'leprosy in the sky.'
Hence, for Wandschneider, nature remains 'logically conceivable' and
'logically structured.' Nature cannot be 'completely undetermined,
formless matter,' otherwise it would be the same as nothing.[32] It is no
accident that Wandschneider's description of nature as the 'Not-Ideal'
immediately brings to mind Fichte's Not-I. Grasping nature negatively,
as that which is not the Idea but which is nonetheless required if
the Idea is to be dialectical, once again reminds us of the Fichtean or
Spinozist problem of natural otherness that I referred to above, a problem of which Hegel was acutely aware.[33]

Although different, both Braun's and Wandschneider's interpretations of *frei entlassen* tend to sacrifice nature's otherness by closely affil-
iating nature to its source in the Idea. I'm not sure, however, if my own
interpretation of *frei entlassen* is any more successful in solving the
problem of natural otherness: how other is nature with regard to
thought? I will nonetheless attempt an interpretation of the expression
before returning to 'the fiery crucible,' namely, what I think is the key
to the question.

I believe we can make more sense of the Idea's 'letting itself go,' if
we take seriously the term Hegel uses in §244 of the *Encyclopedia Logic*
to describe the Absolute Idea's 'decision' to become nature. It is an
error to take this as an act of arbitrary will, as Schelling pretends to do
when he later comments, ironically, that Hegel's Absolute Idea must
decide to become nature out of boredom. In fact, if we take the
verb Hegel actually uses, 'sich entschliesst' (decides), in the quasi-
etymological sense of the term (*ent-* 'de' in the sense of 'out of,' plus
schliessen), we discover a deeper signification. Since one of the meanings of 'schliessen' is to syllogize, 'entschliessen' can be taken as a de-

syllogizing. This in turn can be understood as the syllogism (*Schluss*) releasing its middle term, 'the moment of particularity'[34] that is also the moment of natural contingency.

The Absolute Idea's decision can be seen as a de-syllogizing only if we understand the articulation of the logic as an argument that is itself a syllogism (*Schluss*) moving from the moment of universality (Doctrine of Being) through the moment of essential particularity (Doctrine of Essence) before reaching a culminating and comprehensive moment of absolute or universal singularity: the Absolute Idea. This absolute singularity can be nothing other than the 'punctuality' we find in our aphorism, or the 'absolute uniqueness' that freely 'de-syllogizes' itself at the end of the *Greater Logic*, letting its particularity disperse as nature.[35]

Such a decision must therefore not be seen as an act of free will. It is rather the conclusion of an argument where essence must spill over into existence, where reason, as the Idea, is so absolute it becomes raison d'être, reason *to be*, or as one might say, where the Idea has every reason to be, so it is. We recognize this argument as ontological, and I believe this is the best way to understand what happens at the end of the logic: essence becomes existence following the same 'onto-logic' St Anselm et al. use in deducing the existence of God.

Even if my interpretation of *frei entlassen* is correct, we are still faced with the problem of natural otherness with regard to thought. The notion of the Absolute Idea's essence spilling over into existence still leaves us to wonder how much of the reasonable source has spilled over into nature. This is another way of asking how much of nature can be embraced within a system of science, without reducing its lively contingency to a logical category. In order to understand natural difference in its relation to thought or to systematic science, we have to look at the other half of the Idea's life-course, as we find it portrayed in Hegel's aphoristic myth: the wrath of God, or, in more speculative language, the negativity of the Idea.

This wrath enables us to grasp the radical 'un-godliness' of nature, what might otherwise be expressed as its 'inappropriateness'[36] with regard to the Idea. Indeed, my contention, in referring to Hegel's myth rather than relying exclusively on his speculative texts, is that there is something in the images of God's rage against the ungodliness of nature that helps us understand the dynamism of the Idea's life-course, by feeling the true extent of nature's insult and the power with which it is suppressed.

The ungodly quality of nature is personified in the fragment by
Lucifer, the fallen angel. The inspiration for this analogy is once again
Jakob Böhme.[37] Even without this reference, the Lucifer reference
clearly shows the hybrid aspect of nature itself, its angelic, divine origin in the Idea and its fall[38] to what is furthest removed from godli-
ness: evil. The reference also shows us that, just as Christianity denies
evil any kind of substantial, Manichean reality, nature cannot claim
completely substantial status with regard to the Idea. On the other
hand, although Nature derives its origin from the Idea, it is *not* the
Idea, any more than Lucifer *is* God. As radically ungodly, Lucifer does
not carry within him the immanent trace of his godly origin, any more
than nature carries within it an incipient trace of logic.

Finally, the Lucifer metaphor reveals an even more important element. Just as Christianity sees evil (and good) as a fundamentally
human matter, nature should also be seen in the same light, that is, as a
type of objectivity that pertains to humans. I will come back to this in
a moment.

To return to our aphorism, faced with his natural otherness, with his
rebellious dispersal, God is enraged and directs this wrath 'towards
himself in his otherness.'[39] Far from ineffectual, the wrath God turns
on Himself is greedy and violently destructive. It must 'devour and
swallow up' nature, whose 'bones must be pulverized; [whose] flesh
must be compressed and liquefied,' writes Hegel, enthusiastically. This
rage against natural otherness can be understood as the desire for self-
recovery, for the recovery of that absolute punctuality which has been
lost in natural dispersal. However, we must not lose sight of the violence of this assimilation, where nature is digested in a fiery 'crucible,'
to reappear as a realm of shadows. This re-emerging 'spirit of nature'
arises as 'free spirit,' now purified.[40]

In conceptual terms, the fiery 'crucible' or blast furnace in which the
bones of nature are melted down is the negativity of thought, the dialectical soul of the Idea itself. All otherness, 'its entire extended realm,'
must pass through the fiery crucible of thought in order that the Idea
may recover itself in its now mediated, absolute singularity. For this to
happen, pure, brute, immediate nature must be thought, negated, and
transformed, thereby losing its original character of otherness, of un-
thought. In its new spiritualized form, nature can make up the content
(*Gehalt*) of the philosophy of nature and therefore, of the encyclopedic
system of science.

In the Jena aphorism we have been looking at, Hegel describes the

Idea's movement of self-othering in nature and its subsequent self-recovery through the destruction of that otherness, as 'the life-course of God.' The metaphorical presentation allows us to grasp the essential fact that the relationship between thought and nature is one of process,[41] one that can only be understood in terms of the dynamic, systematic movement Hegel calls science, articulated by logic, nature, and a reconciling third term, spirit. This *Lebenslauf* of the Absolute Idea, on the one hand, is a dynamic, circular movement that implies and indeed requires a scientific or systematic perspective. On the other hand, however, this systematic viewpoint requires protagonistic human content that is thoroughly integral to the action of the Absolute Idea in its self-recovery. This is what Hegel means by spirit. In our aphorism, he refers to this human standpoint as the 'second cycle of the absolute.'

Concretely, this is the point of view of the individual thinker or of human thought actually thinking nature. More specifically, within Hegel's encyclopedic system, it is the work of the natural scientist. From this point of view, what appeared as the wrath of the Idea negating natural otherness in the fiery crucible of thought is incarnated in the actual human quest for knowledge. It is only through this activity that the negativity of the Idea is directed against its otherness. Reciprocally, the individual scientist's hunger for knowledge can be grasped as the personified wrath of the Idea. In fact, this is how individual scientific effort should be seen, as a process where, as Hegel writes in the same passage, individuals literally lose themselves in the quest for knowledge, although like nature itself, they are reborn, as 'second nature' in spirit.[42]

According to my reading, Hegel's philosophy of nature grasps the natural sciences in a systematic way, through a meta-enquiry that does exactly what a true *philosophy* of nature must do. It must go beyond the specific investigations of the particular natural sciences and enquire into the ontological status of both the scientific object itself and the knowing subject. Above all, it must enquire into the relation between the two, that is, between thought and nature. This shows that the speculative, systematic thought of Hegelian science is only what it is insofar as it has content to consider (*überdenken*), content that is supplied by the particular, natural sciences. I believe this is what Hegel means when he writes, 'It is not enough that philosophy corresponds with the experience of nature, but the origin and the formation of philosophical science has as a presupposition and a condition, empirical physics.'[43]

The question of the otherness of nature with regard to thought can only be grasped within a system that is a dynamic, mediated process. This explains why attempts to understand the Hegelian relationship between thought and nature in static terms, for example, in terms of correspondence, fail.[44] By presenting nature as the self-othering of the Absolute Idea, the system presupposes itself as *Wissenschaft*, or presupposes the possibility of knowing all of nature, of the Idea recovering its lost punctuality. However, this 'life-course' of the Idea is only possible through the agency of human thought thinking nature. In other words, the otherness of nature with regard to thought only obtains with regard to human knowing, or with regard to spirit. Without this human agency, there is no question of natural otherness as opposed to thought, just as there would be no system and no science within which the question could be meaningful. Consequently, we can say that the systematically necessary otherness of nature is *for us*, knowing subjects but only to the extent to which we can say the activity of our knowing participates in the systematic movement of the Absolute Idea and its project of knowing all of nature as itself.[45]

When Hegel looked out at the fearful dissymmetry of the night sky, the nauseating multiplicity of the Milky Way, he was looking at nature in its undigested, unmediated form, in a form of radical otherness to thought. In this light, the bitterness of his comment, calling the night sky a gleaming leprosy, reflects, on a human scale, the wrath of the Idea faced with what is still to be known, what has still to pass through the fiery crucible of thought. That there remains nature to be thought, that there is still chaos outside the system, implies an openness to the future. Indeed, from Hegel's notion of science as an absolute process reconciling thought and nature through human agency, a further implication arises: the idea of an open system. This solves the problem we witnessed in other attempts to come to grips with the otherness of nature within the system, which I qualified as Fichtean or Spinozist.

The possibility of an open system, conceived as having recovered natural otherness into itself while remaining open to further otherness outside itself, allows for nature to be both part of the system and outside the system, where this apparent contradiction, rather than being static, powers the process itself. In fact, this dynamic view of the life-course of the Idea sees natural otherness in temporal terms, in terms of the historical process that is the actual human history of the natural sciences. As a temporal process, it also implies the possibility (the necessity) of a future. This is another way of saying that the completion of the system is presupposed and indeed intuited from the absolute point of view (it is always already complete from a logical point of view) but open with regard to the 'second cycle of the absolute,' the human, historical process of knowing.

The view of system as process I am describing must not be collapsed into the 'processional' view I mentioned at the outset, where nature and logic are seen as somehow simply obeying the same dialectical three-step. We now understand that if both the Philosophy of Nature and the *Logics* run along dialectical lines, it is not because nature is somehow pre-programmed to follow these laws. Rather, it is because the Philosophy of Nature represents what obtains after the otherness of nature, dispersed in the infinite multitude of things (*Dinge*), has already been *thought*, that is, negated, liquefied, digested, and reborn as the representations, in fact as the *discourse*, of the natural sciences within the activity of spirit. This is how Yorick's skull fits in.

Yorick's Skull, or What Form Does Natural Otherness Take within the System?

The reference to Hamlet's graveyard scene comes from Hegel's *Phenomenology of Spirit*: 'One can have many thoughts about a skull, as with Hamlet and Yorick's, but the skull-bone itself is such an indifferent, natural thing, that nothing else is to be directly seen in it ... than simply the bone itself.'[46]

The above passage provides us with a vivid illustration of what happens to raw nature when it passes through the crucible of determining, negating, human thought, to be reborn in a spiritualized form and as such, ready to be taken into the system of science. Briefly put, it allows us to see how this spiritualized form of nature is essentially discourse. Only as such can it become a content of Hegel's discursive system of science.

While the *Phenomenology* is usually recognized as one of the great books in the history of philosophy, even by sober-minded analytic philosophers, most readers are puzzled and dismayed when they come upon, in the chapter on Observing Reason, a lengthy discussion of phrenology, in which the philosopher takes a great deal of trouble to demonstrate the specious nature of this pseudo-science. True, at the time, phrenology was, through the writings of Lavater and Gall, fairly well regarded as a science of nature, but surely the great philosopher should have recognized the quack nature of phrenology and not even bothered with it! In protesting against phrenology, Hegel doth seem to protest too much. In other words, that Hegel seems to take phrenology seriously enough to spend valuable pages refuting its axioms merely reinforces the belief that his philosophy of nature is just as dated and wrong-headed as the object of his reflections.

In fact, what Hegel objects to in his discussion of phrenology is the belief that the contingent objects of nature are in themselves meaningful.[47] The idea that the shapes and configurations of a skull immediately signify something that only needs to be deciphered is simply wrong. Its bumps and contours have no inherent significance. As a purely natural form, it does not tell us anything. It is not, as Hegel writes, 'a speaking movement.'[48] It is only when 'thinking is taken as active with regard to objects' that we get beyond the 'infinite mass of singular shapes and appearances' that 'nature offers us.'[49]

Still within the linguistic terms Hegel employs in the passage, the skull-bone is not a meaningful sign that points to something or represents something. Rather, we might say, it is an empty, arbitrary signifier or what Hegel calls elsewhere a 'name' as opposed to a meaningful word.[50] What is important to grasp for our discussion is that, as an empty signifier, the 'name' has the same status as any arbitrary, natural object. As an interchangeable token, the signifier is a naturally formed entity; that is, its present form is the result of a perfectly contingent chain of causes and effects, the same way a pebble has become what it is through centuries of *usage*, as expressed in the dual French meanings of 'wearing away' and 'use.' As Hegel writes: 'Names as such [are] external, senseless entities.'[51] The skull-bone is such an entity. It is an 'immediate being that does not even have the value of a sign.'[52] In order to signify something, it must first be 'worked up by intelligence,'[53] negated in the crucible of thought, in order to be reborn as a meaningful *word* in a discursive context. To say this another way, the skull-bone is only a content of science to the extent that it has been negated by thought and reborn in spirit. This takes the form of words.[54]

As a purely natural object, the skull-bone is an empty signifier waiting to be transformed by thought and given meaning. This is precisely Hegel's point. Yorick's skull-bone is, in itself, a meaningless natural object. It remains so until it is taken up and apostrophized by the character Hamlet. What was formerly a purely natural, contingent object/signifier is thus negated and transformed into a meaningful word within a famous discourse. It is now a 'speaking movement.'

In fact, Yorick's skull is not just part of Hamlet's discourse but part of a Shakespearean tragedy and as such, part of the discourse of great art. In Hegelian terms, we could say that Yorick's skull-bone is now spiritualized to the extent that it is part of world literature. We might even argue that Yorick's skull-bone is reborn in the highest, most spiritualized form, to the extent that the artistic discourse of which it is part is itself incorporated into the discourse of Hegelian science. In this way, the image of Hamlet apostrophizing Yorick's skull enables us to see how an inherently meaningless bone becomes scientifically meaningful, not as a natural thing, but only as a signifier that has been transformed in the crucible of thought and reborn as *logos*. Here, there is no longer an arbitrary link between signified and signifier. The things of nature are the potential words of scientific discourse, but only insofar as they die as 'names' and are reborn as the words of systematic science.[55]

Of course, Yorick's skull, as *artistic* discourse, is not meant to be part of the philosophy of nature. However, the same reasoning applies within the philosophy of nature itself, to the extent that its content is not nature itself, but nature as discourse, nature that has already been negated and spiritualized, reborn as the significant shadow of its former self. This discourse is the representational language of the natural sciences, which perform the same negating/preserving/uplifting operation on natural objects that Hamlet does on Yorick's skull-bone. Just as this natural object does not completely disappear but is taken up into the systematic discourse of Hamlet, so raw nature becomes part of the systematic discourse of Hegelian science, in that it reads and thinks, speculatively, the texts of the natural sciences. In other words, Hegel's philosophy of nature does not observe nature, it reads texts. This is why it is full of references to the natural sciences of his day. The discourses of these sciences, their representations, are the *stuff* of the philosophy of nature, and it is in this *spiritual* content that nature, itself comes to be an integral part of the system.[56]

By stating that Hegel's philosophy of nature takes the discourses of the natural sciences as its content, it is important to understand that I am not saying Hegel's science derives or deduces its categories from the results of particular, empirical research. I am saying that the philosophy of nature is speculative, conceptual thought addressing itself to these writings as content. Far from passively accepting this content into itself, Hegelian thought treats the representational content of these discourses as thought always treats its objects: actively and indeed violently.[57] But thought must encounter something; it must have a content to actively work on. Otherwise, if the categories of the philosophy of nature were completely independent of content, why would they bother referring to 'space' and 'time' at all? Why not simply remain in the sphere of such abstract categories as 'self-externality'?[58] As I hope to have convincingly argued, however, the content of speculative thought is not the sensuous intuitions of raw, undigested nature. If it were, 'animals would, in this way, also be physicists.'[59]

The mediating action of the natural sciences, grinding the bones of raw nature into the discursive content of the philosophy of nature, does nothing to attenuate the shocking otherness of nature itself. That this otherness continues to exist, in spite of the system's logical conclusion (*Schluss*) is proof of the dynamic meaning of identity-in-difference, of speculative thought. In fact, this painful otherness is the condition for any thinking activity at all. In other words, it is only because there *is* natural difference that there is anything for humans to think. The 'gleaming leprosy in the sky' represents the radical, scandalous otherness of nature. It is the chaos outside the system. It represents all that is still left to be thought, all that remains to be said, and perhaps ultimately, for the aging philosopher looking out the window at the night sky, all that will have to go unsaid.

Concluding Unscientific Postscriptum

When we consider Hegel's account of the Absolute Idea and its dispersal in nature, it is hard not to be reminded of certain elements found in contemporary Big-Bang cosmology theory. The chances of anyone involved in the mathematically based physics of today's cosmology considering Hegel relevant are extremely slim, and I am equally sure most Hegel scholars will find such an encounter anachronistic and jejune. Still, I want to consider some of the general concepts of Big-Bang theory in light of Hegel's science. In doing so, I am attempting an example of what I have been claiming Hegel does: I am thinking speculatively the representations of contemporary, positive science.

Singularity

Big-Bang theory postulates the existence of a singularity, out of which the universe exploded, inflated and expanded into its current state. Depending on whom you talk to, the universe will either continue to expand or collapse back onto itself (Big Crunch) into a black hole, leaving once again a singularity.[60] Accounts of the Big Bang tend to look backwards towards the beginning or origin of the universe and therefore toward the original singularity. Most accounts begin in the macrocosmic realm, governed by the theory of relativity and then move back in time. This move back is also, inevitably, a move to the microcosmic realm, governed by the strange principles of quantum physics. As we approach the original singularity, it is generally agreed that the 'laws' of physics 'break down,' to use the words found in most popular accounts of this state. Although physics attempts to look further back toward the beginning, creating super-dense matter in particle accelerators in the belief it will one day find the laws that govern matter at such high densities, the original singularity remains beyond all accounts. There is nothing more to say about it than what can truthfully be said about the Pamenidian One: it is. The reason for this is simply that if the singularity is the beginning, it makes no sense to enquire into the physical conditions or causes that gave rise to it and which might explain it. Otherwise the conditions or causes would precede the singularity, which would therefore no longer be the beginning. So Big-Bang theory must simply begin with the singularity as an axiom. This is another way of saying that physics can never tell us 'why' the Big-Bang occurred.

We can certainly adopt the Heideggerian approach here and simply recognize that what is at stake is the question of being, and dwell within it: why is there something rather than nothing? We can also take the ineffability of the singularity as an esoteric expression of divine agency. Faced with the question of being, even serious cosmologists like Stephen Hawking, whose famous *Brief History of Time* ends with the word 'God,' cannot resist indulging in metaphysics – as I cannot resist indulging in cosmology. However, if we look at the singularity in Hegelian terms, as the punctuality of the Idea, perhaps we can find something meaningful to say about it.

The punctuality of the Absolute Idea arises at the end of the *Logics*. The *Logics* present the articulations of thought as it thinks objectivity as becoming more and more subjective and then thinks subjectivity (or itself) as increasingly objective. The culmination is the absolute identity between objectivity and subjectivity, between reason and being, between thought and being. Here, in such an explosive identity, reason can be nothing other than raison d'être. I expressed this, above, in terms of the ontological argument: essence is so full of itself, it must spill over into existence. As Hegel would express it, the Concept cannot not be, so it is. It is, *because* it is, with the 'because' representing the reason it *is*. Being has every reason to be and so, *is*. How does this pertain to the Big Bang?

If the cosmological singularity is the absolute beginning, if it can have no cause outside itself, then it also must have its own reason within it. Its principle of sufficient reason (the principle by which, according to Leibniz, things are brought into existence) must be within itself. The singularity must be both reason and being or thought and being, as identical.[61] If the singularity is its own reason to be, then it must be. As well, it must *be* absolutely or universally, because it is absolute. There is only one original singularity per universe (I am not counting other entities called 'singularities' that are postulated and indirectly 'observed' in black hole astrophysics) and so the being of that singularity will also be universal, as will its raison d'être.

Contemporary cosmology also postulates a black hole type singularity at the Big Crunch, not in the past but in the future. This ultimate singularity would happen following the collapse of all matter and energy or entropy into what could only be described as the ultimate black hole, one resulting from the gravitational collapse of the entire universe. Of course, this future singularity must be the same as the past singularity. 'Both' are absolute and there is only room for one absolute. In other words, there cannot be two absolute singularities, unless we are talking about more than one universe, which I am not considering. Similarly, we might also say that true singularities are always the same *one* since there is nothing in them to predicate any difference. Consequently, the future singularity is the same as the past singularity and must therefore also be the identity of thought and being. This might explain a problem some contemporary cosmologists raise: the missing information. According to the Big Crunch scenario, the ultimate, universal black hole absorbs all entropy and information within it and then, when there is nothing else to absorb, evaporates. The question is, what happens to all the missing information, all the perceivable, understandable, graspable quanta of the universe? A Hegelian might answer that it subsists as thought, the universal thought we see compressed in the punctuality of the Absolute Idea. It would be, once again, absolute raison d'être or essence so full of itself ('that, than which nothing bigger can be conceived,' as Anselm said) that it could not help but spill over into existence.

Anthropic Principle

In order to explain some of the observable phenomena that seem to throw certain aspects of the Big Bang theory into doubt, *some* cosmologists have come up with the anthropic principle.[62] In its 'strong' form, the principle says the universe is the way it is, for example, relatively smooth and flat, because otherwise we would not be around to perceive, understand, or grasp it. Indeed, if the universe were any different, the physical conditions for our existence would be absent and we would not be able to ask the question of being. Hence, the universe is the way it is, because we are here to think it.

Stated this way, the anthropic principle resonates with Hegel's notion of natural otherness, as I presented it above. For one thing, the principle recognizes the universe as a process and tells us that there is a necessary correlation between the way it is and our ability to think it. Only in a very specific space/time, outside the singularity, is it possible for humans to think the universe. Hegel would define this state as one where nature appears in its otherness to human thought. Only in such a state can nature offer itself up as an object for thought *and* only in such a state is human thought possible. If there is no natural difference, there is no (human) thought and if there is no thought, there is no natural difference. However, while the anthropic principle tends to see human thought and consciousness as a very small window in the general opacity of the universal process, Hegel sees our agency as constitutive of spirit and as such, constitutive of the Absolute Idea's (self-)consciousness, a process that necessarily involves the Idea distinguishing itself with regard to the otherness of nature and then coming to see itself in nature by negating it through (human) thought. If we apply Hegel's life-course of the Idea in a cosmological context, if we see the expanded universe as a moment of difference between thought and nature, where the Absolute (singularity) has reached a point where it can reflect on itself as what it is not, then we arrive at the conclusion that the universe is (self-)conscious. If we accept that, however, we have once again proven the existence of God. For what else could such a thing be?

5 Presenting the Past: Hegel's Epistemological Historiography

The idea that Hegel does a priori speculative history has been largely put to rest, at least for those who care about the philosopher enough to have read him carefully or visited significant scholarship on the question of his philosophy of history.[1] It should now be clear that Hegel's philosophy of history is the history of consciousness and that forms of consciousness are tied to the spirit of the times and places in which they occur and can be witnessed. It should also be clear that Hegel respects the specificity of each epoch. True to the phenomenological method he describes in the *Phenomenology of Spirit*, each historical moment must be allowed to present itself. The philosopher of history must not do violence to this historical content by imposing upon it anachronistic, formal, a priori categories.

The reassuring phenomenological aspect of Hegel's philosophy of history, however, does not entirely cancel out the metaphysical or speculative dimensions of his historical thought, represented in the use of such disquieting concepts as Reason, Spirit, the Idea, the Absolute, and even God. Hegel apologists defending him against the twin-fronted attacks of continental postmodernists and sober-minded analyticals can only wish their philosopher had avoided using such terms altogether. For it is difficult to maintain that a philosophy of history is anything but a priori, speculative, and metaphysical when the philosopher seems to assert that history is driven by Reason, that the events of world history follow the pre-established program of universal Reason itself, and that history can therefore be understood according to inherent dialectical principles of its internal logic. Indeed, certain passages in the famous Introduction to his *Lectures on the Philosophy of History*, posthumously published under the title of *Reason in History*,[2] seem to make such affirmations. I do not believe such assertions adequately reflect Hegel's thought, however. Such misinterpretations are based on misunderstandings of what he actually means by both Reason and history.

The best way to comprehend the role Reason plays in history, and hence to grasp how Hegel actually conceives the philosophy of history, is by considering his epistemology of historiography, his theory of what makes the writing of history true and scientifically significant. It is the epistemology of historiography that is dealt with in the Introduction to the *Lectures on the Philosophy of History* – a fact perhaps obscured by the usual English translation of the term *Geschichtsschreiber*, which occurs throughout the German text, by 'historian' rather than by 'historiographer.' Here, Hegel is discussing nothing other than how the writing of history can be Scientific, in a way that is perfectly coherent with his definition of *Wissenschaft* as the systematic, actual articulation of the objective discourses of human knowledge. In other words, how can history itself be an objectively true discourse of Science?[3]

Exploring the historiographic dimension of what Hegel means by history reveals a different way of understanding its relation to 'Reason,' one that is coherent with Hegel's phenomenological method and evacuates some of the troubling metaphysical elements mentioned above.[4] The historiographic approach invites us to look closer at what Hegel really means by Reason, in the present context. Definition of the term is often taken for granted, or it is simply thought to signify something like 'logically determining' or even 'reasonable.' In fact, Reason has a technical meaning that is best presented by referring to what may be Hegel's last word on the subject, from eponymous chapter in the *Phenomenology of Spirit*: 'Reason is the certainty of being all reality.'[5]

Hegel's historiography does not seek to show how history is logical or reasonable. Rather, it arrives at the truth of history, which is Reason: the recognition that we are 'all reality' and that this reality is historical. To put it another way, the truth of history, attained through historiography, is the recognition that we are what we are through history and that history is what it is through us.[6] The certainty of this recognition is Reason, the truth of history. This is why it is important to see what Hegel means by 'Reason' in the Introduction and why he uses the term, somewhat devalued in the *Phenomenology of Spirit*, rather than Spirit or Idea. For indeed, it is certainly true to Hegel to say that history is the movement of Spirit or that it is the Idea's reappropriation of itself in time. However, neither Spirit nor Idea captures the essential selfness

Hegel ascribes to Reason.[7] From its post-Kantian, dialectical appreciation, Reason's role as a privileged expression of holistic, speculative
truth, for example in the *Differenzschrift*, comes to be usurped by Spirit,
the Idea, and more formally the Concept, leaving Reason a humbler,
more human destiny. It is the mutual recognition between the self and
the world that defines what Hegel means by the term. This recognition
is also the outcome of philosophical history.

It is only through the realization of this truth that something as
apparently arbitrary and chaotic as history can become part of Science.
The deeply epistemological question addressed in Hegelian historiography, which asks how history can become part of Science, must
involve the recognition of what history truly is: Reason, or the mutual
recognition between consciousness and the world as *having been*,
where history is seen as the story of the self (of freedom) and the self is
grasped as historical. The actuality of this apprehension, the embodiment of this co-habitation of consciousness and history, which is the
goal of the philosophy of history, *takes place* in the system of Science.
The historiographical aspect of this philosophy, whose content is
formed by original and reflective historiography, helps us understand
how its Scientific embodiment is essentially language, whether expressed in the *Lectures on the Philosophy of History*, in the *Philosophy of
Right* or in the Objective Spirit section of the *Encyclopedia*. History may
be many things, but unless it is language, it is nothing to Science.

To understand Hegel's epistemology of historiography, as he presents it in the first pages of the Introduction to his *Lectures*, it is necessary to be aware of the process of mutual recognition that takes place
between consciousness and its past, between the self and its world, not
as something static and immediate, but as a path of discovery. Hegel's
historiography is a pedagogical process that leads us to philosophical
history or to the truth of Reason and hence, to Science. The path itself is
a progression in historiography, in the writing of history, leading from
original history, through reflective history. These ways of doing history
are not to be taken as alternative 'methods' to philosophical history, as
the invented subtitle in *Reason in History* ('Methods of Writing History') may lead us believe, nor as 'Varieties of Historical Writing,' as
we find in another English translation[8] but rather as integral, constitutive 'errors,' as Hegel uses the term in the Introduction to the *Phenomenology of Spirit*. Original and reflective historiography are necessarily
experienced and subsumed moments without which philosophical
history would have no content and be therefore abstract and a priori.

The different types of historiography outlined in the opening pages of the Introduction to the *Lectures on the Philosophy of History* (or to *Reason in History*) correspond to different levels of consciousness presented in the first three chapters of the *Phenomenology*. This is not surprising, because for Hegel levels of consciousness represent different knowing relationships between subjectivity and objectivity. Historiography is a way of knowing the objectivity of history and is therefore consciousness. More specifically, original history, reflective history, and philosophical history reflect the knowing relationships (forms of consciousness) that appear in the *Phenomenology*, as well as in the *Encyclopedia*'s Philosophy of Subjective Spirit, under three main determinations: as sensible intuitions, as the reflective products of the understanding, and as mutual recognition.[9] Just as all knowing must begin with and go on to subsume immediate (unreflected) empirical knowledge, historiography must begin with original history.

The intuitive dimension of original historiography is, in fact, double. First, the original historiographer is the eyewitness of the world he describes. Second, he presents, or represents, this world before the eyes of those reading his account. This is possible because the original historiographers 'transform the events, actions, and situations present to them into a work of representation,'[10] which is essentially discourse.

There are epistemological conditions governing this first level of historiographical science. In other words, there are conditions governing the scientific truth of these original narratives or, in more Hegelian terminology, conditions whereby certain original accounts may form the content of Science, as Hegel understands it. Such truth conditions cannot be adequately grasped in terms of contemporary epistemological issues of historical realism and constructivism,[11] where the question is ultimately whether the truth of historical discourse is grounded in correspondence to facts or in its coherence within itself and to other accounts. As is typical when such unilateral options present themselves, as those offered by correspondence or coherence theories of truth, Hegel's solution seems to involve both. There is a certain amount of constructivism in the original historiographer's narrative, which Hegel likens to that of the poet, and yet the immediate presence of the historian's witnessing guarantees a necessary realism.[12]

While the original historiographer's narrative work shares the poet's use of imagination (production of images) and *Phantasie* (production of linguistic signs), these instances must be understood in the technical, psychological sense Hegel ascribes to them as central moments in the representing process (*Vorstellen*) itself, as Hegel describes it in the *Encyclopedia*'s Subjective Spirit section.[13] However, the content of the language produced by the historian is distinctively derived from witnessed 'actions, events, and conditions,'[14] which are transformed into images by the imagination and then stored as memories in the mind's subconscious (*Schacht* – mine), to be remembered and represented in language. That the images are derived through external, empirical perceptions makes them different from purely poetical constructions derived from inner emotions.[15] This is why Hegel protests against Niebuhr's idea that original history is derived from popular folk tales and songs.[16] Such an origin would place original historiography in the realm of poetry and deprive it of any grounding in reality. Since original historiography is the primary, fundamental content of history as it participates in Science, depriving it of its reality would deprive it of its specificity as (world) history. It would be (history of) art.

The original historiographer is immediately present in the epoch he describes, and his participation in the events and conditions, along with a certain degree of artistic *Phantasie* in the ability to represent this 'second nature' in discourse, combine to ensure the writing is *anschaulich*, which may be translated as 'having intuitive liveliness.'[17] Indeed, this 'intuitiveness' may be seen as Hegel's epistemological truth condition governing original historiographical accounts, which we might say combines both elements of realism and constructivism to attain something higher. This 'something higher,' this artful intuitiveness reflects a deeper truth than either that which stems from pure correspondence to facts or truth involving coherency of narrative. Intuitiveness means that the account captures the spirit (*Geist*) of its time. It may do so because the original historiographer is an actual participant in the events he describes. This immediate participation confers an immediate (non-mediated) actuality on his account and on his discourse, and ensures that his narrative is the spiritual embodiment of the epoch he is writing about.

It is necessary to insist upon the completely actual nature of this discourse, which lies at the heart of what Hegel means by *anschaulich*. Only by grasping the significance of this immediate narrative actuality can we grasp the mediated actuality of historical discourse as it reoccurs or takes place in systematic Science, through the presence of philosophical history. As we will see, this mediation is effected in the second level of historiographical knowledge, reflective history. First, I want to say a word about the actuality of original historiography.

We must understand this actuality as the stemming from the mutual presence of the historiographer and his world. In other words, the immediate knowing relationship between the knowing subject (historiographer) and the objectivity he is describing is represented in the actual historical account. The historiography is itself an objective expression of the spirit of the age. In fact, original historiography must be seen as really objective and existing, as the active embodiment of a certain form of spirit. Hegel expresses this powerfully in his comments on the original historiographer Thucydides, who re-presents the discourse of Pericles. It makes no difference whether Thucydides provides a faithful account of Pericles' actual words, since the former is just as much a participant in the *Zeitgeist* of classical Greece as is the latter. Thucydides' narrative is therefore just as real, just as much an 'action' (*Handlung*) as the event (the speech) it recounts.[18] It is discourse that is indistinct from the *Sittlichkeit*, the ethical life it describes. The ethical (in the Hegelian sense) actuality of Thucydides' discourse is the immediate, 'effective' expression of the participatory liveliness scientific discourse should accomplish, and when Hegel writes, 'In these orations these men expressed the maxims of their people, of their own personality, the consciousness of their political situation, and the principles of their ethical and spiritual nature, of their aims and actions,'[19] we may perhaps intuit the consummation Hegel reserves for (his own) Scientific discourse. I will return to this below.

Original historiography, the written, first-hand representations of participants in the spirit of their time, is for Hegel the stuff (*Stoff*) of history. Although the ancients provided some of the best models of this type of writing, it is important to see that original history is not exclusively ancient history. If it were, there would be no other history, and philosophical history would only have ancient Greece and Rome as subject matter. Medieval historiography can be found in the chronicles of bishops and humble monks, and more contemporary examples of original historiographers are Cardinal von Retz and Frederick the Great. Further, says Hegel, even 'today' original history continues to be written, in the form of 'reports' or accounts, some of which are 'excellent.'[20] This ongoing original historiography is significant because it means there will always be enough of what we might call 'primary source material' to reflect on, even if this material has become principally journalistic, which Hegel seems to be indicating when he speaks of 'reports' (*Berichte*), something he could certainly value as a former journalist. As well, having original historiography to reflect on is at least a necessary condition for any further philosophical history, an idea which may impugn what might be referred to as the 'strong version' of Hegel's 'end of history' thesis.[21]

The account of original historiography does, however, end with a reference to historians who, like Frederick the Great, because of their 'high social position' have a synoptic, more general view of their time than do those who 'peer up from below through a small opening.'[22] The synthesizing of individual points of view into a more general perspective represents a typical Hegelian *Übergang*, a transition or passage where one moment is pushed to its maximum and thus moves into its dialectical 'opposite.' Here, the dialectical nature of the transition is another indication that we are meant to grasp the different ways of doing historiography not as alternative methods but as levels of knowledge in an organic progression. Original history is not reflective; it is the immediate representation from an individual point of view. In a way, we can say that this individual point of view comes to contradict itself by becoming more general, leading to the subsequent, first level of reflective history, which is one of generalization.

The goal of historical science is to make history actual, to bring the past to the present in such a way that we may recognize ourselves in the past and the past in ourselves (Reason), so that the actuality of history may 'take place' in the effectivity of Scientific discourse. In this way, we can say that historical discourse comes to rediscover the effectivity it first enjoyed as immediate 'action' in the discourses of Pericles, as represented by Thucydides, but now enriched through mediation. This mediation takes place in reflective history, whose goal can thus be seen as a historiographical process, a way of writing history that takes the immediate representations of original history and makes them ours.

In general (not universal) history, the first form of reflective history, historiographers work on the immediate 'historical material,' the primary sources provided by the original historiographers, in order to provide the synoptic or general view of the history of a people or a country or the world. The general historiographer reflects on the material he is presented with and compiles it, synthesizes it or, in more Hegelian language, thinks it and sublates it into a newer, more thought-ful and therefore more spiritual representation. This reference to 'spirit' is not gratuitous. Since the reflective, general historiographer is representing past historiographical accounts 'for us,' for a contemporary time that is *not* that of the original account, his work necessarily means the investment of this newer time or spirit into the old material. Thus, 'Livy makes his old Roman kings, consuls, and generals speak in the fashion of accomplished lawyers of the Livian era.'[23] More suc- cinctly, the generalizing compilations make the past more present by re-presenting them in the spirit of a newer age. The best of these accounts are those that do not attempt to ape or imitate the particulari- ties of the original epoch (as, e.g., Johannes von Müller), which only serve to give the writing a 'stilted, hollowly solemn, pedantic charac- ter,' but rather those like Livy's that allow the more reflective writer's spirit to penetrate the original material and thus make it more actual. Once again, we see how Hegel's epistemological criterion of lively intuitiveness is directly related to spirit. Here, the *anschaulich* aspect of the reflective historiographical account is derived from the fact that its spirit is represented, and made present to us, in its discourse.

Pragmatic history, the next form of reflection on historical accounts continues this work of 'presenting the past' by making it present. (It seems that pragmatic history may reflect on either original or general historiography.) Although it claims to use the past in order to teach us moral or perhaps ethical lessons about the present, so that we may 'learn from the past,' in fact, as Hegel writes, the only thing we can really learn from past events is that the specificity of their conditions means they can teach us nothing useful. Rather than using the past to inform the present, pragmatic history does the exact opposite; it virtu- ally does away with the past altogether. 'It sublates the past and makes the given event present'[24] by investing it with the spirit of the reflective historian who seeks to impose on the rich chaos of the past his own universal, moral principles. In the best cases, where the writer is steeped in the spirit of his own epoch, he may do as the French do and 'spiritedly create a present for [himself] and refer the past to the present state of affairs.'[25] That the liveliness of these accounts depends so directly on the 'spirit of the writer' means they tend to arbitrariness, where 'each [writer] can think himself able to arrange and elaborate [the histories] and inject his spirit into them as the spirit of the ages.'[26] This subjective arbitrariness, which is, for Hegel, always present where morality is concerned, provides the dialectical *Übergang* or transition to the next form of reflective history, where personal arbitrariness is fully instantiated, critical history.

It is tempting to see Hegel's take on critical history as a kind of metacritique, a critique of the critique. Certainly, to the extent criticism is associated with Kantian idealism and more definitively and perhaps unjustly with Friedrich Schlegel's theory of irony, Hegel tends to see it as dangerously subjective and arbitrary. Indeed, the language Hegel uses in describing critical history, which produces 'unhistorical monstrosities of pure imagination' and 'subjective fancies – fancies which are held to be more excellent, the bolder they are' takes up expressions he uses elsewhere to qualify Schlegel's critical irony and makes it probable that his historical works are Hegel's target here.[27] This is interesting because Schlegel stands here accused of what Hegel is usually charged with: ignoring the 'factual basis,' the 'definite facts of history.' We must understand, however, that for Hegel, as I have shown, these 'facts' are only meaningful to the extent they are embodied in the discourse of history – in historiography, that they take place in narratives. To the extent that the critical historian does not take these accounts (*Erzählungen*) 'at their word,' but seeks only to look at them hermeneutically, one might say, there can no longer be any factual basis for historical science itself. The same result occurs as the one we witnessed with Niebuhr's idea that Livy's historiography is derived from popular folk songs, rather than from the accounts of original historiographers; history loses its textual foundation.[28]

Given Hegel's critical stance towards critical history and its 'subjective fancies,' how can it be part of the dialectical historiographical process that I am putting forward, one that affirms that the different 'methods' of historiography are different levels of historical knowing or consciousness, leading to Reason and Science? There are several answers to this, but I believe the main one can be stated as follows. For history to be actual, for it to be present to us, for us moderns (postmoderns?) to be able to recognize ourselves in it, it must also embody that which makes us who we are, modern, individual subjectivity. Critical history puts us in the story. To put it another way, pure freedom or pure subjectivity must be part of any historiographical process meant to lead to the actuality of mutual recognition.

On a more systematic level, absolute criticism provides the necessary dose of negativity, which is the animating soul of the dialectical movement the historiographical process follows. This dynamic is played out in other Hegelian contexts: the negating freedom of scepticism dissolves and renders fluid the uncompromising substantiality of the stoic world, just as, in another area, individual, moral freedom (*Moralität*) comes to break down the immediate unity of the Greek city-state. In order for historical knowledge to become speculative, in the true Hegelian sense of a systematic unity incorporating difference, it must integrate the difference between present consciousness and the past. This is also the space of our freedom, the fact that we are neither absolutely crystallized in the present nor determined by the causal chains of the past. Critical history is a necessary spacing between our past and our present, the separation without which the mutual recognition and reconciliation of Reason (self-knowledge through otherness) would be inoperable or meaningless.

As Reason, historical knowing is ultimately philosophical.[29] The final reflective form of historiography demonstrates this. History is a process of knowing. To say there is Reason in history is to say that history is the phenomenological story of the gradual co-penetration and mutual recognition of the knowing subject and the known object. We only know ourselves through history, and history is only something in that it is known. Furthermore, if historical knowledge is ultimately self-knowledge in otherness and self-knowledge in otherness is the goal of philosophy, history is necessarily philosophical. The final *Übergang* or dialectical transition that takes place in Hegel's epistemological historiography is found in the ultimate form of *reflective* history, that is, in its maximized form, where it actually becomes something else, *philosophy* of history.[30] In fact, this final form of reflective history is already, in truth, philosophy.

Unfortunately, this fact is 'lost in translation' when the final section of reflective history is referred to as 'fragmentary.'[31] A more appropriate title would be 'conceptual history,' to borrow the phrase from within Hegel's text itself. This is because the point of the passage is to show how the specific histories dealt with by this type of historical account (e.g., history of art, of law, or of religion), when they are fully carried out, must be grasped according to the movement of the concept, the same movement that we see played out in historical knowledge itself as it moves from the immediate intuitions of original history, through the mediating representations of reflective history, to their philosophical truth, incorporated into the system of Science. Thus, we can say that the history of art, as a discourse presenting (making present and indeed actual)' the historical knowledge of art, becomes the *philosophy* of art, the same way history, in general, becomes philosophy of history. This is why Hegel's extensive philosophies of art and religion and law (world history or history of state constitutions)[32] are all histories, philosophical histories of their subject matter. To these histories, we may add that of philosophy itself. The history of philosophy is, above all, philosophy. As is the case with historiography in general and with the specific histories of art, religion, and law, the goal is ultimately the knowledge or recognition that 'we are what we are through history,'[33] which also implies that history is what it is through us. Consciousness recognizes itself as historical and history recognizes itself as the path of consciousness, which is the most we can expect from Reason.

As Hegel writes in the Introduction to the *Phenomenology*, there is no distance between the method of philosophical knowing as it moves through phenomenological forms of consciousness and the actual content of knowledge. The form of knowing is always determined by what is known and vice versa. Similarly, we can see that the 'method' of historiography Hegel outlines in the Introduction to the philosophy of history is not to be separated from the content of history. Since this method implies different ways of representing history in language, we must conclude that history is fundamentally historiographical, that it is meaningless unless it is written. It is through this re-presentation that history *presents* itself to us as actual. Only as such discourse can history be part of Science.

If these affirmations have a postmodernist, constructivist flavor, it is not entirely because they refer to history as textual in nature. It is above all because joining together the epistemology of historical science (methods of knowing history), and historiography (methods of writing of history) and conflating both with what we generally mean by history itself is a thoroughly postmodern way of doing history. Frank R. Ankersmit describes the postmodern relation between epistemology and history in these terms: 'Epistemology is ... historicized in that the history of historical writing has now become the foundation of epistemology.'[34] Such affirmations echo what Hegel says about critical history, which 'is not history itself ... but rather history of historiography,'[35] which leads me to reaffirm the pivotal role of critical-reflective history in Hegel's philosophy of history. Without it, we would perhaps not be able to see that historical method, ways of knowing history, are integral to history. The fact that we do understand history as a historiographical process that is inherently epistemological provides support for my belief that Hegel's critical-reflective history is a necessary element in *our* ability to recognize ourselves in history, as it is represented to us. In order to preserve us from falling into the spurious portrayal of a postmodern Hegel, we simply have to recall that reflective history is only part of the story. It is preceded, on one side, by the empirical content of original historiography, and followed, on the other, by history's integration into systematic Science, the fact that history becomes philosophy (of history) and philosophy becomes Science. Those looking for the Hegelian 'end of history,' need look no further than this: history ends in Science.

I will conclude with several comments on history as it is related to systematic Science. This relation is essential. For if indeed the epistemological dimension of Hegel's historiography is inseparable from historical content and if, as I wrote above, the epistemological issue is how history can be Scientific, then what history actually is depends on its relation to Science. As well, while showing how Reason in history means it becomes *present* to us, in such as way that we recognize ourselves in it as mutually constitutive, I stated that the actuality of this recognition takes place in Science. So, it is necessary to look at the Scientific actuality of history.

In the final section of reflective history, what I called 'conceptual history,' it becomes apparent that the specific histories of art, law, and religion, when pushed to their maximum, when thoroughly grasped or conceived, become philosophy, namely the philosophies of art, of law, of religion. The end of art is the philosophy of art; the end of religion is the philosophy of religion; the end of law is the philosophy of law (right). This does not mean that there is no more art, religion, or law. It simply means that their histories necessarily end in philosophical discourse that integrates immediate intuitions and further reflections in present recognition. That all histories end in philosophy does not drown out their rich specificity in a night of black cows, and this is because these 'specialized' philosophies are integrated into Science. It is the systematic nature of fully articulated Science that preserves the specificity of the different historical contents. It is because the philosophies of art, religion, and law (world history) are part of the *Encyclopedia of Philosophical Sciences* that the specificity of their histories is maintained. Further, the actuality of these histories, the re-presented presence of their discourses, 'takes place' in the actuality of Science.

There is no reason the historiographical trail we have followed, leading from original historiography, to reflective historiography, to the texts of philosophical history (of art, of religion, of law), should not include the path's final embodiment in systematic Science. Indeed, this is the final locus of these 'conceptual' historical/philosophical discourses: in the book known as the *Encyclopedia of Philosophical Sciences*. This book was essentially conceived as a teaching manual and this reveals the truth of Scientific actuality, and of the historical/philosophical discourses that are part of it. That the content of Science was meant to be taught, and thus to actually take place in the world, reveals the performative or effective nature of historical/philosophical discourses within the State. The actuality of Science is its pedagogical destiny, which lies in its ability to form the world in which it is read and pronounced. We must not forget that all Hegel's writings on history, his historiography, are expressed either in actual lessons or in teaching manuals, within the university setting. In this actual world of Science, historiography rediscovers the vivacity and effectivity of its original accounts. No longer immediate, but re-presented now through reflective mediation, historical discourse within Science is the contemporary language of Thucydides, 'speeches that are actions among men.'[36]

Of course, by accepting the actuality of Hegelian Science in its own time, its presence in its epoch, we must also accept its temporal nature. It thus becomes an original account for us to reflect upon historically. In doing so, we make it part of history, part of us.

6 The State University: The University of Berlin and Its Founding Contradictions

The creation of the University of Berlin, in 1810, was the result of inter-action between the state and philosophy, two human expressions whose relationship, at least since Socrates' death and Aristotle's exile, has tended to be problematical. That university, which became an important model for North American institutions of higher learning, was from the outset a state university; it was designed and run by the state, as opposed to what had previously been the rule: institutions dependent on the church or princes.[1] The bind, of course, is that this idea of a modern university, defined by its independence from ecclesi-astical and private interests, must depend on the state to guarantee its independence. This dilemma is already apparent in the philosophical ideas at work in the University of Berlin's early evolution.

The ideas embodied in the Prussian state university project, through the consultative and administrative participation of Johann Gottlieb Fichte, Friedrich Daniel Ernst Schleiermacher, and Hegel, are in them-selves profoundly contradictory. Indeed, this modern notion of a state university seems to rest on two opposing currents of thought that engender two different conceptions of the state and the university's place within it. This contradiction necessarily involves the question of freedom. In the first part of this essay, I will trace the initial philosoph-ical tendency at work in the University of Berlin project; in the second part, I will show how Hegel, arriving at the university only eight years after its founding, stood opposed to this tendency.[2] The original con-tradiction is still pertinent in contemporary discussion of the univer-sity, since it is inevitably considered in relation to the state.

It is through the notion of *Bildung*, generally translated as 'culture' or 'education,' that I would like to approach the conceptual currents at work in the creation of the University of Berlin. *Bildung*, in its eighteenth-century philosophical acceptance, carries a Gnostic, even Neoplatonic etymological connotation, through its root *Bild* (image or picture), a reference to *energeia*, the radiant light of the good, the beautiful, and the true, illuminating the illuminated ones, regardless of their distance from the light's source. In fact, it is the tension between being *in* the truth and at the same time being removed from it that is essential to the notion of *Bildung* as grasped by the first theorists of the state university: Fichte, Humboldt, and Schleiermacher.[3]

The theoretical dimensions of *Bildung* these thinkers inherited through such loosely defined 'movements' as the *Aufklärung*, the *Sturm und Drang*, early German romanticism, and speculative idealism, are, to say the least, complex. Nonetheless, a brief genealogy of the concept can be traced using the Leibnizian monad as a point of departure. The monad is a pertinent model since it reflects the tension I see as essential to notions of *Bildung* from the period in question, that is, the tension between perceiving the light of truth and remaining removed from it. Indeed, the monad, which is defined as nothing other than perception and appetite, is essentially a perception of the truth and an aspiration towards it. The conceptual model of the monad is germane to the two distinct currents of thought I will examine, each of which holds its own notion of *Bildung*.

One current, stemming from the *Aufklärung*, interprets the monad's perceptive aspect in terms of universal reason, as we later find it developed in Kant and Lessing. This fundamentally rationalist view of the human soul produces a universal expression of 'humanity': a community of rational beings to which every human belongs, a priori. The apologists of universal reason understand the appetitive aspect of the monad as a *Streben*, a tendency and ultimately the 'infinite progress' of reason, and therefore of humanity, towards the true, the good, and the beautiful, the three unconditioned instances at the heart of Kant's three *Critiques*.[4]

The other current stems from the rejection of *Aufklärung* ideals that characterizes the multifaceted and evanescent *Sturm und Drang* movement. This involves, above all, a refusal to consider reason as an instrument capable of adequately perceiving the truth. Representatives of this movement, tired of the endless wait implied by the notion of infinite progress, find another means to achieve an edifying vision of absolute truth; the immediate knowledge implied in *feeling* is adopted as an important aspect of *Sturm und Drang* thought, and along with feeling, the promotion of nature as an expression of truth itself. This idea is radically opposed to the Kantian or Hegelian idea of supernatural, and even counternatural reason.

However, far from abandoning the monadic model with its double axis of perception and appetite, *Sturm und Drang* thinkers reinterpret it to come up with a new notion of *Bildung*. No longer related to reason, the perceiving aspect of the monadic soul becomes a pure 'pathos.' It is the *immediate* feeling of truth as nature. This immediacy is possible since there is no distance between nature and the feeling soul. They co-penetrate and identify with each other. In fact, the soul becomes nature and nature becomes a soul. The appetitive element of the monad is expressed within this sentimentalist *Sturm und Drang* approach to *Bildung* as a natural instinct. In other words, the natural soul is attributed a *Trieb* or a pulsion. Borrowed from the natural sciences of the time, the notion of *Trieb* applies to the soul as a thoroughly natural entity.

Since nature *is* truth and the soul is a natural entity that knows the truth immediately through feeling, this instinct towards truth may seem superfluous. However, in this context *Trieb* has to be understood as the very soul or animus of nature itself. It is an infinite instinct that is the pulse of nature and therefore the pulse of the human soul as natural. This pulse is expressed in the concept of genius, an entirely natural and therefore creative quality that expresses itself in humanity through art and feeling.[5]

Although nature as *truth* can readily be understood to express itself, through sentimental genius, in the *beautiful*, an expression of the common *good* appears to be missing. This is because the link the *Aufklärung* thinkers establish between universal reason and the good seems to underlie any coherent notion of community. Rejecting universal reason seems to simultaneously preclude any possibility of universal recognition, and therefore any possibility of concrete, ethical good. Indeed, theories of genius and feeling remain essentially individualistic, even solipsistic; they refer to the individual and his or her natural, interior universality. What is missing is worldly particularity, a necessary although not sufficient condition for ethical good.

Herder's concept of the genius of a people can be seen as a *Sturm und Drang* response to the need for a theoretical instance of ethical or common good. As perhaps the most illustrious representative of this movement, if we except the young Goethe, Herder developed the concept of a people as a natural, shared, or specific expression of cultural tradition. If a people remains a unique, singular whole, it is because within it nature is expressed in each individual in a common fashion.

In this context, the monadic appetite for or towards the good is translated into an expression and ultimately an affirmation. The genius of the individual expresses the genius of the people and the genius of the people is expressed in its self-affirmation before other peoples. This self-affirmation is especially manifest in a people's attempts to rediscover its own properties, its 'original' myths, traditions, and linguistic forms, by purging them of exotic expressions that are the properties of other peoples.

In the late 1700s, this notion of a people's cultural self-affirmation constitutes a new definition of *Bildung*, conceived in terms of a natural impulse or drive, a *Bildungstrieb* directed towards a Golden Age 'of nature,' more authentic (good, beautiful, and true) than the present. This notion of *Bildung* is radically different from the one associated with the *Aufklärung*. For although both involve monadic tension – of being in the truth (perceiving it) while still being removed from it (tending towards it) – the *Bildung* defined by the natural self-affirmation of a people is not the infinite progress of universal reason. For the latter, nature remains something external, constraining, a resistance against which reason in its freedom must fight in order to enforce its laws. Conversely, according to the new conception of *Bildung*, it is reason itself that appears as something external, constraining, and unnatural.

Two opposing notions of the state and liberty emerge from these two intellectual currents. The notion of a people stemming from the naturalist conception of *Bildung* is 'naturally' opposed to the essentially rational idea of the state that arises from the *Aufklärung*. The naturalist conception sees the state as essentially external and mechanical; it is a clockwork assembly, more or less effective, and related more to necessity than to freedom. Thus, for both Herder and Fichte, it is the nation and not the state that expresses the genius of a people.

The concept of freedom, however, proves problematical for the naturalist, *Sturm und Drang*, and ultimately romantic current; in rejecting *Aufklärung* reason, these thinkers have to also refuse any idea of freedom that flows from it, whether this means freedom conceived as free will or as Kant's practical reason. In both cases, freedom is based on the primacy of reason and its power to determine nature for the good. The problem is that while the legislative and 'liberating' power of reason (against natural determinism) may also be understood as a repressive and heteronomous element, it is not immediately clear how the other pole, nature and natural sentiment, can provide a foundation for the concept of freedom, not only because nature had always been thought of in terms of necessity, but also because the immediacy of the nature-soul relation implies an immediate determination between natural feeling and the source of that feeling: nature. Briefly put, this relation seems to annul any distance and therefore any possibility of decision. In the ethical field, this implies that the soul of a people will be a purely natural entity, immediately determined by nature, a condition apparently irreconcilable with any expression of freedom, a fundamental principle of ethical good.

Although they interpret it rather freely, early German romantics find in Fichte's *Doctrine of Science* a theoretical structure able to support a new expression of freedom. In the Fichtean context, freedom appears as the self-positing of the *I*, simultaneously positing a not-*I* by which it limits itself. Perhaps inspired by Spinoza's idea that the Substance's freedom consists in its self-determination (self-limitation), Fichte discovers freedom in the self-positing (self-limiting) of the *I*, a movement he applies exclusively to the subjectivity of consciousness but which the romantics ascribe to nature as a whole. Nature is thus attributed subjectivity. In other words, national genius and national freedom can now be expressed as self-positing, or natural self-determination. A people's freedom is its self-affirming self-definition, defining itself through its affirmation. This movement is expressed as *Bildung*, not a state's but a nation's. This is the first current of thought participating in the creation of the University of Berlin.

The problem then becomes the apparently paradoxical role of the state in this creation. Indeed, in espousing the *Bildung* project of the German nation, the Prussian State, because of its own perceived 'mechanical,' unnatural 'nature,' seems, at the same time, to divorce itself from the project. This ambiguity is obvious with Fichte himself. In 1793, before the *Doctrine of Science*, he refuses all state participation in the work of *Bildung*, attributing the educative function to society in general, to the private sphere and particularly to the family, while in 1807, when he was called to the Prussian ministry of education to participate in the creation of the University of Berlin, he then accords the main educative role to the state.[6] However, in taking on this role, the state is nonetheless meant to fill a purely instrumental function, perfectly adapted to its mechanical nature, thus serving the German nation in its self-actualization through *Bildung*.

This expression of *Bildung* still draws from the Gnostic or Neoplatonic source I referred to above; universal truth is revealed in a particular people striving to regain the Absolute. Since the state university is grasped as an essentially *national* institution, it requires a special ontological status. With reference to the monadic model I've been using, the state university represents the place where the Absolute is clearly perceived and where the appetite for attaining it is strongest. Fichte's acceptance speech, upon becoming Rector of the University of Berlin in 1811, is remarkable in this regard. Here, the university is seen as nothing less than 'the most important institution, and the most sacred thing possessed by humankind.' Fichte continues: 'Since the communication that takes place there maintains and transmits ... everything divine that has ever occurred in humanity, within [the university] lives humanity's true being, its uninterrupted life, sundered from all decay, and the university is the visible presentation of our species' immortality, the visible presentation of the unity of the world, as a divine manifestation, as God Himself.'[7]

When the university project is defined in these terms, it is easy to understand why the philosophical research of that time, grappling with the Absolute, was the worthiest of academic disciplines; it embodied the very expression of that project itself. In any case, the university's unique ontological status implies several founding principles. Their trace can still be observed in the university as it is largely conceived in the West, today. These principles are rooted in the romantic conception of *Bildung*, as I have been examining it.

One, the university, an expression of national freedom, must have absolute freedom in relation to the mechanistic state. Moreover, the state must put itself in the service of the university. Thus, Fichte's 1811 University of Berlin speech demands 'complete freedom, academic freedom in the broadest sense of the word,'[8] for the University, an autonomy declared primarily from any strictly utilitarian ends the state might try to impose on it. The university should not become a professional training school for state functionaries, for example. Even if the German university was, de facto, a place where civil servants were educated, the program was not conceived *in view of* this end. Instead, a university education was meant to cultivate in them an appreciation for the *Bildung* project and thus adapt them to the state's assigned role, in the service of this project. In any case, the result was a class of particularly cultivated civil servants. In the same way, although the traditional faculties of medicine, law, and theology provided careers in the professional world, these professions remained subservient to the national project.

Two, the university is above all a place for pure research. The idea that the individual efforts of each researcher express a genuine cultural drive (*Bildungstrieb*), and therefore participate in the national project, gave rise to a university system that encouraged innovators. At Berlin, the *Privatdozenten* and the *Extraordinariis*, directly remunerated by students attending their classes, and not by the State, were young researchers/doctors appointed, but not employed, by the university to develop and disseminate the fruits of their personal research and participate in university life while waiting to be hired by the state as professors.

From its beginnings, the University of Berlin was consequently defined as superior to and independent of the state that created it. Philosophy, that is, science, as represented by Fichte, Schelling, Schleiermacher, Humboldt, and Pestalozzi, not only provided the theoretical underpinnings of the institution but expressed its very spirit, its freedom conceived as an expression of self-determination taking place within a broader expression of national self-affirmation.[9] When he arrived in Berlin in 1818, Hegel strongly challenged these philosophical foundations and their attendant notion of freedom, along with the ontological status of the university itself. By examining Hegel's conception of the state university here, I not only want to show how his vision is opposed to the original one, but how his contrasting vision is also constitutive of the state university institution.

Hegelian philosophy is a philosophy of state insofar as the state is a manifestation of spirit's objective truth rather than nature's; the purely natural is radically devalued by Hegel. He remains fundamentally inspired by the *Aufklärung*, by universal Reason as he found the notion in his youthful readings of Lessing, where it largely surpasses any purely calculative, ratiocinative definition. In Hegel, Reason, which evolves into the concept of spirit, must be grasped as the activity (the life) of thought manifesting itself in the world as the human oeuvre: the state, religion, art, and, above all, the ultimate work that comprehends all the others, philosophy. Nature only makes up the raw material for the activity of human thinking. Nature is pure exteriority, devoid of all self-movement and life. As long as nature remains unpenetrated, unworked and unfashioned by thinking, it remains lifeless. Thinking (and human action is also a manifestation of thinking) 'kills' this *nature morte* and thus breathes life into it, the true life of spirit.[10] Consequently, *Bildung*, human culture, is an expression of neither nature nor the fundamentally natural entity that is the nation. *Bildung* is a particular form of objective spirit, situated within a more general manifestation of objective spirit: the state.

Hegel does not deny that *Bildung* has a natural element: the ethical training a child receives in the bosom of the family, the customs, the traditions, and the national language, all stem from the natural element in that they are determined by nature in an immediate unreflected way. But this natural aspect is only a moment, the first in a dialectical movement of mediation through civil society, that is, the bourgeois life of production and possession within a system of needs. This movement, as a movement of thought, negates the natural aspect of *Bildung* and thus mediates its immediateness. Education represents the dissolution of the family, the child's first entry into the system of needs.[11] The child leaves home, goes to school where the family's particular and selfish interests are mediated or subsumed (but also conserved, according to the economy of *Aufhebung*) to the more universal interests of civil society.[12] This universality (or generality) only appears as such, however, in relation to the family's singular or individual interests. In fact, this relative generality proves to be no more than particular, on the level of the genus or the corporate. Indeed, society is divided into corporations, each one representing a particular interest or need of civil society.

The third moment of this dialectic of objective spirit, of Reason in the world, is that of the state, although this must be grasped as the result of the two preceding moments, family and civil society; the result preserves them as subsumed but still at work within itself. Thus the concept of state in Hegel is essentially organic rather than mechanistic. It is not only the culmination of a dialectical process, but the manifestation of the whole syllogism of ethical substance in its genuine generality. As with the *Aufklärung* thinkers, the state is defined in terms of reason, but instead of being reduced to a rational mechanism, Hegel's state is Reason itself, the life of spirit in its objective moment. Moreover, the state represents *actual* freedom, more concrete than the formal, abstract freedom of civil society with its juridical or contractual references to the 'person.' In the context of the state, freedom proves concrete, actualized in institutions. In other words, in state institutions, singular will recognizes general will as its own.

In Hegel, *Bildung* represents an intermediary instance rather than the final, recapitulating moment of objective spirit that is the state.

The university moment, which is part of *Bildung*, only acquires meaning within the passage from the natural immediacy of family to the generality of state.[13] The university is not, as we saw with Fichte, the crowning of a monadic project both *in* and *towards* the absolute. The university is, rather, a preparation for active involvement, a place where man learns formally what he will effect in earnest within the public sphere, that is, within the state taken as the expression of actual freedom. From this viewpoint, academic freedom can only be relative and abstract. Even if the educational process carries, as its significant content, the moments through which it has passed, the moments of family and school, the process remains empty and abstract if it is not completed in the actual, professional life of a corporation of the organic state. To put it another way, in order to participate in the really general freedom of the state, academic freedom must be relativized. Far from serving the university, with its absolutist pretensions, the state has the right to demand that this *particular* corporation recognize its own intermediary role as subordinate to the *general* interest of the state.

It is therefore understandable how Hegelian philosophy became, at the University of Berlin, the official philosophy of this State institution. Indeed, this is not only because of the ultimate right Hegel accords the state and its institutions, but, on a less theoretical level, because of the friendly and professional relations that Hegel enjoyed with Prussian Minister of Education, Karl von Altenstein, and the secretaries Johannes Schultze and Friedrich von Raumer.[14] Already in Nuremberg, Hegel scrupulously fulfilled the many administrative responsibilities that went with his teaching activities, although he did so more from a sense of duty than enthusiasm, and won the admiration of the Bavarian authorities. Of course, Hegel's dedication earned him additional responsibilities and in 1813 he became education secretary for the city. By the time he left Nuremberg, Hegel had already been a state civil servant (of Bavaria) for eight years.[15]

Hegel, however, saw himself as more a pedagogue than an administrator and he tended to consider the latter responsibilities as impediments to the former function.[16] In fact, his own teaching experience provided the basis for his ideas concerning the teaching of philosophy: that it could form a content the learned professor could convey to unlearned students, that philosophy could be taught. The belief that philosophy has real content, which 'the master possesses, considers beforehand [and which] the students consider afterwards,'[17] denotes a pedagogical attitude radically opposed to the one inspired by Kantian critical thinking, according to which philosophy cannot be taught, only 'philosophizing'[18] can. It is against this idea and the related sceptical tendency that Hegel argues, in an increasingly polemical fashion, in his pedagogical writings from the Nuremberg and Berlin periods. In fact, the critical trend Hegel encounters at Berlin derives from the romantic notion of *Bildung* I described above. Hegel's assertion that philosophy can (and must) be taught implies another notion of *Bildung*, which ultimately determines philosophy's place within the university and the university's place within the state.

For Hegel, the teaching content of philosophy is the content of philosophy itself. As such, this content is articulated in three moments: as content derived through the acquisition of factual knowledge stemming from the understanding, with the subject-object split this entails; logical or dialectical training where formal contradictions engender negating doubt, which dissolves the hard unilaterality of the first moment of factual knowledge so that the third recapitulating moment can take place, the identity of identity and difference, or the system of speculative philosophy as a whole. However, the 'soul' of this movement, its animus, is in no way different from the method by which it is taught, which evolves naturally from the content itself. In other words, philosophical content itself moves through these three moments. Teaching has only to follow it.[19] To understand the position philosophy occupies within the university and how the university relates to the state, it is necessary to take a closer look at this content.

Philosophical content, in its initial moment, must be introduced at the *Gymnasium* level,[20] through the teaching of law, ethics, and religion. This content is not yet, in fact, philosophy as such, but only the content of philosophy *in itself*, which will later develop along speculative lines (in and for itself). Studying law and ethics means acquiring relatively formal knowledge, by studying the texts of Greek and Roman culture as well as Christian doctrine and dogma. This acquired textual content is the real substance of philosophy, without which it would be no more than empty, abstract reasoning. This is how we should understand the objective claim of Hegelian philosophy, its opposition to any purely subjective, metaphysical construction. According to Hegel's conception, philosophy is nothing as long as it is not philosophy *of* something. This 'something' is the content of philosophy. It is not a matter of subjective elaborations, and ideas 'thrown into my mind like stones.'[21] The determinations of philosophy, its textual content, must be learned, and this training (or apprenticeship) is the necessary first moment of philosophical education.

The second stage of Hegelian philosophical training, still at the *Gymnasium*, is the one ascribed to the dialectical moment, that is, to the moment of negativity, of radical scepticism that comes to dissolve the fixed, unilateral knowledge of the initial moment of the understanding we just looked at. Here, then, the term 'dialectic' reclaims its ancient meaning, found in Zeno: the confronting of two antithetical and paradoxical assertions in such a way that they contradict each other. Besides the 'dialectics of the ancient Eleates,'[22] the Hegelian program included, with some reservations, the Kantian antinomies as well as Aristotelian and Leibnizian logics. The passage between the first moment of formal understanding and second dialectical moment happens quite naturally in that, according to Hegel, the unilateral content of the first moment actually does contradict itself, or rather, the content is, because of its unilaterality, self-contradictory. Learning dialectical thought merely elucidates the contradictory truth inherent in the understanding's way of thinking, in order that it may come to grasp itself speculatively. This is the final, crowning moment of philosophy's teaching; as philosophy per se it comprises, within itself, the other moments and their contents, now fully deployed. Speculative philosophy, which fulfils at the university the two preceding stages, suspends any possibility of becoming stuck in one or the other; such a fixation would lead to either a purely formal philosophy of subjective understanding or to a radical scepticism, or involve an unresolved dichotomy of both. Hegel recognizes that the speculative level of philosophy is 'naturally what is most difficult,'[23] and this, for a very specific reason: it is the truth. The place where truth is *taught* is the university.

The difficulties of philosophical instruction, according to Hegel, are to some extent those of teaching the 'other sciences,'[24] that is, the practical difficulty involved in combining 'clarity with depth and an appropriately detailed development' while also requiring that the instruction fall within 'time constraints, generally a semester, which must be stretched or shortened depending on the science taught.'[25] On the other hand, presenting philosophy at the speculative or university level has its own specific difficulties. For as philosophy forms the systematic totality of knowing, the truth, it must comprise all the particular sciences within itself. Rather than simply articulating 'several universal formulae,'[26] it must penetrate and deploy itself in theology, law, natural sciences, art, and history in order that these sciences acquire their 'remoulding and their acceptance into the new [speculative] idea.'[27] Thus the 'former material,'[28] the older sciences, must not be abandoned, and the new 'materials of the specific sciences'[29] must not be ignored; the ultimate meaning and truth of all this material depend on its becoming the object and content of philosophical science. In Hegel, this objective content is contained in his university-level teaching manual, the *Encyclopedia of Philosophical Sciences*, the most complete articulation of 'his' system.

In fact, the possessive pronoun 'his' is completely at odds with Hegel's intention. As opposed to designating a purely subjective construction, the *Encyclopedia* is meant to form the system or the science (the two terms are virtually synonymous in Hegel) of human spirit, the fruits of human thought. Thus philosophy is 'a systematic complex of sciences full of content,'[30] and studying it involves the difficulty, the enormous labour, of learning the content of the 'positive sciences.'[31] As Hegel puts it, 'the study of these sciences is necessary for a profound insight into philosophy.'[32] This labour of learning was certainly not foreign to Hegel himself. A voracious reader, a keeper of 'file cards' from the age of fourteen, he could perhaps claim universal knowledge at a time, no doubt the last, when this remained possible. In other words, he possessed a general culture, a *Bildung*, which, in most cases, his students seemed to be lacking, a factor representing, in his eyes, the biggest impediment to the teaching of philosophy. This 'lack of knowledge, the ignorance'[33] he noticed in his students was not the result of mere gaps in their education, but rather it stemmed from a misguided philosophical conception, widespread at that time: a notion of *Bildung* completely different from the one implied by a general culture, formed through knowledge of objective truth, painstakingly acquired.

In his pedagogical texts, Hegel takes a clear polemical stand against the romantic conception of *Bildung*, which represents, in his view, an obstacle to the development of the speculative Idea. By asserting that 'the possession of specific and varied knowledge is superfluous for the Idea and even beneath it,'[34] *Bildung* understood as self-affirmation ignores genuine content and contradicts true philosophy defined as the objective totality of knowledge. It is this notion of *Bildung* that lies at the heart of the pseudo-philosophies of critical thinking and sentiment. These are purely subjective and formal expressions of selfish, abstract freedom and represent what Hegel refers to as a 'thinking-for-oneself.'[35] This essentially solipsistic thinking leads to the 'absurd madness ... according to which everyone wants his own system.'[36] It can only be expressed in 'the form of feeling, imagination, confused concepts'[37] printed on 'one or two pages that supposedly contain everything essential about all of philosophy or one of the particular sciences it contains.'[38] In his letter to von Raumer on teaching philosophy at university, Hegel takes up the same argument he used ten years earlier in the Preface to the *Phenomenology of Spirit*. Immediate knowledge of the truth is ultimately subjective and empty. Thinking-for-oneself, exclusive of true objective content, is nothing more than a thinking-*of-oneself*.

What Hegel is targeting in his criticism of philosophical teaching at the university is therefore ultimately the conception of *Bildung* as the *I*'s self-affirming genius, which, reflecting itself in a people, in the nation, is expressing Nature as absolute freedom. To this conception of subjective, individual, and national freedom, Hegel opposes concrete freedom, the shared, particularized freedom within the organic state.

The polemical character apparent in certain of Hegel's Berlin writings attests to this opposition. Within the University of Berlin itself, where Hegel was at odds with Schleiermacher, the 'theologian of feeling,' this conflict was exacerbated by the murder of the writer-diplomat August Friedrich Kotzebue, in Mannheim in 1819, by the theology student Karl Ludwig Sand, who was enroled at the University of Jena. As this fanatical patriot belonged to a *Burschenschaft*, a liberal, nationalist student association, his criminal act provoked severe police repression from the State, which was to stifle university life in Germany for years to come.[39] When Professor Wilhelm Martin De Wette in Berlin appeared to excuse Sand's crime (in a letter to his mother), the State relieved him of his teaching responsibilities. Hegel, contrary to Schleiermacher, spoke out in favor of the State's right to do so, 'providing it leaves him [De Wette] his salary,' an opinion that Schleiermacher judged as 'pitiful.'[40]

No doubt, from Hegel's point of view, Sand's action was an extreme expression of purely subjective, abstract freedom, the actualizing of the 'philosophy' of thinking-for-oneself. Such an action rips apart the organic wholeness of the state, to the extent that it reacts, as would an external, mechanistic power, against one of its corporations and certain individuals. This is the state's right because it is ultimately seeking to re-establish its lost wholeness. The teaching of philosophy must preserve the state from such rips in its fabric, for what is in fact taught is freedom, not the abstract, subjective variety but freedom engendered by the reciprocal recognition at work in the organic state in which the university is a particular corporation.

A corollary to this is that Hegel's extensive pedagogical activity is itself sufficient reason to refute any thesis that, according to him, the world has already arrived at the end of its history or actualized absolute knowledge. On the contrary, as long as the teaching of philosophy is felt to be what he called 'a need of the time,' history is not finished, and the lesson of freedom has still to be learned.

I have attempted to show how two opposing notions of *Bildung* give rise to two opposing ideas of freedom, of the state and of the university's situation within it. In Hegel, although the university can be seen as the embodiment of systematic philosophy and its contents, it remains a specific corporation where this objective content, which has already been grasped by speculative science, is taught. In such a context, academic freedom is relative. Conversely, the other tendency conceives of the university as a place where the truth reveals itself through pure research. In this context, both academic freedom and the ontological status of the university tend towards the absolute.

However, in spite of its corporate status within the organic state, Hegel's university, as the embodiment of the philosophical sciences, can be seen as determining the form of the underlying system of education and its institutions. After all, the purpose of this system is to provide students of the *Encyclopedia* the content necessary for their speculative reflections.

7 Music and Monosyllables: The Language of Pleasure and Necessity

In the *Phenomenology of Spirit*, in the less-discussed Reason section, there is a short subchapter called 'Pleasure and Necessity.' In 'Reason,' consciousness, on its journey of self-discovery, arrives at a stage where it seeks to find itself not just in one other individual but in the world, in 'all reality.'[1] After first attempting to recognize itself immediately in nature, by observing it theoretically, consciousness now seeks this self-recognition in otherness through different levels of practical (moral) engagement in the world.

This passage from theoretical to moral reasoning retraces the logic of what Hegel calls subjective idealism, as found in both Kant and Fichte. In both cases, the strivings of theoretical reason become moral in their endless efforts for accomplishment. In Kant, the unconditioned thing-in-itself eludes theoretical knowledge, only to be formulated in the Categorical Imperative, where the moral law is postulated as a universal law of nature. In Fichte, the theoretical, self-reflecting *I* engenders a Not-*I* against which it measures itself ethically. For Hegel, of course, the abstractions of subjective idealism, whether theoretical or moral, will always remain on the level of immediate self-reflection. Subjective moral consciousness will prove just as unsuccessful as theoretical consciousness in its attempts to actually be in the world and, therefore, to find itself in the world. For this to happen, moral self-reflection must give over into real ethical activity.

In 'Pleasure and Necessity,' Hegel is claiming that the first level of moral self-reflection is through feeling, perhaps inspired in this by both Kant (the feeling of respect for the moral law) and Rousseau (pity). However, the feeling that Hegel is referring to is sexual. The first stage of morality, and therefore the first step towards real ethical activity, involves the attempt to immediately find oneself at home in the world through erotic agency and the feeling of sexual satisfaction. This is what the erotic pleasure-seeking individual is really after: the immediate feeling of union in otherness through which he recognizes himself as all of reality. Needless to say, the very immediacy of this self-knowledge, its absolutely sensual nature, means it must fail, but it does not do so because it is wrong or false or morally bad. Sexual pleasure fails simply because it is immediate or unmediated by real activity of a more communal nature. In fact, the immediate erotic satisfaction of feeling oneself in the other actually prefigures intuitively the final ecstatic moment of the *Phenomenology of Spirit*, the ultimate satisfaction of truth as represented in the closing image of the foaming chalice of spirit. However, here the satisfaction has been mediated over the entire epic of consciousness and spirit. The danger, as always in this work, is premature satisfaction, endless repose in the arms of Circe, forgoing the efforts of mediation.

I want to look closer at why the feeling of erotic satisfaction fails. This is interesting because, according to the dialectical logic that we find in the *Phenomenology*, self-knowledge through sexual pleasure will not fail because of some external idea, some better idea, which, when compared with sexual satisfaction, shows it to be deficient. Carnal knowledge must fall on its own accord. It must bring about its own demise, and this is what happens in the passage called 'Pleasure and Necessity.' Pleasure comes up against a type of necessity that causes it to go under. Although this necessity at first appears alien to pleasure, it must show itself to be inherent in sexual pleasure itself. Consequently, looking at the failure of sexual satisfaction as a form of knowing allows us to see how something in the structure of erotic pleasure itself causes its demise. We can only discover what this is by understanding what Hegel means by necessity in this context.

The literary reference in the 'Pleasure and Necessity' subsection is Goethe's first published version of *Faust*, the so-called *Faust-Fragment*, from which Hegel quotes.[2] Using this reference as a key to understanding pleasure and necessity is of limited help, I believe, partly because of the inevitable ambiguity in the rather elliptical literary work itself and partly because of the esoteric nature of Hegel's reference to it. Besides a few quoted lines, there is nothing explicit in the passage from the *Phenomenology of Spirit* to tie it further to Goethe's work. I say this in full recognition of the fact that H.S. Harris, in his commanding commentary on the *Phenomenology*, claims to find a number of hidden references in the text, leading him to assert that 'Hegel specifies unmistakedly that the concrete Gestalt which answers to [this form of reason] is the Faust of Goethe's Faust-Fragment.'[3] Nonetheless, it is entirely possible that Hegel is as helpful in explaining Goethe as Goethe is in understanding Hegel.

The oblique references that Harris is such a master at uncovering are, indeed, illuminating in showing how Mephistopheles and then Faust turn their backs on purely theoretical, observational reason in order to indulge in the sensual life of the *Erdgeist* (earthly spirit), but beyond this point, the hermeneutical use of the *Faust-Fragment* becomes less successful and less convincing. It seems to me that exclusive reference to this work, as an exegetical tool, is neither justified by the Hegel text itself, nor completely helpful. In fact, this reliance may veil other aspects essential to understanding how Hegel presents sexual pleasure and the true nature of its self-destructive necessity.

Harris encounters this difficulty when he seeks to use the early *Faust* to explain necessity, which he ambiguously portrays as representing the social world, the natural world, abstract reason, and blind fate. Thus, Gretchen's pregnancy is significant in that it can be said to represent both natural necessity and the inevitability of social reprobation. However, relying on Gretchen's fate as a key to understanding Hegel's idea of necessity is unsatisfying from a philosophical point of view. That lovers inevitably run up against natural and social barriers that are (to them) the unexpected consequences of their sexual pleasure may work dramatically, but philosophically this idea does not resonate very deeply, in spite of its truth. There must be a deeper, less external reason for sexual pleasure's necessary culmination and failure, an essential element that underlies both the natural and social aspects of pleasure-seeking's unhappy fate. I believe the underlying philosophical dimension of Hegel's 'Pleasure and Necessity' takes place in what might be described, at least in a preliminary way, as the unmediated encounter between the singular individual and the universal. This encounter is not mute. It has its own language, and once we have identified it, we can hear it echoed in other rooms and corridors of the *Phenomenology of Spirit*, where similar encounters are playing themselves out.

I intend to approach the question of necessity through reference to Mozart's opera *Don Giovanni* and its Kierkegaardian interpretation.[4] This is not only because the necessary outcome of the opera's story reflects the destiny of the singular individual in its unmediated relation to the universal but also because the logic of this encounter has its own type of utterance, one that is best expressed in the language of monosyllables and, therefore, is particularly resonant in musical notes. We will see how this language is articulated in the actual musical score, near the end of the opera, when the hero meets his fate in the form of the unavoidable stone statue: the Commendatore.

On a more mundane level, reference to *Don Giovanni* is justified by the fact that Hegel saw it performed at least twice in his lifetime and felt it was a significant work.[5] Before getting to the music, however, I want to look more closely at Hegel's dialectic of pleasure and necessity.

What the individual seeks, in this section of the Reason chapter, is the immediate reflection of itself in the other, the 'I am I.'[6] In sexual pleasure, this reflection is sought through the immediate feeling of satisfaction arising from sexual union with the other. Such a feeling of union and wholeness seems, at first, to meet the stated requirements of Reason: 'the certitude that [consciousness] is all reality'.[7] This sensual certitude is not, however, the truth.

For Hegel, sexual pleasure (*Lust*) involves desire (*Begierde*) and, therefore, the natural imbalance between subject and object. Pleasure or satisfaction arises from the overcoming of this imbalance. In raw appetitive desire, the subject seeks to redress this imbalance by destroying and consuming the alien object, as animals do with their food. Of course, in sexual pleasure, desire does not seek to annihilate its object, the other self-consciousness. Sexual pleasure involves finding oneself in the other, being at home in the other, and this requires maintaining the otherness of the other. Erotic pleasure, therefore, depends on a representation of the other as independent. Erotic desire seeks to overcome this independence without destroying the object.

Structurally, sexual pleasure is not different from the other satisfactions that we encounter throughout the *Phenomenology of Spirit*, where each form of knowing, or form of consciousness, involves finding oneself in the other and the satisfaction that this affords. These satisfactions are only partial, however, and as such they lead to the ultimate ecstasy where self-consciousness is fully at home in absolute spirit and when absolute spirit is self-conscious. As an isolated figure of consciousness, the pleasure-seeking individual remains fixated at the level of carnal knowledge, which reveals itself to be contradictory and unsatisfactory. Indeed, if it were completely satisfactory, there would be no need to continue on to the satisfaction of spirit.

In the feeling of sexual enjoyment, the problem is that rather than feeling *itself* (the 'I am I'), what the individual feels is the absolute unity of the two self-consciousnesses. In other words, instead of finding itself at home in the other, the individual finds itself dissolved in an empty universal or undifferentiated intuition of 'all of life,' as Hegel writes in a fragment on erotic love from 1797, to which I will return.[8] Consequently, in attempting to find its individuality in the other, the pleasure-seeking individual actually experiences the *loss* of its individuality, a loss that appears to it in the form of an abstract universal, in the feeling of wholeness or oneness that it experiences in satisfaction. This feeling of self-loss can be understood as the intuition of dissolution or death.

The feeling of dissolution or death appears to the pleasure-seeking consciousness as the result of an 'abstract necessity,' an 'empty and alien necessity,' a 'lifeless necessity' on which the individual is 'pulverized.'[9] We may say that the feeling of *petite mort* that arises in sexual satisfaction is actually this very intuition, the inevitability of death as a biological necessity, natural death as an imposed fate. The alien aspect of this mortal fate is radically distinguished, in Hegel, from the 'death' of consciousness, proper to the self in its never-ending self-overcoming, on the path of spirit.[10] For the feeling of death as a natural necessity to become spiritual, it must be internalized. This is what happens at the end of 'Pleasure and Necessity,' where the feeling of death as an alien necessity is taken into the self, becoming an essential moral element.

In truth, the pleasure-seeker's fate is not alien. It is in the structure of sexual pleasure itself. The feeling of self-loss as a deathly necessity is actually the feeling of its own universality, its own principle of necessity, its own concept. In other words, at the end of 'Pleasure and Necessity,' the empty universal of death and necessity, which appeared as an alien fate, is grasped as an internal principle, as a universal moment within the self. It is grasped as its own essence, as pure (empty) universality or negativity. This is similar to the form of unhappy consciousness in the *Phenomenology of Spirit*, where a universal moment is brought into the self as its true, unchanging essence, in contradiction with the contingent nature of individual life. However, here, at the end of 'Pleasure and Necessity,' the universal, unchanging moment is felt as a 'law of the heart,' the title of the following subsection. Hegel's dialectic of sexual pleasure arrives at the surprising conclusion that singular pleasure carries within it the intuition of its own natural death, which is then internalized as the intuition of a pure, universal essence. Or, conversely, the feeling of 'something pure' within us is the internalized feeling of our own natural death, and this arises out of the failure of sexual pleasure as a form of knowledge.

The outcome is perfectly coherent with the logic that Hegel announces in the Introduction to the *Phenomenology of Spirit*, as driving the progression from one form of consciousness to the next: the truth or essence or in-itself of one form of knowing, which is first thought to be in the object of knowledge, is then grasped as being in the subject, leading to a higher form of consciousness. Here, what first appears as my external fate or necessity is revealed as an internal principle or essence, leading to a higher form of moral consciousness. The abstract universal of death, encountered through sexual pleasure, becomes, in 'The Law of the Heart,' a moral instance, a kind of superego. Or, as Kierkegaard would later say, the esthetic stage leads dialectically to the moral stage of existence.

From this rather dense account of the dialectic at work in 'Pleasure and Necessity,' we already have the presentiment that the latter term has a deeper, richer meaning than the discovery that pleasure-seeking inevitably leads to a social or natural dead end. To further elucidate this deeper meaning, I want to return to and tarry a while with the erotic-pleasure-seeking individual as an isolated, or fixated form. I want to do this by briefly referring to Hegel's 1797 fragment on erotic love. Reference to this work will shed light on the dialectic of pleasure and necessity by placing it in the context of other, logically similar forms, where the individual encounters the universal without any mediation.

On 22 March 1797, Hegel wrote to his friend and correspondent Nanette Endel from Frankfurt. At the end of the letter, he tells her excitedly that he is going to see Mozart's *Don Giovanni* the next day and that he is very much looking forward to the event. Sometime in November of the same year, he wrote his fragment on sexual love, which he would later revise and incorporate into his essay on the 'Spirit of Christianity.' In the fragment, we find: 'In order to suppress this feeling of separation, what is mortal feels, touches, penetrates the other ... but this unification is just a point [*Punkt*] ... what is separable returns to the state of separation.'[11]

We have seen how in sexual satisfaction, the pleasure involved in union inevitably leads to a feeling of self-loss in the empty universal. The Hegel fragment from 1797 shows that, for the erotic pleasure seeker, the feeling of union is merely punctual, that it constitutes 'a point,' and that this point is again followed by a feeling of separation, which in turn, leads to the reawakening of desire. In other words, the fragment intimates a repetitive cycle of instantaneous satisfaction and renewed desire. This oscillating movement is driven by the recurrent consciousness, following the ecstatic feeling of union, of the other as a natural object, in other words, as a separate body.[12] In the fragment, the resurgence of individual 'separateness' brings about a feeling of post-coital modesty, which again gives birth to desire, as an imbalance between the subjective and the objective.

The repetitive and punctual nature of erotic pleasure is reiterated by Hegel in other, later texts, in the *System of Ethical Life*[13] and elsewhere in the *Phenomenology of Spirit*, where we find that, in sexual satisfaction, self-consciousness 'produces the object again, and the desire as well.'[14] Indeed, it appears that this repetitive and punctual aspect is very much the fate of the individual who remains caught in the cycle of erotic pleasure seeking and satisfaction, a truth that is perhaps later found in Freud's principle of repetition and its relation to eros. In any case, the compulsive, metronomic dimension of pleasure seeking seems to provide us with another meaning of Hegel's 'alien necessity,' in the 'Pleasure and Necessity' section. The erotic form of consciousness, attempting to find itself immediately in the other, loses itself in an endless series, in a mechanistic, bad infinity that appears to it as a foreign, inevitable destiny, as a form of lifeless necessity.

On the one hand, therefore, we have seen how, in the feeling of union and wholeness, individual consciousness feels its loss in the universal. On the other hand, this self-loss may be understood as the dissolution of the individual into an endless series of similar, singular acts, in the incessant oscillation between desire and satisfaction. It is crucial to realize that both cases are ultimately the same. For Hegel, a bad infinity of singular instances is just another expression of the unmediated universal, ultimately an expression of nature itself, whose universality is comprised of an unnumbered mass of indifferent singularities. Without the mediating middle term of particularity, of species, individual 'ones' collapse immediately into the One. Indeed, that is their destiny, which the seeker of sexual satisfaction feels as prefiguring death as an alien destiny.[15]

This is what Hegel means when he writes: 'in taking hold of life, [the pleasure-seeking individual really] lays hold on death.'[16]

The compulsive, repetitive aspect of pleasure seeking and its speculative truth, that unmediated singularities collapse into the universal, is clearly in tune with the story of Don Juan and especially with his musical incarnation in Mozart's *Don Giovanni*, where Leporello boasts of his master's 1,003 conquests. The absurdity of this elevated and arbitrary figure, which Kierkegaard stresses in his brilliant essay on the opera in *Either/Or*, is an eloquent expression of the punctual nature of sexual satisfaction and its futility as a form of knowledge.[17]

It is significant that for Kierkegaard the story of Don Giovanni can only be expressed adequately in music – and expressed perfectly by Mozart. Other written expressions (Molière, Byron, etc.) must fail because they are not musical and, therefore, not erotic.[18] For Hegel, as well, it appears that the truth of desire and satisfaction is best expressed in musical terms, since music, like sexual pleasure itself, is essentially punctual. Indeed, the pointlike individuality of the musical note is explicitly affirmed in the *Esthetics*, where we find that music 'suspends the indifferent exteriority of space and idealizes it in the individual unit of the point.'[19]

The essential punctuality of music, the fact that its notes are points, is significant to how we understand the figure of the Commendatore, the stone statue that appears near the end of the opera and seals Don Giovanni's fate. In fact, the Commendatore *is* Don Giovanni's fate. His granitic, alien, lifeless immobility is the perfect expression of the dead necessity, the alien fate, against which the individual pleasure-seeker runs up and is 'pulverized [*zerstäubt*].'[20] The stone statue is the end of the living individual, the inflexible destiny, or, to use the expression Hegel that employs in 'Pleasure and Necessity,' the 'uncomprehended power of universality on which individuality is smashed to pieces [*zersmettert*].'[21]

In Mozart's opera, the statue is not only the figurative but, above all, the *musical* embodiment of the pulverizing universal, of the individual's dispersal into a cloud of similar atoms. In the scene where Don Giovanni meets his fate, the unrelenting nature of this necessity is reflected in the repetitive, punctual character of the actual notes that the statue sings. In fact, in the short but crucial excerpt shown below, the Commendatore (K.) sings only one note (monotonous), which is repeated in a series of dotted quarters and eighths, a recalcitrant rhythm that is reiterated throughout the scene and reinforced by other instruments, here, by the first and second violins, the viola, the cello, and the double bass.[22] Towards the end of this scene, the statue's abbreviated, repetitive phrases gradually dissolve into longer monosyllabic utterances, first as repeated half notes ('Yes! ... Yes! ... Yes!') and

finally as five repeated whole notes, which underscore the Commendatore's last words to Don Giovanni, 'Now your time has come.'

I want to look at two other contexts in the *Phenomenology of Spirit* that involve the same logic that is found in 'Pleasure and Necessity,' where the unmediated singular is dissolved in the universal. Each of these contexts gives rise to a form of monosyllabic utterance, similar to the musical line iterated by the stone statue. Such expressions are significant because they are the objective language of a certain (impoverished) type of reality within the work's economy, a world devoid of particular mediation between atomic individuals and the whole.

The well-known dialectic of sense certainty in the *Phenomenology of Spirit* can easily be seen in this light. The naive sort of empiricism that reduces reality to an endless stream of individual sense impressions can only give rise to the monosyllabic utterances of 'here' and 'now.' As words, these are meant to express singular impressions, in all their uniqueness. Each impression certainly takes place here and now. However, the temporal adverbs 'here' and 'now' that articulate these experiences cannot help but reduce the individual sensations to a punctual, repetitive sameness that is essentially universal in nature. Thus, the monosyllables 'here' and 'now' express the destiny of sense impressions, their dissolution in the universal, and the loss of their individuality per se, where unmediated diversity collapses into indifference.

The 'Absolute Freedom and Terror' section of the *Phenomenology of Spirit* provides another, logically similar context that produces its own distinctive form of punctual, repetitive discourse, the objective language of a certain (impoverished) type of reality, one that has seen the 'destruction of the actual organization of the world.'[23] The truth of this absolute or empty freedom manifests itself in the language of the Terror, which Hegel describes explicitly as the 'monosyllabic' reiteration of the guillotine's blade.[24] Here again, the individual is lost in a sea of indifference, this time, in universal freedom, whose 'sole work and deed ... is therefore death.'[25]

It is inevitable that such monosyllabic expressions as 'here and now,' the stupid thud of the guillotine's blade, or the repetitive notes of the stone statue bespeak an impoverished level of reality. Truly rich (*gehaltvoll*) forms of discourse are only found in the particular, mediating objectivity of the State, Religion, Art, History, and the human and natural sciences. In a world where the individual has 'thrown off all community with others,'[26] in a world of atomistic singularities, 'universal works of language or of reality' cannot take place.[27] The reality of discourse can be no richer than the objectivity it embodies.

It is significant that in Hegel such moments of immediacy and indifference are the stuff of comedy, a point that can be grasped with reference to its opposite, tragedy. Over against tragic difference, comedy appears as a sort of decadence. This is especially true when particular differences appear to be erased in an exterior arbitrary fashion, by the fateful hand of Zeus, for example. Thus, in the *Phenomenology*'s 'Spiritual Work of Art' chapter, 'higher language' (here, classical tragedy) breaks down into a culture of comedy when the Zeus of *Antigone* is seen to incarnate alien, manipulative fate, where '[n]ecessity has ... the characteristic of being the negative power of all the shapes that appear, a power in which they do not recognize themselves [and] perish.'[28] In 'Sense-certainty,' 'Absolute Freedom and Terror,' and 'Pleasure and Necessity,' where all mediating forms of particularity or community are absent,[29] the universal appears as an alien necessity or fate annihilating the individual. Fate's work is 'merely the nothingness of individuality.'[30]

This means that the unmediated relationship between the individual and the universal and the state of general indifference into which the relationship dissolves are just as easily the stuff of comedy as terror, but they are *not* the stuff of tragedy. In this way, the absolute terror with which the individual character Don Giovanni meets his fate[31] can still be thought of as no more significant than the lopping off of a head of cabbage. A strange mixture of comedy and terror seems essential to any truthful account of the erotic pleasure seeker and his destiny, such as the one we find in Hegel's 'Pleasure and Necessity.'[32]

The final scene of the opera *Don Giovanni* reinforces the impression of comic indifference. Following Don Giovanni's flaming fall into Hell, Zerlina and Masetto decide to go home for dinner. Donna Anna tells her fiancé Don Ottavio that they can still be married, given a little time. Donna Elvira will get herself to a nunnery, and Leporello, the faithful servant, decides to go to the local inn and find 'a better master.' As a chorus, the remaining characters incant a reassuring ode to banality: 'We good people will daily sing the ancient moral: this is the evildoers' end'; then they all go about their business, apparently forgetting the life and death of Don Giovanni. It is as if he has never lived. Of course, this indifference with regard to the fate of the individual is terrible. But ultimately, we must remember, *Don Giovanni* is comedy.

8 Hegel's Critique of Solger: The Problem of Scientific Communication

In 1828, Hegel published two long, consecutive articles in the *Annals of Scientific Criticism* in Berlin,[1] a review of the recently published, posthumous writings and correspondence of Karl Wilhelm Ferdinand Solger, 'theoretician of romantic irony.'[2] To the question of why Hegel dedicated such a lengthy text (the articles occupy seventy pages in the Suhrkamp edition of the complete works) to this philosopher, who was never important in his lifetime and is largely forgotten today,[3] a purely historical answer might be supplied. The articles may be seen as a posthumous gift of gratitude that Hegel made to his late colleague at the University of Berlin, for it was at least partly thanks to Solger that Hegel was hired at Berlin in 1818, just a year before Solger's death.[4] A more philosophical reason, however, can be found in the important question that arises within Hegel's review itself, a text that seems to have, for the most part, shared the fate of the philosopher to whom it was dedicated.[5]

The essential question is developed out of a distinction that Hegel makes, in his review, between irony from the *Athenäum* period[6] and irony as Solger defines it. While severely criticizing Friedrich Schlegel's ironic position, Hegel recognizes at the heart of Solgerian irony the same dialectical beat that animates his own system, together with the fact that both philosophies share the same fundamental speculative content: the self-positing of the Absolute Idea through the negation of a negation. Indeed, Hegel admits that on the level of what he calls 'the most abstract speculative summit,'[7] where identity includes both itself and difference, his philosophy is virtually indistinguishable from Solger's. The review's central question is, consequently, how to grasp a philosophy that apprehends true speculative content but where this essential content is articulated in a way that is non-scientific or even antiscientific, in the Hegelian sense of systematic *Wissenschaft*. Asking the same question from a different angle, how is it that Solger's philosophy fails, in spite of its intuition of the truth – a failure evidenced in the 'public silence'[8] repeatedly referred to in his correspondence, and the apparent incomprehension that even his friends shared when reading him?[9]

For Hegel, Solger's inability to communicate the truth can be explained by the form of expression that he applies to speculative content. Hegel's review shows how the only expression adequate to speculative truth is a discourse that is itself the concrete expression of truth. Taking this idea of objective discourse to a more radical level, Hegel's critique of Solger shows how discourse engenders the world in which it makes itself heard.

The Hegel of 1828, who writes the review of Solger's posthumous works and correspondence, that is, the professor at the height of his career, respected, influential, and eminent, seems intrigued by the failure of this serious colleague[10] whose fundamental view of things is so akin to his own. This failure is all the more intriguing given Solger's constant and vain search to disseminate his ideas through 'popular' literary forms such as manifestos and philosophical dialogues. Hegel is sensitive to the ironic futility of Solger's project, where the means of expression calculated to appeal to almost anyone, to 'the uneducated, women and teenagers,'[11] remained virtually inaccessible to everyone, even to his own educated friends. Hegel quotes one of them, who admits in a letter to Solger, 'Up to now, I have a better understanding of the Cathedral of Strasbourg than I do of your [philosophical dialogue] *Irwin*.'[12] We might be tempted ourselves to indulge in irony, observing how Hegel, a philosopher not always known for clarity of expression, allows himself to refer repeatedly to the difficulty of Solger's texts. However, it is more fruitful to try to understand the reasons to which Hegel attributes Solger's difficulty in communicating his ideas, his incapacity to develop a discourse capable of making others grasp what must, therefore, remain a speculative intuition.[13]

In his review, Hegel approaches the problem of Solgerian discourse from three related critical angles. The first concerns what Hegel refers to as 'etiolated representations' that 'do not deal with content.'[14] Hegel actually begins this attack by borrowing the words of Solger himself, before turning them back on him, for Solger levels exactly the same criticism at Friedrich Schlegel, regarding his writings on Indian religion.[15] Thus, when Solger writes that it is 'essential to abandon right away all the inherited terminology: emanation, pantheism, dualism, etc. [because] no people, no man has ever seriously entertained these unilateral and empty concepts,'[16] Hegel adopts this judgment but turns it against its author. In fact, for Hegel the terms frequently found in Solger's pronouncements, like 'mysticism,' 'inner life,' 'poesy,' and even 'religion' and 'philosophy'[17] are just as empty as the 'etiolated representations' found in Schlegel. In both cases, these representations are symptomatic of a certain type of discourse that Hegel refers to as formal or judging, a discourse that 'cruelly anatomizes living knowledge.'[18] Formal judging refers to the subjective language of the understanding, associated with the ratiocinating thought of the *Aufklärung*. Such a language can be abstract and empty (formal), because here the understanding places itself outside the object or content that it judges and analyses. Consequently, the sole content of this language's representations is unilaterally derived from the judging subject, and since pure subjectivity is nothing but an empty form, as rightly established in both Kant and Fichte, its representations are equally empty. Briefly put, the language of the judging understanding proves to be the language of appearances (Kantian phenomena), deprived of objective reality in the Hegelian sense.

This type of expression is opposed to what might be called, in Hegel, the language of the Thing, in the sense of the German word *Sache* (affair, matter at hand, case),[19] rather than *Ding* (individual, empirically observed phenomenon). The language of the Thing is the objectification of thought, real words that are possessed and uplifted by thought. Insofar as the agreement between thought and being is generally how truth is defined, we can see how the language of the Thing can be seen as embodying truth.[20] Its words are to be taken as the objective embodiment of being and thought. However, the language of formal judgment is not only inadequate for the language of the Thing,[21] but judgments also tend to rip apart objectively true language. Thus, the language of judgment not only 'pushes away ... the Thing of religions and philosophies, with the help of abstractions,'[22] or empty representations, but its judgments actually rip apart what they address.

Judgment, as the form of predicative statements or propositions, must be seen, in this context, through an etymological interpretation of the German word *urteilen*, an act of original division. While this act is at the origin of thought, of the concept, in that *urteilen* posits the essential difference between subject and object, when its divisive action is aimed at what Hegel calls, 'the Thing of religions and philosophies,' at the objective discourses of these forms, then judgment proves to be destructive of the truly objective. Thus, in this case, understanding 'cruelly anatomizes' 'living knowledge,' which is ultimately the organic whole of Science.

When Hegel writes that the form of judgment, with its empty representations, constitutes a 'decidedly negative tendency against objectivity,'[23] he is not referring to just any, everyday objectivity but to the objectivity of the Thing, objective thought embodied in words.[24] More specifically, the 'Thing of religions' refers to actual religious doctrine, which forms the objective content of theology whose texts provide content for the discourses of philosophy of religion. The 'Thing of philosophies' refers to the great philosophical texts, which come to form the objective content of the discourse of history of philosophy. In this way, both philosophy of religion and history of philosophy are ultimately objective contents of systematic Science. For philosophical discourses to be objective, they must incorporate the language of the Thing, that is, certain 'doctrinal' objectivity as their content. This is what (Hegelian) scientific discourse claims to do. However, any discourse that 'holds itself above the Thing'[25] behaves 'negatively' against the *logos* of Science. Therefore, by employing etiolated representations in his discourse, Solger is falling into a form of discourse that is opposed to the speculative truth that he means to communicate. In fact, Solger's judging discourse, in its negative behaviour to religion and philosophy, reproduces the ironic form of discourse of Fr. Schlegel, which according to Hegel does not even recognize speculative truth. When he borrows Solger's criticism of Fr. Schlegel but turns it back on its author, Hegel's point is devastatingly subtle: Solger's discourse is an ironic self-contradiction.

A second critical approach Hegel takes to the problem of scientific communication in Solger concerns what is referred to as undeveloped categories. Hegel sees this as a problem of development between what are, for him, truly logical categories (e.g., being, nothingness, or appearance) and what he calls 'concrete representations,' words that are not part of the logical vocabulary but do represent real entities (e.g., God, evil, or Man). The problem, ultimately, is how the language of Science can relate the logical and the ontological spheres: 'Just as disturbing for the act of philosophizing as for exposition and comprehension is the constant mixing, in the cited ideas, of concrete representations such as God, self-sacrificing, Man, knowing, evil etc. and abstractions such as being, nothingness, appearance etc.'[26]

It may be tempting to understand Hegel's statements as simple affirmations of good methodological sense, stating that to do successful philosophy one must first define the terms used. However, the development of the categories has a much deeper meaning within Hegelian logic, where the categories, traditionally 'what is affirmed *of* being,'[27] reveal themselves objectively as the being-essence that is *logos*, that is, as being that affirms *itself*. Hegelian logic represents the course of the development from the most abstract categories of thought, for example, the categories of being, of nothingness, of appearance, to the most objective, the categories of the true, the good, the Absolute Idea.

Within the economy of Hegel's logic, the development of the categories occurs through the mediation carried out in the Doctrine of Essence. This doctrine presents the middle term, where the abstract logical forms come to address particular objective content and become ontological. Objectivity becomes the Thing of scientific language. It is only through the mediation in the Doctrine of Essence that the language of logic can come to express (and not represent) such absolutely objective realities as those we find at the end of the *Logic*: the true, the good, and the Absolute Idea. Similarly, it is only through the *Logic*'s development that the language of logic can come to express the same ontological content that we find in Solger's 'concrete representations': God, Good, Man. By reproaching Solger for a lack of development in the categories, Hegel is again making a criticism that is linguistic in nature. Only through such a progression as the one found in the *Logic*, where abstract categories take on greater and greater objectivity and truth until they come to embody the greatest ontological presence, can God be replaced by the Absolute Idea. Without this progression or development, logic remains divorced from ontology, and the highest levels of being can only be expressed in 'concrete representations,' as pictures rather than as concepts.

As well, the Hegelian critique of undeveloped categories is noteworthy because it helps us apprehend the double nature of the understanding and the ambiguity of its role in Science. As we saw, Hegel criticizes Solger for adopting a mode of expression that is specific to the understanding, the form of the simple predicative judgment, and yet the proposed Hegelian development of the categories, their passage from abstract thought to essential being, is also the business of the understanding. Here, however, the understanding is not a terminal stand-point (*Ver-stand*) but fills a transitory role in the conceptual movement. The development *by* the understanding of the immediate categories *of* the understanding, in Hegel's review, makes the language of simple predicative judgment pass over into speculative and scientific language, without really being something else. It is simply propositional language pushed to the maximum, where through self-development, it is both itself and something new, discourse that is onto-logical, thought and being.

The third criticism of the Solgerian discourse in Hegel's review is aimed at the dialogue form, which Solger espouses in a number of his writings. Hegel attributes this 'error' on Solger's part to the fact he maintains a 'hiatus ... between scientific thought and the existence of truth in the [knowing] subject.'[28] The subsequent divorce between Science, on the one hand, and knowledge of the truth, on the other, leads Solger to believe that philosophy's task is to 'infuse the life of the Idea in [knowing] subjects,'[29] as if this life were not the result of real human scientific activity. Ultimately, for Solger, truth has a separate, transcendent ontological reality that must be conveyed to humans through an exterior artful form if scientific knowledge is to take place. However, applying an exterior, 'lively' expression to the Idea is, for Hegel, deeply unscientific, since Science is ultimately the actual discourse where truth and knowledge are equally at home. The actual space where this discourse *takes place* is the state university.

Solger's dialogical efforts are, for Hegel, more related to religion or art, where representations of truth are meant to *inspire* the general public, rather than constitute the living language of scholars working in the different university faculties, whose discourses may become the content of philosophical Science. In seeking to 'infuse the life of the Idea in [knowing] subjects,' Solger mistakenly takes 'popularity as an essential goal,' which in terms of the truth or the Idea, really means that his goal is more religious than scientific and aims at 'moving the heart of the world.'[30] To carry out this project, Solger borrows the representational form that he feels is the most effective for 'attracting men's looks to that which is the most elevated,'[31] namely, 'the artistic form of dialogue.'

In using the artistic form of dialogue, Solger contradicts Hegel's idea of scientific *logos* in a more fundamental way. Hegel recognizes that for Solger art is essentially symbolic, in that individual productions can do no more than act as symbols for the divine Idea that has taken possession of them. Art is the production of religious symbols that must represent the Infinite, either in its tragic act of becoming the finite or in its comic act of suppressing its own finitude. In terms of an artistic form of expression like the dialogue, the symbolic dimension implies a notion of language where words are never more than signs, represent-ing something alien to them.[32]

A linguistic notion supposing a radical separation between the signi-fier, as the finite, empty sign, and that which is signified, understood as pure essence or truth, is inimical to Hegel's idea of scientific lan-guage.[33] Furthermore, for Hegel, Solgerian symbolic discourse actually engenders a world distinct from that of Science. The words of this world, the subjective arbitrary relationship between sign and signified, actually form an objectivity that is other than the world in which scien-tific truth may take place. In the case of artistically conceived dis-course, as in the case of subjective, predicative judgments, holistic reality is reduced to an empirical horde,[34] emptied of all consistency. Only within such a world is it possible to conceive of what Hegel means by the public, namely, a swarm of empty 'signs' waiting to be 'infused with truth.'

Solger's failure to communicate is, therefore, inevitable. The public whom his discourse addresses, and that it engenders, is incompatible with the only (Hegelian) language that may adequately express specu-lative content and the world where it may be heard. The notion of sci-entific communication that underlies the Hegelian critique of Solger implies a community producing real, positive content, which specula-tive philosophy reflects on and elevates to the level of philosophy (of art, of religion, of law, of nature, etc.), incorporated into systematic Sci-ence. In concrete terms, as we find in Hegel's pedagogical writings,[35] philosophers, educated within the state school system, must first acquire the hard content of Science, which is then rendered fluid and dialectical through an apprenticeship in Eleatic logic. Only then are students deemed capable of studying speculative philosophy, at the university. This is certainly not the public.

This scientific exclusion of the public and its discourse, however, tends to give a false impression of Hegel, the man. Indeed, within his *Review of Solger's Posthumous Writings and Correspondence*, there is a passage containing what might be called a positive ethics regarding the non-scientific public, an ethics directly inspired by Hegel's own social life in Berlin. Far from refusing purely sociable relations[36] or 'avoiding all relations and all meetings where the banality and the uncultured character of such phenomena' manifest themselves 'heavily,'[37] one should simply be careful to distinguish between the serious scientific domain and the public arena, the place of entertainment. One must be able to 'orient one's activity and work uniquely in that area worthy of them,'[38] that is, to those people capable of understanding scientific development because they are part of it.

The world in general, however, the public as an empirical horde, should be an object of neither seduction nor disdain. In fact, the public world is closer to the unreflected natural sphere than to the domain of Spirit. As such, the public may form an object for Science, but this does not mean that Science is for the public and certainly not that its general world *is* Science, a false belief held by those who misrepresent Hegel as the philosopher who finds Reason in everything around him. Nature does not accede to the status of Spirit until it has been thought, that is, articulated in a language whose highest expression takes place in speculative discourse within the university. This discourse addresses the general public only indirectly, through the work of those formed by the institution, who leave school to participate in the public life of the state.

9 On Schleiermacher and Postmodernity

The contretemps between Hegel and Schleiermacher at the University of Berlin is well known.[1] The nature of their struggle for influence, the latter's refusal to admit the former into the Berlin Academy, and Hegel's reciprocal distancing of Schleiermacher from his critical *Annals* have been well documented and explored. In fact, Hegel's antipathy towards Schleiermacher stems from the latter's early association with Friedrich Schlegel, whom Schleiermacher had defended in his 'anonymous' letter in support of the 'scandalous' novel *Lucinde* in 1800. Schlegel's novel, which seemed an apology for free love, the ambivalence of male and female sexual roles, and a blending of literature and philosophy, could not but offend Hegel's sense of propriety, both with regard to his belief in the institution of marriage and his Platonic promotion of philosophy as science over poetry. Pastor Schleiermacher's defence of Schlegel's apparently loose sexual mores seems to have struck Hegel in a visceral way, as hypocritical, which explains the parson's inclusion in the long addition to paragraph 140 of the *Philosophy of Right* where hypocrisy, through 'probabilism,' is linked to romantic irony and Schlegel.[2] In this light, it is not surprising to see Schleiermacher appear as the 'Tartuffe'[3] in the same passage. That it was written some twenty years after the Jena period reveals the depth of feeling underlying Hegel's antipathy.

What concerns me here is how Schleiermacher's theology of feeling came to represent, for Hegel, an exemplary expression of contemporary malaise that is presented as the manifest culmination of the history of Christianity. This is interesting for several reasons. First, the actual (*wirklich*) character that Hegel attributes to Schleiermacher's theology of feeling shows us how Hegel comes to understand it in terms of a worldly, historical development. This approach allows him to overcome genealogically what was initially a deeply felt theoretical dilemma between the enlightened and dogmatic views of Christianity. Second, the contemporary nature of the malaise represented in his rival's theology shows that, far from seeing the world around him as the comforting realization of his own system, Hegel feels the presence of something new, something inimical to the world of Science.[4] Third, insofar as we may recognize in Hegel's description of contemporary malaise something of our own condition and to the extent that we understand our epoch as postmodern, we can take his critique of Schleiermacher as telling us something about ourselves. I believe this is indeed the case and that Hegel has something new to say about the postmodern condition.

Hegel seems to have discovered the symptoms of malaise retrospectively, in the parson's influential *Speeches on Religion*, and particularly in the undiluted first edition of the work (1799), where Schleiermacher's 'theology of feeling/intuition' is initially articulated.[5] I say 'retrospectively' because Hegel's early take on the theologian's *Speeches* is far more positive than the polemical critique we find during the Berlin period, for example, in the *Philosophy of Right* (1820) and in Hegel's Preface to Hinrichs's work on religion (1822).[6] This Preface is particularly important, since it represents one clear instance where Hegel's thoughts on religion are not confined to his published lectures. He actually *wrote* the Preface.

The Preface represents Hegel's ultimate pronouncement on his rival and brings to light the first aspect of interest I mentioned above: how Hegel comes to resolve a deeply felt contradiction between dogmatic faith and the reasonable religion of the Enlightenment, what was called 'natural religion' at the time, through the dialectical movement of the history of Christianity. It is only in the light of this historical movement that we can understand, by contrast, how Schleiermacher's religion of feeling stands in opposition to such a movement – as the static, unresolved expression of the contradiction between faith and reason, where the movement stalls without realizing integration into the wholeness of Hegelian Science. Before looking at the Preface, however, it is necessary to see how Hegel's grasp of his Berlin rival evolved in light of his own attempts to reconcile this fundamental contradiction.

We can trace the origins of Hegel's dilemma between dogmatic faith and Enlightenment religion back to his college days at Tübingen in the late 1780s, where he was caught up between two very distinct currents of theological debate. In one corner stood Professor of Theology Gottlob Storr, a proponent of orthodox faith and the unquestioning acceptance of religious truth as divine Revelation. Opposite was the incendiary young Carl Immanuel Diez, leader of the Tübingen 'Kant-Klub' that included Schelling and Hölderlin, but not Hegel. Diez represented an extreme Enlightenment view of Christianity, so radical that it dispensed with the divinity of Revelation and Christ altogether. Curiously, both Storr and Diez based their opposing doctrines on equally opposing interpretations of Kant. For Storr, the impossibility of noumenal knowledge simply proved that extrasensory truth must be conveyed by Divine Revelation and grasped directly through faith. Diez argued that the impossibility of knowing the thing-in-itself simply showed that Revelation itself, falling beyond sensual intuition, was impossible to know and thus best forgotten. As Kant had 'shown' in his second *Critique*, free reason, postulating its own principles, was a sufficient basis for determining the Good.[7]

That Hegel was torn between these two viewpoints is evident in his subsequent writings on Christianity, in Berne and Frankfurt. First he embraces the *Aufklärung* view of natural religion, in his essay 'The Life of Jesus,' where Christ is seen as a moral teacher, a kind of archetypal embodiment of Kant's moral philosophy or *Postulatlehre*. Then, Hegel essays the more orthodox route in his 'Spirit of Christianity,' where Christ is the perfect instance of Divine Revelation and dogma is sacred. Ultimately, the reconciliation of these two unilateral positions, to use Hegel's language, only happens within systematic (Hegelian) philosophy, in other words, where religion becomes philosophy of religion, and philosophy becomes absolute knowing. The first attempt at this reconciliation between faith and knowing is attempted in 1802, specifically in the published work of that title: *Glauben und Wissen*. Here, the 'synthesis' is largely understood in terms of an intellectual intuition, an immediate seizing of the *absolute* unity, that is, the one that includes both intuitive identity and conceptual differentiation. I believe one could argue, although I won't do it here, that the *Phenomenology* and the final system of the *Encyclopedia of Philosophical Sciences* embrace, in different ways, the same project, namely, how to reconcile the intuitive, felt content of faith with the demands of knowing.

Just as Hegel sees philosophical *logos* as reconciling this conflict, he sees Schleiermacher's theology as an aborted state of affairs, where the two poles become fixated in their opposition. Such a fixation must therefore also represent, for Hegel, a *logos* opposing that of philosophical science. To the extent that philosophical science (his own) was meant to embody objective truth and enjoy a certain actuality, in that it was professed at the University of Berlin, Schleiermacher's theology could only represent a reality that stood in opposition to the world of Hegelian *Wissenschaft*. This is ultimately how Schleiermacher comes to represent, for Hegel, a generalized malaise. Hegel's judgment of Schleiermacher evolves according to the dynamic interplay in his own mind between the poles of faith and reason, or rather, in this context, between intuition and understanding. In fact, Schleiermacher's progressive fall from Hegelian grace reflects the progression of Hegel's own take on intuition, from his early espousal of Schelling's vision of intellectual intuition, to his later reading of intuition as essentially subjective feeling.

An early judgment on the *Speeches* can be found in Hegel's article on 'The Difference Between the Systems of Fichte and Schelling' (1801). In this context, with Hegel himself still very much under the influence of the latter, Schleiermacher's publication is welcomed, with some reservations, as sharing a common speculative project: the synthesis of reflective understanding and (particular) intuition within an intellectual (universal) intuition. Schleiermacher's 'intuition of the Universe' is seen as seeking to redress the injustice Kant and Fichte perpetrate on nature,[8] where nature is deprived of any essential substance and where objectivity is no more than a subjective phenomenon. What Schleiermacher clearly promotes in the *Speeches* as an individual, subjective feeling of the universe as God,[9] Hegel interprets in terms of his and Schelling's systematic project. Rejecting this alien interpretation may account for the fact that, in subsequent editions of his work, Schleiermacher largely replaces the term 'intuition' with 'feeling.' Ironically, in doing so he mirrors the progression of Hegel's own thought as I just described it, away from an attachment to intellectual intuition, towards an understanding of it as purely subjective and hence arbitrary feeling. This is how Schleiermacher, who initially is taken for a fellow proponent of intellectual intuition, will later be characterized as the 'theologian of feeling.'[10]

Already one year later, in *Glauben und Wissen*, Hegel somewhat revises his earlier positive appraisal of the *Speeches*. Here, Schleiermacher is distinguished from Jacobi, who is understood, with regard to objectivity, in Kantian or Fichtean terms: essence (the thing-in-itself) has been divorced from objectivity and sent 'beyond', where it is the object of yearning (*Sehnsucht* or *Streben*). 'On the other hand, in the *Speeches*,' writes Hegel, 'nature, as a collection of finite realities [*Wirk-*

lichkeiten] recognized as the Universe, is destroyed [and] the infinite effort [*Streben*] is satisfied in intuition.'[11]

Whereas in the earlier writing Schleiermacher's intuition of the universe 'appeased' nature, now it is seen as destroying it. Hegel has come to see universal intuition in terms of a pantheism where the universal is present in everything. This puts an end to the painful yearning towards an other-worldly essence; however, this is at the expense of true objectivity, which loses its particular reality and becomes absorbed in a melting pot of pure sentiment. A universal intuition of everything as absolute essence cannot but do away with things in their particular individuality. What is missing in pure intuition is its polar opposite: reflexive understanding, which alone makes the particular distinctions necessary for the understanding of 'finite realities.'

Several conclusions can be drawn from this summary look at Hegel's early writings on Schleiermacher. First, it is noteworthy that neither passage can be described as polemical. Even though in *Faith and Knowing* universal intuition is accused of destroying nature, it nonetheless puts an end to the condition of romantic yearning.

Second, Hegel's views are centred around Schleiermacher's relation to objectivity. In the earlier passage, intuition is seen as saving nature from the mistreatment it undergoes at the hands of reflexive understanding. Then, intuition seems to turn on objectivity and abolish it. In other words, when reflexive understanding mistreats objectivity, intuition saves it, and when intuition destroys objectivity, only reflexive understanding can rescue it. The conclusion to this apparent contradiction is simply that the unilaterality of either moment is pernicious to objectivity, and without a mediating middle term, consciousness oscillates endlessly from one extreme to the other.

Third, it should be noted that up to this point Hegel considers Schleiermacher himself solely in terms of intuition or feeling. Reflexive understanding is remarkable in its absence. As we will see, only later, in the Preface, does this moment come to be ascribed to his Berlin rival, through a historical movement that is meant to show how the theology of feeling comes about. This movement, therefore, involves an important new distinction. Dogmatic faith comes to be seen as a historical expression of (dogmatic) understanding and not of intuition. As we will see, this frees feeling from faith, giving the former a life of its own.

As a final remark, before looking at the Preface, we should also note that the objectivity in question in both of the passages we just looked at is presented in an ambiguous fashion: as both purely natural phenomena devoid of essence (which understanding has relegated to the 'beyond' as the thing-in-itself) and as something essential that must be preserved. Indeed, reading the two passages in question, we cannot but feel Hegel's struggle. On the one hand, we find that objectivity must exist as something substantial and essential; otherwise its mistreatment and destruction at the hands of universal intuition would be of no concern. On the other hand, when objectivity is preserved by reflexive understanding, it is no longer essential, since reflexive understanding can do no more than apprehend objectivity as a subjective phenomenon, divorced of its true essence. There is a fundamental ambiguity involved in these positions, which I believe is only resolved with Hegel's subsequent grasp of objectivity as Spirit and ultimately as scientific *logos*. Without this *elenchus*, however, the objective world is sapped of its truth, both by understanding (or reason or knowing) acting alone, and by intuition acting alone. It is this state of affairs that Schleiermacher comes to represent.

In his Preface to Hinrichs's work on religion, Hegel puts forward a genealogy of the contemporary condition, in which the paradigmatic or symptomatic figure of Schleiermacher appears, along with his 'religion of feeling.' This genealogical approach to Schleiermacher's position supports my argument that, far from perceiving this figure as an individual peculiarity, Hegel sees it as an actual, contemporary condition of malaise, at odds with Hegel's own conception of scientific objectivity as the *logos* of the Idea. The protagonist in this story is thought itself, or rather what Hegel calls reflexive thought, the thought of subjective understanding (*Verstand*). It should now come as no surprise that the 'antagonist' in this story is dogmatic, religious faith. What is surprising is that, as I mentioned above, dogmatic faith is now historically presented as a form of dogmatic understanding rather than as an expression of intuition. This is why, in the Preface, the agency of reflexive thought is first presented in the religious context of the pre-Renaissance world, where ratiocinating understanding is under the sway of religious faith and entirely taken up with the casuistic concerns of Church scholarship. In this context, understanding finds absolute truth in the objects of faith, in the immediate and finite objectivity presented as 'the stories, events, circumstances, and commandments'[12] of positive religion. The truth of these things (*Dinge*) is imposed dogmatically. In fact, this 'holding-for-true' (*Fürwahrhalten*) of finite things that is characteristic of Scholastic understanding is structurally identical to the dogmatic empiricism that Hegel ascribes to Jacobi, empirical certainty grounded in religious faith. The truth of what I perceive is guaranteed by my faith in God.

It is significant that the 'finite things' Hegel is dealing with here are of a textual nature; he refers to 'stories, events, circumstances, and commandments' that are recounted or written. In other words, reflexive understanding does not necessarily involve direct perception of objectivity. It can operate through a dogmatic language of predication where words have the same status as merely natural things. This is the language of 'sterile erudition and orthodoxy,'[13] where dogmatic understanding expresses itself in 'letters' (*Buchstaben*), in an 'external, historical account' (*aüsserliche Historische*), in order to have the 'last word' (*Hauptwort*) on divine truth.[14] So here, Hegel presents the unilateral position of dogmatic faith as a certain historical moment of thought, that of Late Medieval Scholasticism, where the data of Revelation must be accepted as true, leaving thought the job of 'sterile erudition and orthodoxy.' This position might also reflect, to a certain extent, the orthodox theology of Hegel's old Tübingen professor, Gottlob Storr.

Dogmatic, orthodox religion, however, is the architect of its own demise. By allowing understanding to promote itself through theological erudition, for example, as arbitrator on the veracity of Biblical accounts, the 'infinite energy'[15] of pure thought, which is inherent in reflexive thought, is liberated. In fact, in Hegelian terms, pure thought is synonymous with abstract freedom, the negativity powering dialectical movement, or the systematic (scientific) scepticism that thought brings to fixed, sclerotic positions, dissolving them into movement.[16] In this way, reflexive understanding turns on itself, or rather on its own dogmatic and orthodox approach to finite objectivity. Historically, the power of thought promoted in Scholasticism unleashes itself in the Enlightenment. Hegel presents this as a kind of bacchanal of free thinking, where thought turns against its own hitherto held dogmatic positions.

In religious terms, this means the 'histories,' 'commandments,' and so on, are simply not believed anymore. The words recounting them are emptied of all significance or essence. Biblical texts are no longer sacred, but rather are treated hermeneutically, as a system of linguistic signifiers. In fact, Biblical texts share the fate of 'mistreated' nature as I invoked it above: they become the phenomena of subjective idealism à la Kant and Fichte; they are mere appearances (*Scheine*). Regarding objectivity, the shift from dogmatic Christianity to the *Aufklärung* mirrors what might be thought of as a passage from dogmatic empiricism, as expressed in Jacobi, to Kantian empiricism. Both expressions remain those of reflexive understanding, although the former, by an act of faith, places essence in finite, natural reality, whereas the latter relegates essence to the great noumenal beyond.

According to this new way of looking at things, the data of Revelation and worldly objectivity, in general, consist of subjectively formulated appearances; essence, or truth, is now an unattainable (through *understanding*) thing-in-itself. The radical scepticism I mentioned above, which always haunts reflexive understanding and accounts for its restlessness, is expressed, in Kantian empiricism, in the assertion that the truth, as the thing-in-itself, cannot be *known*. This clears the way for the sort of radical Enlightenment posture espoused by the other emblematic figure of Hegel's Tübingen days, Carl Immanuel Diez, who had once argued that even the Apostles could have no real *knowledge* of Christ's divinity, since such a knowledge would not be empirical.

That the truth cannot be *known* means it cannot be attained by reflexive understanding. It can only be, as Kant asserted, the object of faith, which, in the present context, means subjective intuition or feeling. Schleiermacher's religion of feeling appears precisely in this light, as the corollary to his hermeneutical approach to religious doctrine and to the facts of Revelation. Reflexive understanding grasps objectivity, including text itself, as a swarm of finite, natural things that are the phenomena (*Scheine*) of subjective thinking.[17] This objectivity is inessential. Things are no more than arbitrary signifiers or 'names,' emptied of all inherent significance. What this means is that essence or truth, as beyond understanding, can only be the object of *feeling*. To use Hegel's words, theology is 'reduced to historical [i.e., hermeneutical] erudition and then to the deficient exposition of certain subjective feelings.'[18] Thus, 'feeling is the sole mode in which religion can be present.'[19] This is how Schleiermacher is presented in the Preface, as one of those 'ratiocinating theologians ... who set religion in subjective feelings.'[20] As such, he appears as a 'contemporary representation' (*Zeitvorstellung*) of 'the culture in our time.'[21]

Hegel sees this culture as a condition of malaise, a condition where unilateral positions are sclerotically fixed and, therefore, impediments to the life or movement of thought and, ultimately, to the holistic conception of Spirit. This condition of malaise is manifest in what Hegel refers to as the three 'absolute presuppositions' or 'truths' of 'our time,'[22] all of which are represented in Schleiermacher's theology.

The first contemporary presupposition is the sceptical assertion that 'man knows nothing of the truth.'[23] As we have seen, this attitude is deduced from the empiricism of Kantian critical philosophy, which 'has presented to understanding the correct consciousness of itself: that it is incapable of knowing the truth.'[24] This modern sceptical attitude is the one we saw arise in the Enlightenment, the bacchanal of doubt that was historically responsible for overturning and emptying the data of Revelation of their truth.

This attitude leads directly to the second universal presupposition of our times, 'that spirit ... can only deal with appearances and finite things.'[25] In other words, generalized scepticism has collapsed into generalized empiricism, as we saw it historically come on the scene with the Enlightenment. Following Hume and Kant, objectivity is now necessarily empirical, consisting of *inherently* meaningless, that is, subjectively determined, phenomena.

Out of these empirical and sceptical attitudes towards truth arises the third 'universal prejudice' of our time, 'the opinion that feeling constitutes the veritable and even sole form in which religiosity conserves its authenticity.'[26] Schleiermacher's theology of feeling is thus explained as the natural outcome of attendant positions of empiricism and scepticism. In other words, Schleiermacher's theology is symptomatic of a modern condition where objectivity has been reduced to empirical, subjectively determinable sense data, where scepticism is generalized and where feeling is seen as the only way to experience a truth that is necessarily grasped as 'out there.' Needless to say, this contemporary condition is not the one traditionally associated with Hegel's supposed 'end of history,' and indeed, it helps explode the myth that the philosopher believed this had come about, in Berlin, around the time that he moved there.

The contradiction that Hegel had first experienced powerfully in his youth, between dogmatic faith and enlightened understanding, is therefore presented as two moments in the history of thought. These two positions are meant to be reconciled in Hegel's encyclopedic system, where, in 'Absolute Spirit,' the true objectivity of philosophy is expressed as the overcoming and suspension of art and religion. Schleiermacher, however – who, of course, refuses this Hegelian speculative reconciliation – comes to represent the same two moments fixed in their unresolved, unilateral opposition. Similarly, since Hegel uses Schleiermacher to represent this refusal of reconciliation, we may also understand the generalized, contemporary malaise he represents in terms of a refusal of speculative reconciliation. In Berlin, towards the premature end of his life, Hegel came to see himself as living in a culture that was inimical to his holistic, reconciling vision of Science. He presents this contemporary condition as a culture of fixed, unreconciled positions of empiricism, scepticism, and feeling.

I now want to return to the question addressed at the beginning of this essay. Is there anything in Hegel's description of contemporary malaise that reflects our own postmodern condition, and if so, does Hegel's reading tell us anything new? I will address this double-barrelled question, briefly, in two parts.

First, in order to see if we can recognize something of our own postmodern condition in the 'three absolute presuppositions' of Hegel's contemporary world, I will refer to those authors who seem to have best described our condition, beginning with a pioneer in this area, Jean-François Lyotard. I choose Lyotard not only because of the ground-breaking nature of *La condition postmoderne*, and its undeniable pertinence, but because the framework of his investigations is identical to that of Hegel: forms of knowing as expressions of a historical, cultural moment that Lyotard calls postmodern. Moreover, the French philosopher actually refers to Hegel's systematic philosophy as abrogated by a crucial postmodern tendency, one that echoes Hegel's own 'postmodern' diagnostic.

In his chapter 'La délégitimation,'[27] Lyotard evokes precisely the overarching scepticism that Hegel expresses as the first universal presupposition, that 'nothing is true.' Lyotard presents this generalized scepticism as the end of the 'great narratives' of progress and science, particularly as these are embodied in Hegel's systematic philosophy. In fact, Lyotard explains the eclipse of such great narratives in Nietzschean terms, by saying that these discourses carried the germs of nihilism within themselves and more or less self-destructed by turning onto themselves their own extravagant demands for truth criteria. Regardless of the cause ascribed to the scepticism that brings about the end of the great narratives, this breakdown ushers in a type of postmodern knowledge that echoes the second of Hegel's universal presuppositions 'of the times,' that spirit can only know finite things.

Lyotard expresses this knowledge of the finite as an *éclatement*, a dispersal into a multitude of empirical subsciences, a particularization or 'parcelling' of scientific domains according to their finite objects. This parcelling is accompanied by the breakdown of scientific discourse into ever smaller units, finally reaching 'languages-machines' or 'bits' of information. In fact, it is with this 'hegemony of computer science'[28] and the transformation of knowledge into 'quantities of information' that Lyotard begins his report on postmodern 'knowing,' contrasting the traditional idea of the acquisition of knowledge as '*Bildung* of spirit and even the person' with the postmodern notion of information as a product for consumption.

This 'consumer' aspect can be related back to Hegel's statement of one of the pivotal contemporary presuppositions, namely, that knowledge deals with only finite things. Perhaps we may also recall that the form of knowing he describes as 'natural consciousness' is very much an individual consumer of the 'world' in the form of finite sense phenomena.[29] What is pertinent to my argument is the fact that Lyotard describes the postmodern condition of science as Hegel describes the spirit of his own epoch: the sceptical breakdown of systematic truth fractures and disperses in finite forms and objects of knowledge. This is particularly important because for Hegel (and I believe for Lyotard) objectivity only *is* as the object of knowledge. When the systematic objectivity of the great narratives breaks down, all that is left is the 'bad infinity' of individual, finite things (*Dinge*). For both philosophers, these finite things are the potential objects of knowledge and/or consumption.

This view of fractured, dispersed objectivity and its consumption, whether as information or as actual objects, is present in other important portrayals of the postmodern condition. Jean Baudrillard eloquently expresses the *éclatement* or dispersal underlying the *Société de consommation* as a loss of transcendence: 'In the specific mode of consumerism, there is no more transcendence ... there is only the immanence in the order of signs ... there is logical calculus of signs and absorption into the system of signs.'[30] For Gilles Lipovetsky, 'postmodern society no longer has ... a mobilizing historical project[;] now we are governed by emptiness.'[31] This is the emptiness of generalized consumerism, of constant hunger for more 'objects or information.'[32] The same logic can be found in Hannah Arendt's observations on the contemporary world, where we find that the great narrative of 'hope that inspired Marx' has broken down to show the 'fallacy of this reasoning; the spare time of the *animal laborans* is never spent in anything but consumption, and the more time left to him, the greedier and the more craving his appetites.'[33] If I were asked to find additional testimonials, I might also mention Michel Foucault's 'analytic of finitude' and the end of metaphysics.[34]

What I believe all these accounts have in common is the movement that we find in Hegel's description of his 'present age': overarching scepticism has caused the disintegration of systematic objectivity, whether this is understood as the system of Science or its objective contents, namely, the Philosophy of Nature, the State, History, Art, and Religion. Knowledge, or what Hegel calls the negativity of thought, can now only understand (*verstehen*) or consume the bad infinity of finite remains.[35] This plays significantly on how we grasp our philosopher, not as the satisfied herald of the end of history, but as the anxious observer of something new and antagonistic to his notion of *Wissenschaft*. Beyond this scholarly significance, however, Hegel's perceptive and prescient account may actually tell us something new about the postmodern condition that we live in. I find this insight in his third 'universal presupposition of our time,' that the only way to the truth is through feeling.

The only diagnosis of the postmodern world I have found that refers to something like this is Charles Taylor's reference to our contemporary desire for authenticity. Taylor even juxtaposes this contemporary search for inwardness with the pervasive aspect of selfish individualism, whose instrumental reason supposes the same fractured, consumable objectivity common to the other accounts of the postmodern condition referred to above.[36] Taylor's idea of the contemporary aspiration towards authenticity, as an inward-directed search for truth, certainly does not contradict Hegel's third universal presupposition of the age, but I think the idea of *feeling* has a broader interpretive field, and in this sense, it is even more fruitful.

Uncovering the expressions of feeling in the postmodern world would itself be an encyclopedic undertaking. It would involve looking at such phenomena as the contemporary explosion of religious forms, not in terms of the fracturing and dispersal of the larger religions, but in terms of the reliance on individual feeling rather than on dogma that seems typical of the new religious forms. It would involve analysing the growth of New Age superstitions and their eschewal of reason and science. Such an investigation might also look into certain ecological expressions, into popular psychologies and self-help techniques. It might enquire into the contemporary willingness to embrace references to God within political, patriotic discourse, divorced from any appeal to organized religion and its doctrines.

Even without embarking on such an enterprise, however, we can still derive contemporary relevance from Hegel's idea of feeling as the third universal presupposition of the times. The idea is simple and insightful. The expressions of 'feeling' that are so present in our world should be seen as an integral part of what constitutes postmodernity. Reliance on feeling is not a reaction against the contemporary expressions of individualization that we readily observe in both the subjects and the objects of knowledge and/or consumption. Rather, the contemporary culture of feeling is the direct consequence of this sister culture. The sceptical breakdown of the great narrative structures that typified modernity brings about a condition where instrumental reason can only tell us about finite things. Any project for truth in terms of an overall, systematic, and scientific 'summing up' is considered hopeless, leaving behind an arbitrarily requited yearning (*Sehnsucht*) for the transcendent, through various forms of feeling.

We might test this correlation of Hegel's by applying it to a given society. If the correlation works, we should witness the following: the more a given culture treats objects of knowledge (and objectivity in general) as consumable, digestible 'bits,' the more that culture will manifest expressions of sentimentality. But I am not a sociologist.

Last Words

Within the system that Hegel calls Science, language is the objective middle term between thought and being. This means that the words that make up scientific discourse are the real embodiment of thought as it takes possession and inhabits linguistic signs, forming a richer, more spiritual reality than what is immediately present. The empty sign, the 'name,' as Hegel calls it, is meaningless until it is given determined content, just as a name is insignificant until it is attributed to someone we know. In fact, the empty sign has no more inherent significance than do pebbles in a stream, and just as centuries of water rushing over them gradually and arbitrarily fashion their forms, the linguistic signs we use, over time, are rubbed into their present shapes by the streams of usage they undergo. The empty sign is an impoverished, naturally formed, arbitrary thing. As a pure signifier, it may be inhabited by any thought, assigned any meaning subjective whimsy chooses to bestow or to withdraw. Where the relation between signifier and signified is entirely symbolic, words are no more than the sepulchres of dead, alien meaning.

The real words of scientific discourse do not have this lifeless character: there is no arbitrary distance between signifier and signified. The words of Science are the organic embodiment of their meaning. Within this context, words are objectively true and truly objective. They are thought and being, the real content of Science itself, substantiating its ultimate objectivity. In this way, the content of Hegel's Philosophy of Nature is found in the discourses of the natural sciences of his day. The content of the Philosophy of Art takes place in the real words of classical tragedy; a Philosophy of Religion is only possible because religious doctrine and dogma can be taken as objective content. Similarly, the laws of the state become the objective content of a Philosophy of Right and the Philosophy of History, substantiated in the evolution of governing constitutions, can rely on the actual words of historical narrative.

These contents are expressed in acts of predication or judgments that are more than the arbitrary pronouncements of a self-positing I. Within systematic Science, the objectivity of judgments is guaranteed by the larger syllogistic forms they make up, just as these syllogistic forms derive their objectivity from the real content embodied in their middle terms. This is not begging the question. In Hegel, we have a circular epistemology where the presupposition of organic completeness confers meaning on any specific research undertaken. Without this guarantee of narrative completeness, human knowledge becomes aimless, a haphazard string of affirmations, which may just as easily run in one direction as in another, an endless series of discoveries amounting to nothing. Science must always be able to recapitulate. Otherwise, there is no remembering and, therefore, no accumulation of knowledge building on what went before. To recapitulate, Science must logically or, one might say, grammatically presuppose systematic completeness, while remaining open to new positive content.

The notion of real language has ethical – in the Hegelian sense of *Sittlichkeit* – implications. If language, within the systematic articulation of Science, is the objective and true embodiment of thought, then it must participate in ethical life. Further, ethical life must, to some degree, be constituted by real linguistic expressions. The social reality of the world we live in and know must be, at least in part, engendered by certain discourses, the objective languages that are found in the contents of Hegel's *Encyclopedia of Philosophical Sciences*, the discourses of law, religion, art, the natural and human sciences. This means that social institutions such as universities, the courts, government ministries, regulatory bodies, religious entities, and so on are the embodiments of these discourses. Indeed, without their charters, doctrines, constitutions, publications, mission statements, regulations, minutes, and laws these institutions are sapped of their substance. The thought that creates and animates social institutions is effective through language, but only if this language is taken as being truly objective and not merely arbitrary.

What are we to make of such an ethical vision, one that sees true meaning or objective truth in the institutions and their linguistic constitutions, rather than in the subjective choices of individual moral agents, their identities, struggles, claims, and demands? Few today would tend to promote institutional language over the pronouncements of the individual. Indeed, institutional language is generally seen as a sclerotic bureaucratese, a *langue de bois* standing opposed to the earnest self-expression of the individual. That which is personal and heartfelt tends to strike us as authentic and true, not what is found in dogma, charters, and laws. Such a romantic point of view only obtains, however, when we see our state institutions as divorced from the linguistic participation of the citizens, when individual discourses are seen as having nothing to do with the political reality in which we live. Only in this way do we no longer recognize ourselves in the languages of our own institutions.

Hegel's ideal of *vita activa* is essentially Athenian. The perfect linguistic embodiment of this city is classical tragedy – above all, *Antigone*. Here, the essential conflict within all political bodies, the conflict between the private and the public spheres, is expressed in objectively real language, playing itself out in the public forum, taking place in the community, in a civic ritual where the two opposing spheres are actually reconciled. Significantly, when the world of tragedy disappears, it is replaced by the monosyllabic indifference of comedy and terror. Now, the objective linguistic bonds of community, the institutions of society where dialogues of difference make sense, no longer have meaning. They are supplanted by a new social 'reality,' new discourses where any true difference is either laughable or annihilated. The utterances of indifference are always singular and punctual. They are personal judgments, exclamations, and feelings that can never attain coherence, since all general structures of relevance have been abolished.

Significantly, what threatens the rich language of tragedy is not difference and opposition, which is the very stuff of tragedy, but rather the language of irony. Irony renders the most meaningful conflicts indifferent, creating a state where nothing really matters, where the structures brought about through objectively true discourse dissolve into a sea of atomic individuals and utterances. Devoid of all inner coherence, these monadic sands may be sculpted by any breeze, surrendering any possibility of direction to the external hand of fate, to a deus ex machina who may take the comic form of capricious, bearded Zeus or the terrible form of an equally arbitrary Robespierre.

In his review of K.W.F. Solger's work, Hegel defines romantic irony as a *Vereitelung*, a rendering vain or emptying of all that matters, all that is of substantial interest, the objective discourses of the state in its most organic, ethical articulation. Irony as *Vereitelung* is purely subjective. Its judgments are a pure self-positing, a vain self-reflection that can best be expressed in the Fichtean formula of I = I. The judgments of the ironic individual are not, however, harmlessly solipsistic. They are words aimed at the very expressions Hegel sees as constituting objective truth, namely, the discourses of religion, art, science, law, and history. Irony decimates the ethical life of the world and the language that constitutes it. Its judgments break apart the words of Science, the holistic embodiment of thought and being, leaving, on the one hand, disembodied thought, the transcendental signified, and on the other, mere names that have no more meaning than pebbles or stones.

One may be tempted to see irony as the discourse of difference and opposition, as a discourse standing against the totalizing tendency of the system. In fact, however, irony as *Vereitelung*, as the vanity that renders everything vain, is a discourse that makes any meaningful difference impossible, drowning all opposition in a sea of indifference, bringing forth a world of comedy and terror.

Notes

1. The Objective Discourse of Science

1 See Adriaan Peperzak's insightful article 'Second Nature: Place and Significance of Objective Spirit in Hegel's Encyclopedia,' *Owl of Minerva* (hereafter *OM*) 27, 1 (1995): 51–66.

2 This is particularly true with overviews of Hegel's philosophy. Two examples: Charles Taylor's book on Hegel contains only ten pages on the philosophy of nature; none of the fourteen contributions making up *The Cambridge Companion to Hegel*, ed. Frederick C. Beiser (Cambridge: Cambridge University Press, 1993) deals directly with the philosophy of nature.

3 This is precisely Friedrich Engels's misconception, as can be found in his essay, *Ludwig Feuerbach*: '[Dialectical philosophy] reveals the transitory character of everything and in everything; nothing can endure before it except the uninterrupted process of becoming and of passing away; of endless ascendancy from the lower to the higher. And dialectical philosophy itself is nothing more than the mere reflection of this process in the thinking brain' (New York: International Publishers, 1941, 12). For a succinct contemporary expression of this misconception, see Alison Stone's 'Hegel's Philosophy of Nature: Overcoming the Division between Matter and Thought,' *Dialogue* 39, 4 (2000): 725–43. Stone claims to discover a 'theory' of nature 'according to which nature progresses in a rationally necessary series of stages from an initial division between its two constituent elements, thought and matter, to their eventual unification.' She proceeds to show this progression through 'an extended comparison between the Philosophy of Nature and the Philosophy of Spirit' (725–6). I am arguing that if objectivity, whether natural or human, moves according to such a progression, it is *because it has been invested with thought* and thought is dialectical,

i.e., it moves from original unity, through separation (*Urteilen*) to reconciliation. In Hegel, pure, undigested, pre-negated nature does not move on its own accord. Indeed, it is unmoving, lifeless, and dead.

4 See John McCumber's rewarding discussion of Hegelian truth, *The Company of Words: Hegel, Language, and Systematic Philosophy* (Evanston, IL: Northwestern University Press, 1993), 33–117.

5 In *Glauben und Wissen*, e.g., Hegel credits the *influence* of Locke and Hume with having 'dragged down' the subjective idealism of Kant, Jacobi, Fichte into the realm of 'finitude and subjectivity.' *Werke in 20 Bänden*, vol. 2, ed. Eva Moldenhauer and Karl Markus Michel (Frankfurt am Main: Suhrkamp, 1970), 376–7; hereafter *Werke* followed by volume number).

6 See below.

7 Daniel Cook, in reviewing David Lamb's book *Language and Perception in Hegel and Wittgenstein* (New York: St Martin's Press, 1979), agrees that both Hegel and Wittgenstein argue against the empirical account of the relationship between language and reality and the resultant 'atomic facts.' However, both commentators share the belief that we can still 'make sense of our sense experience' through 'certain contextual relations.' 'Review of *Language and Perception in Hegel and Wittgenstein*,' *OM* 14, 2 (1982): 2–3. In her article 'Can Hegel Refer to Particulars?' *OM* 17, 2 (1986): 181–94, Katharina Dulckeit also sees sense certainty in the *Phenomenology of Spirit* (hereafter *PS*) as a thesis about linguistic reference; by proving that Hegelian discourse can refer to particulars, she apparently seeks to show that, for Hegel, scientific knowledge is empirically grounded.

8 Investigations such as Dulckeit's article 'Can Hegel Refer to Particulars' fail to grasp the distinction that I am making between referential, reflective language and the language of science, just as they fail to distinguish between indiscriminate objectivity (Dulckeit is referring to the miscellaneous objects of sense certainty in the *PS*) and the objects of scientific discourse.

9 Frank Schalow, in his article 'The Question of Being and the Recovery of Language within Hegelian Thought,' *OM* 24, 2 (1993): 163–80, writes: 'In an amorphous way, Hegel (like Kant) formulated the problem of the relation between being and thought, but not so decisively as to view language as having an even greater importance in forming an essential link between the two' (164). I am arguing that the language of science is precisely that: the essential embodiment of being and thought. For Schalow, language can only reflect or 'make visible' the mediation between thought and being. The relation between objective truth and language thus remains referential and ultimately, according to Hegel, subjective. 'Through its own activity,

language makes visible the mediation of opposites, and thereby exemplifies the form of determinateness essential to thought' (165). In other words, scientific language remains merely analogous to truth itself (the union of thought and being). In fact, as early as 1802, in *Glauben und Wissen*, Hegel defines the discourse of Reason as that in which subject and predicate express the identity of thought and being (*Werke* 2: 304).

10 *Encyclopedia of Philosophical Sciences* (hereafter *EPS*), §464 (*Werke* 10: 282). Unless otherwise indicated, the translations in this book are mine.

11 McCumber's insightful and detailed analysis of this portion of the *EPS* (§§451–64) explores Hegel's use of the 'name' as linguistic 'sign' and reveals its entirely natural and singular objectivity (*Company of Words*, 220–38).

12 '[N]ames as such [are] *external, senseless entities*, which only have significance as *signs*.' *EPS*, 'Philosophy of Spirit,' §459 (*Werke* 10: 274). In this paragraph, Hegel argues against the Herderian notion of words, as natural objects, having some inherent sense, i.e., that they naturally imitate certain sounds. For Hegel, purely natural entities have no inherent sense. Even though they may be formed by the interplay of natural causes and effects, they remain, in themselves, arbitrary. They are meaningless 'names' or empty signs waiting to be signified by intelligence. This also explains Hegel's argument against phrenology, in the *Phenomenology*. Skulls, as purely natural entities, do not express some inherent meaning which needs only be deciphered.

13 McCumber, *Company of Words*, 233.

14 McCumber uses the term 'sign' as something signifying. I am using it as a synonym for 'name,' a mere, empty token waiting to be invested with meaning or *Gehalt*. As such, it is still insignificant.

15 The 1817 version of this paragraph included the sentence, 'Names, there are many of them, and, as such, they are contingent names with regard to one another.' The contingency of the actual sign, divorced from any signification, simply means that 'lion,' e.g., could well have evolved to be written and pronounced otherwise, as 'leo,' e.g., just as I personally might have been *named* 'Gregory' instead of 'Jeffrey,' which could also have been spelled 'Geoffrey.'

16 'Sense-certainty, then, though indeed expelled from the object, is not yet thereby overcome, but only driven back into the "I."' *Phenomenology of Spirit* (*PS*), trans. A.V. Miller (Oxford: Oxford University Press, 1977) §100 (*Werke* 3: 86).

17 This, then, is why the thing (*Sache*) appears, in the 'Doctrine of Essence,' under the heading 'The Thing's Emergence into Existence' and why James Wilkinson's proposed translation of *die Sache* as 'engendering,' though

somewhat awkward, does make sense. 'On Translating *Sache* in Hegel's Texts: A Response,' *OM* 27, 2 (1996): 211–30.

18 For Hegel, there is no (universal) philosophical science without the particular sciences as content. Thus, in his letter/report to von Raumer, on education, he complains that 'the materials of the particular sciences have not yet attained their reorganization and adoption into the new idea' (*Werke* 4: 419). Hegel sees the particular, positive sciences as a (written) canon of work to be first learned and assimilated, and then reconsidered conceptually. 'This content of understanding, this systematic mass of abstract concepts [i.e., predicative statements] rich in significance [*gehaltvoller Begriffe*] are immediately the stuff of Philosophy.' Report to Niethammer on education (414). This content, reworked dialectically, is how Hegel defines science: 'The content grasped conceptually [*Das Begriffene*] is alone what is philosophical [as it is present] in the form of the Concept.' (415). The scientific whole is 'only grasped through the elaboration of the parts' (420).

19 More importantly, the concept of the content-rich, scientific word enables us to understand how, for Hegel, formally common language, with its (almost) everyday vocabulary and predication-based grammar can ultimately attain to an expression of *logos* in its deepest, richest meanings: as the word of science, as reason and reality, and as the Word of God. It can do so because it is capable of embodying thought and being, and thereby embracing true, objective content and becoming, itself, true objectivity.

20 *EPS*, §491 (*Werke* 10: 307).

21 *PS*, §§61–6 (*Werke* 3: 59–62).

22 Jere Paul Surber, 'Hegel's Speculative Sentence,' *Hegel-Studien* 10 (1975): 222.

23 McCumber, *Company of Words*, 260. Also, Cook's review of Lamb's *Language and Perception*, 2. Both Cook and Lamb share, to some extent, the Wittgenstein idea of contextuality.

24 For Hegel, philosophical discourse is university discourse, and not destined for public consumption; see his critique of Solger in this regard (*Werke* 11: 266–71). Cf. my French translation of Hegel's review of Solger's work: *Hegel: L'ironie romantique* (Paris: Vrin, 1997).

25 *Science of Logic* (hereafter *SL*), Doctrine of the Concept, §I, chapters 2, 3.

26 Discussion of the copula arises in a Kantian context (i.e., in *Faith and Knowing*) and can be seen as a reaction to Kant's belittling of the copula in his dismissal of the ontological argument, in the first *Critique*. The copula is again discussed in the section on judgment in the *Systementwürfe* (1804–5), in *Gesammelte Werke*, vol. 7, ed. R.P. Horstmann and J.H. Trede (Hamburg: Meiner, 1968), 80–93. Hegel's discussions of the copula can be understood

only with further reference to Fichte's 'I am I,' to Hölderlin's thoughts on judgment (*Sämtliche Werke*, vol. 4, ed. F. Beissner [Stuttgart: Kohlhammer, 1962], 226–7) and to Schelling's philosophy of identity. Perhaps Hegel's earliest thoughts on the speculative nature of judgment and the copula are found in the Frankfurt fragment '*Glauben is die Art...*' in ed. Herman Nohl, *Hegels theologische Jugendschriften* (Tübingen: Mohr, 1907), 382–5.

27 See *Wissenschaft der Logik, Die Lehre von Sein*, ed. H.J. Gawoll (Hamburg: Meiner, 1986), 54: 'The proposition (*Satz*) is in no way immediately suited to express speculative truths.'

28 *SL*, Doctrine of the Concept *(Werke* 6: 304). This understanding of judgment as an 'original dividing' is explicitly stated and referred to as an 'Ur-Teilung' in Hölderlin's short text 'Urteil und Sein' (*Sämtliche Werke*, 226–7).

29 Surber, 'Hegel's Speculative Sentence,' points out how Hegel asks us to accept 'subject' in both its grammatical sense and as individual consciousness (214–15). Again, I refer to Hölderlin, *Sämtliche Werke*, apparently written in the Frankfurt period, when he and Hegel were reunited. Here, Hölderlin describes judgment as the original separation that makes 'subject and object possible,' thus conflating the grammatical and 'consciousness' senses of the subject. In fact, in Hegel's later, polemical writings, judgment or predication becomes increasingly associated with the pronouncements of individual (ironic) subjectivity in its position against scientific objectivity, thus referring judgment to Fichte's 'I am I,' as indeed Hölderlin does. See Hegel's *Review of Solger's Posthumous Writings and Correspondence*, where Hegel deals with Friedrich Schlegel. Here, the language of judgment is seen as operating, as irony, against objectivity. 'Judging is a decidedly negative tendency against objectivity ... [S]uch judgments do not take contents into account, but rather vacuous representations that reject the thing [*Sache*] of religions and philosophies' (*Werke* 11: 233). The ironic assault on true objectivity is effectuated through an evacuation of content from meaningful, scientific language. Briefly put, the 'word,' as the very foundation of that discourse, is sapped of its thought-content and relegated to the status of the always arbitrary 'name.' Ironic discourse sunders being and thought. For an elaboration, see my introduction to *Hegel – L'ironie romantique* (Paris: Vrin, 1997), an annotated translation of Hegel's *Review of Solger's ... Writings*.

30 *SL* (*Werke* 6: 302).

31 Ibid., 309.

32 Ibid., 310.

33 Hegel, *PS*, §464 (*Werke* 10: 282).

34 *Werke* 6: 354.

35 This is why the thing (*Sache*) appears, in the *Logic*'s Doctrine of Essence, under the title, 'The Thing's Emergence into Existence.' *Die Sache* should be understood as the objective manifestation of essence. I am arguing for its linguistic nature in Hegel, i.e., its status as *logos*, both in the Greek sense of a reasoned discourse and in the Christian sense of God's revelation.

36 *EPS*, §493 (*Werke* 10: 308).

37 Ibid., §494.

38 *SL*, Doctrine of Essence (*Werke* 6: 13).

39 *PS* (*Werke* 3: 169).

40 *PS*, §489 (*Werke* 10: 307).

41 *EPS*, §494 (*Werke* 10: 308).

42 I will deal with this crucial 'performative' or actual aspect of scientific language below. For now, it is important to understand that ethical life (*Sittlichkeit*) can only constitute an object (i.e., a content) for science in terms of what I have been describing as content-ful language. Discussions on Habermasean language-based ethics and their opposition to Hegelian intersubjectivity should be re-examined in this light. Obviously, my account of Hegel's scientific language implies that this opposition is largely unfounded, since it seems based on 'Habermas's attention to the linguistic dimension of ... autonomy, and Hegel's neglect of that dimension,' as Robert Pippin summarizes the problem in *Idealism as Modernism* (Cambridge: Cambridge University Press, 1997, 180). I want to stress, however, that the linguistic dimension I am referring to is that of language as it pertains to the objects (contents) of science. This most emphatically does not mean conversation or the exchange of personal opinions. In terms of intersubjectivity, as I hope to show in this section on 'Objective Spirit,' it might well mean mutual recognition through mutually recognized text.

43 Shlomo Avineri points out how the expression 'what is rational is actual and what is actual is rational' (which is another way of expressing the conjunction of thought and being) first appears in Hegel's Heidelberg lectures (1817–18) in the context of the (written) constitution. Avineri quotes Hegel: 'What is rational must happen (*muss geschehen*) since the constitution is after all its development,' 'The Discovery of Hegel's Early Lectures on the Philosophy of Right,' *OM* 16, 2 (1985): 203.

44 As Hegel maintains in §549 of the *EPS*, history is essentially historiography, the objective, yet still formal expressions of which are: (1) original and (2) reflective. History itself becomes *rational* (i.e., dialectical) only in that it is then understood and expressed speculatively in the philosophy of history. This view is obviously at odds with the interpretation of Hegelian objectivity that I am arguing against, which holds history (i.e., historical events) to

be, in itself, dialectical. Marx understood this difference better than many have done since.

45 This reflects a deeply personal penchant of Hegel's, who was, by all accounts, a voracious and methodical reader from his very youth. Hegel's predilection for nature in its digested, determined form is also reflected in his account of his youthful trip to the Alps, where his primary interest seems to have been in finding locations whose descriptions he had previously read.

46 See, e.g., John Burbidge, 'Hegel on Galvanism,' in *Hegel on the Modern World*, ed. Ardis B. Collins (Albany: SUNY Press, 1995), 111–24. The article shows how Hegel relies on the writings of his time to develop the theory of galvanism which we find in §330 of the *Encyclopedia*. Burbidge also shows how Hegel, in choosing his scientific content, prefers those where the form of speculative thought is best seen. The article by Alison Stone, 'Hegel's Philosophy of Nature,' which argues for a Hegelian 'theory' of nature, must necessarily misunderstand the importance of objective content in Hegel's science. Indeed, Stone attributes much of the difficulty of the Philosophy of Nature to the fact that Hegel's arguments are 'submerged amidst [his] lengthy discussions of now-unfamiliar works' (725).

47 The word has a particularly elevated status in Hegel's aesthetics. 'The object corresponding to [poetry] is the infinite sphere of spirit'; thus the word is 'that most constructive material [*bildsamste Material*], which immediately hears spirit and is most capable of grasping its interests and movements into its inner liveliness' (*Lectures on Aesthetics, Werke* 15: 239).

48 '[T]he true content of religion is first present to the mind in words and letters ... in words and writings' (Preface to H.F.W. Hinrich's *Science of Religion, Werke* 11: 44). Hegel's position is radically opposed to Schleiermacher, for whom 'all sacred writing is a mausoleum for religion'; see the 1st ed. of *Discourses on Religion, Kritische Gesamtausgabe*, vol. 1, part 2, ed. H. Peiter, J. Birkner, et al. (New York, Berlin: de Gruyter, 1980) 242.

49 Hegel's 1802 polemical essay against the philosopher W.T. Krug, who had asked speculative philosophers to deduce his pen, is meant to show that philosophy does not deal with individual, 'natural' objects.

50 *Philosophy of Right* §330.

51 *Werke* 11: 265; cf. Reid, *Hegel: L'ironie romantique*, §52.

52 *Werke* 11: 233; cf. Reid, *Hegel: L'ironie romantique* §23. It should be stated here that Hegel's definition of romantic irony is in no way dependent on the various definitions that Schlegel comes up with in the *Athenäum*, e.g., 'Irony is the clear consciousness of the eternal agility of infinitely fecund chaos.' *Kritische Friedrich-Schlegel-Ausgabe* (35 vols.), vol. 2, ed. E. Behler (Munich:

Schöningh, 1958–85), 263. According to Hegel, the choice of the word 'irony,' by its theorists, is purely arbitrary.
53 *EPS*, Philosophy of Spirit, §467 Add. (*Werke* 10: 286).
54 *Werke* 11: 233.

2. The Ontological Grasp of Judgment

1 In the *Science of Logic* (*SL*): 'Judgment is the division of the concept through itself.' 'It is thus the original dividing [*ursprüngliche Teilung*] of the original identity' (*Werke* 6: 304). See also *Encyclopedia Logic* (hereafter *EL*), §166: 'The etymological meaning of judgment in our language is deeper and expresses the unity of the concept as what is first, and its differentiation as the original dividing, what judgment is in truth.'

2 *SL*, 301–1. See also Hegel's analysis of the speculative proposition, in the Preface to the *Phenomenology of Spirit* (*Werke* 3: 57–63). 'Thus as well, in philosophical propositions, the identity of the subject and the predicate should not abolish the difference within, which the form of the proposition expresses, but rather their identity should present itself as a harmony.' (59).

3 *EL*, §166: 'The copula "is" comes from the nature of the concept, of being, in its alienation, identical with itself.' As we will see, the destiny or fulfilment of the copula is the moment of particularity, the existing and essential middle term of the Hegelian syllogism, where '[t]he determined and filled [or fulfilled] copula, which before was formed by the abstract *is*, but has subsequently been further constituted as the foundation in general, is now present' (*SL*, 350–1). Andreas Graeser refuses to consider this fulfilment that is already present in judgment; but persists in seeing the judgment form as only a deficient iteration of identity, citing Hegel's *EL*, §31. While, for Hegel, the propositional form of judgment is, *in itself* or on its own, incapable of articulating speculative truth, i.e., it is not yet the syllogism, when it is grasped speculatively, it is seen to contain within itself the germ of speculative truth, of both identity and difference. In Hegel's words, 'The etymological meaning of judgment in our language is deeper and expresses the unity of the concept as what is first, and its differentiation as the original dividing, what judgment is in truth' (*EL*, §166). This essay seeks to show that, for Hegel, propositions are only speculative, or objectively true, within the system of science, which is syllogistic in form. See Andreas Graeser, 'Hegel über die Rede vom Absoluten. Teil 1: Urteil, Statz und spekulativer Gehalt,' *Zeitschrift für philosophische Forschung* 44 (1990): 175–93.

4 Jere Paul Surber, 'Hegel's Speculative Sentence,' *Hegel-Studien* 10 (1975):

214–15. Surber's ground-breaking article is an exegesis of the above cited passage from the Preface to the *Phenomenology*. Graeser seems to understand the homonymous use of 'Subjekt' as an unfortunate vagueness or ambiguity. In fact, 'das Subjekt ist kein Subjekt.' See Andreas Graeser, 'Hölderlin über Urteil und Sein,' *Freiburger Zeitschrift für Philosophie und Theologie* 38 (1991): 117. This point of view seems untenable in light of subsequent passages that we find in Hegel, where both meanings of 'subject' are clearly present. In *EL*, §166, e.g., Hegel writes: 'However, in that the copula "is" states the predicate of the subject, this exterior, subjective subsumption is in its turn suppressed, and the judgment is taken as a determination of the *object* itself.' For Graeser, the speculative sentence is not really speculative: 'the so-called speculative proposition is a proposition, and nothing more' Graeser, 'Hegel über die Rede,' 176. See also Jere Paul Surber, 'The Problems of Language in German Idealism,' in O.K. Wiegand et al., eds., *Phenomenology on Kant, German Idealism, Hermeneutics and Logic* (Netherlands: Kluwer, 2000), 305–36, where he refers to 'the Idealists' reflections upon *Urteil and Satz* as fundamental to their understanding of the relations among logic, language and consciousness' (336). See, as well, J.P. Surber, 'Satz and Urteil in Kant and Fichte,' in *New Essays in Fichte's Foundation of the Entire Doctrine of Scientific Knowledge*, ed. D. Breazeale and T. Rockmore (Amherst, N.Y.: Humanities Press, 2001).

5　In terms of classical truth theories, Hegel eschews truth by correspondence. 'Hegel is rejecting any form of the correspondence view of truth.' Tom Rockmore, *Cognition: An Introduction to Hegel's Phenomenology of Spirit* (Berkeley: University of California Press, 1997), 3. One might then turn to the coherence theory of truth, but this is only completely effective with formal systems and their statements. Hegel's system makes statements about reality, and so the question arises as to how these statements can be true without being so by correspondence.

6　Surber points out how this idea of language as both being and thought is found in Schelling's idea of language as art, the incarnation of the absolute ('The Problems of Language,' 322–3).

7　'The Logos, by tradition ... signifies the identity of thinking and Being – or, in modern terms, of subjectivity and objectivity.' Werner Marx, *Hegel's Phenomenology of Spirit*, trans. P. Heath (New York: Harper and Row, 1975), xxii.

8　*SL*, 351: '[The regained unity of the concept] is the fulfilled or content-full copula of judgment ... Through this fulfillment of the copula, judgment has become the syllogism.' This is what Hegel means when he writes that the judgment form, or the proposition, is 'unsuited to expressing what is concrete (and the truth is concrete) and speculative.' (*EL*, §31). To express truth, propositions must be part of a system. 'The true form in which the truth exists can only be as the scientific system of itself.' *PS*, (*Werke* 3: 14).

9 Pierre Aubenque, *Le problème de l'être chez Aristote* (Paris: Presses Universitaires de France, 1962), 291.

10 *Lessons on Esthetics* (*Werke* 13: 211). Also, ibid., 96.

11 *EPS*, §404 (*Werke* 10: 203–4). Recent work on madness and Hegel includes Jon Mills, 'Hegel on the Unconscious Abyss: Implications for Psychoanalysis,' *OM* 28, 1 (1996): 59–75; the same author's book on the same topic, *The Unconscious Abyss: Hegel's Anticipation of Psychoanalysis* (Albany: SUNY Press, 2002); Kirk Pillow, 'Habituating Madness and Phantasying Art in Hegel's Encyclopedia,' *OM* 28, 2 (1997): 183–215; J. Rozenberg, 'Physiologie, embryologie et psychopathologie: Une mise à l'épreuve de la conceptualité hégélienne,' *Archives de Philosophie* 60, 2 (1997): 243–54. On Novalis and madness, see D.F. Krell's *Contagion: Sexuality, Disease and Death in German Idealism and Romanticism* (Bloomington: Indiana University Press, 1998).

12 *EPS*, §404. Here, Hegel describes mental illness as 'state where the development of the soul, already having achieved, in its later determination, consciousness and understanding, can once again fall.'

13 Ibid.

14 This is the original meaning of the Latin term 'genius,' a spirit presiding at the birth of an individual, determining its destiny.

15 *EPS*, §405.

16 Ibid., §404.

17 Ibid., §405.

18 Ibid., §410.

19 Hegel says that the adolescent seeks a male authority figure but he does not say this figure has to be his biological father. This seems to indicate that the father's role in the child's genesis and upbringing is extra-natural (*Encyclopedia* §397 add.). The movement from soul to consciousness can be seen as a struggle for liberation, as we find in Hans-Christian Lucas, 'The Sovereign Ingratitude of Spirit toward Nature,' *OM* 23, 2 (1992): 131–50, or Lydia Moland, 'Inheriting, Earning and Owning: The Source of Practical Identity in Hegel's Anthropology,' *OM* 34, 2 (2003): 139–70. In psychological terms, this liberation from nature should perhaps also be seen as a liberation from the maternal. In this way, the fall into madness is, in the proper sense of the word, hysteria. Other important commentaries on the Subjective Spirit portion of the *EPS* include Allen Olsen, *Hegel and the Spirit* (Princeton: Princeton University Press, 1992); Murray Greene, *Hegel on the Soul* (The Hague: Martinus Nijhoff, 1972); I. Fetscher, *Hegels Lehre vom Menschen* (Stuttgart: Friedrich-Frommann Verlag, 1970); and the thematic issue of *Hegel-Studien*

19 (1979), edited by Dieter Henrich, *Hegels Philosophische Psychologie*.
20 *EPS*, §405 (*Werke* 10: 125–6).
21 *EPS*, §403 (*Werke* 10: 122).
22 I had the honour of studying with the late Jacques Rivelaygue at L'université de Paris IV-Sorbonne: some of his later students edited his incomparable *leçons*.
23 I am translating. Jacques Rivelaygue, *Leçons de métaphysique allemande*, vol. 1 (Paris: Grasset, 1990), 191–92.
24 It may have been written on the inside cover of Hölderlin's copy of the first edition of Fichte's *Wissenschaftslehre*. Hölderlin, *Sämtliche Werke*, 4: 226–7; see also Beissner's commentary, ibid., 391–2.
25 Hölderlin, *Sämtliche Werke*, 4: 226.
26 Hegel uses the expression I = I, in too many places to mention, to denote subjective or personal identity, a solipsistic self-reflection that cannot include real, worldly difference. See below.
27 *EL*, §84. '[Undetermined] being is the concept only in itself.'
28 *Wissenschaft der Logik, Die Lehre von Sein* (1832), ed. Hans Jürgen Gawoll (Hamburg: Meiner, 1990), 72.
29 Hölderlin, *Sämtliche Werke*, 4: 227.
30 The text was published in 1961 by Beissner and was apparently written in early 1795. See Graeser, 'Hölderlin über Urteil und Sein,' 111.
31 Hegel, *Briefe von und an Hegel*, vol. 1, ed. Johannes Hoffmeister (Hamburg: Meiner, 1961), letter 9. Cf. Vincente Serrano-Marin, 'Sobre Hölderlin y los comienzos del Idealismo alemand,' *Anales del Seminario de Historia de la Filosofia* 10 (1993): 173–94.
32 In this fragment, Hegel refers to the question of judgment and being, although he expresses it in terms of a reunion of differences: 'Reunion and being have the same signification; in each proposition the binding word 'is' expresses the reunion of subject and predicate – a being' (*Werke* 1: 251). See notes by O. Depré in the French translation, Hegel, *Premiers écrits* (Paris: Vrin, 1997), 137. See also P. Kondylis, *Die Enstehung der Dialektik* (Stuttgart: Klett-Cotta, 1979), 467.
33 Hölderlin, *Sämtliche Werke*, 4: .
34 In his article on 'Hegel in Canada,' John Burbidge rightly notes a reluctance among Canadian Hegel scholars to use 'absolute' as a noun. *OM* 25, 2 (1994): 215–19. In fact, I would say there is a general reluctance among contemporary Hegel scholars to consider the 'absolutist' dimensions of Hegel's thought. I believe it is impossible to understand Hegel's systematic claims without considering the Idea as an absolute subject. At the end of the *EPS*, §577, Hegel refers to 'the subjective activity of the Idea.'

35 The expression is found at the end of the *EL*, §244: 'The absolute freedom of the Idea is, however, that it ... decides in the absolute truth of itself ... to freely let itself go out of itself as nature.' A similar expression is found at the end of the *Science of Logic*. In *EL*, §219, Hegel calls this 'letting itself go' the 'judgment of the concept' that produces 'objectivity as an independent totality ... an inorganic nature it is faced with.'

36 *WL*, 573.

37 In both the Greek sense of *logos*, the creative Word at the beginning of Hegel's favourite Gospel, and a reasoned discourse. In these rarified realms of the absolute subject, it is hard not to think of God. Indeed, it is difficult not to understand a proposition in which an absolute subject, called the Idea, posits its essence as the existence of the predicate as something akin to the ontological argument, which claims to express the singular case where an idea can do nothing other than posit itself as existing. Such an interpretation would certainly not be false. It would simply be, in Hegelian terms, a depiction or representation of a more complex, scientific, or speculative truth. Such an interpretation would also explain why Hegel took pains to save the ontological argument from Kant's critique. After all, can anything be more radically opposed to Hegel's ontological notion of judgment than Kant's devastating refutation of the argument, saying that existence cannot be *predicated*?

38 In *EL*, §171, Hegel writes that the destiny of judgment, through the filled or fulfilled (*sich erfüllt*) copula is to become the syllogism. In the *SL*, Hegel writes: 'Through the filling/fulfillment of the copula, judgment has become the syllogism' (*Werke* 6: 351). Cf. ibid. 309. The copula is 'filled' or is *inhaltsvolle* because it is the actual determination of both subject and predicate, or, it is the moment of particularity between the universal singular (subject) and the universal predicate. As determined particularity, we can say it fulfils its meaning, which is 'to be.' The copula thus becomes the middle term in the syllogism. We might say that Hegel reinterprets what every philosophy student knows on a purely formal level: the truth must not simply be asserted in a proposition; it must be expressed in a valid argument form, e.g., a syllogism.

39 Preface to the *PS* (*Werke* 3: 61).

40 Not seeing the homonymous nature of 'subject' in Hegel's notion of judgment leads Richard Dien Winfield to ask '[E]ven if judgment relates only two terms why should the independent conceptual factors resulting from individuality be specifically related as subject and predicate? The subject-predicate relation seems to be not just bipolar, but non-transitive.' 'From Concept to Judgment: Rethinking Hegel's Overcoming of Formal Logic,'

Dialogue 40, 1 (2001): 70. Winfield's answer to his own question implies that Hegel arbitrarily adopts the judgment form because it is an adequate reflection of a true state of affairs existing outside the language of science itself. I don't believe Hegel's idea of scientific language admits such arbitrariness. 'Subject and predicate are appropriate qualifiers insofar as they capture the salient features that the immediate individual and the abstract universal possess in the relationship by which the copula joins them' (72).

41 F. Schlegel is, for Hegel, the paradigm of this sort of judging. *Philosophy of Right*, §140 add. Also, *Werke* 13: 93–5, and *Werke* 11: 233–4. Hegel also associates non-speculative judgment with the calculative reasoning of the understanding, where it is, again, destructive of the organic whole. 'Judging means putting to death, presenting *the individual* not *what matters* (*die Sache*), as if the living were the individual, not the *truth*' (*Werke* 2: 560). Graeser fails to see this distinction between personal judgment and speculative judgments within the system of science.

42 *History of Philosophy* (*Werke* 20: 415–16). *EPS*, §424. See T.M. Knox's commentary to §35 of the *Philosophy of Right*. 'Knowledge of the self in abstraction from all objects and determinate experiences is the knowledge that 'I am I.' Here the object known, the self, is identical with the knower, the abstract and infinite ego' (Oxford: Oxford University Press, 1967), 320.

3. Why Hegel Didn't Join the 'Kant-Klub': Reason and Speculative Discourse

1 H.S. Harris, *Hegel's Development*, vol. 1, *Toward the Sunlight* (Oxford: Oxford University Press, 1972), 98n3; Terry Pinkard, *Hegel: A Biography* (Cambridge: Cambridge University Press, 2000), 33–6, where I found the expression 'Kant-Klub'; Günther Nicolin, ed., *Hegel in Berichten seiner Zeitgenossen* (Hamburg: Meiner, 1970), 12.

2 Pinkard, *Hegel*, 33; Harris, *Hegel's Development*, 83n1.

3 Nicolin, *Hegel in Berichten*, 10–13.

4 Ibid., documents 5, 6, 8, 9; Harris, *Hegel's Development*, 1: 98.

5 The expression is from Leutwein. Nicolin, *Hegel in Berichten*, document 8.

6 The source of this opinion is perhaps the account by C.T. Schwab: Hegel 'wouldn't put up with Storr's dogmatics' (ibid., 16). Cf. the correspondence between Hegel and Schelling five years later (*Briefe von und an Hegel*, ed. J. Hoffmeister (Hamburg: Felix Meiner, 1953), vol. 1, letters 7 and 8) where Hegel refers to the 'philosophico-kantian' orthodoxy of Tübingen. 'Storr was Hegel's, Hölderlin's and Schelling's teacher and a figure against whom all of them reacted' (Pinkard, *Hegel*, 34–5). Frederick Beiser writes of Flatt, Storr's disciple at Tübingen, that 'Hegel, Hölderlin and Schelling bitterly

resented his compulsory lectures. The three saw Flatt as a reactionary, opposed to the ideas of Kant, Reinhold and Fichte.' Frederick C. Beiser, *The Fate of Reason: German Philosophy from Kant to Fichte* (Cambridge: Harvard University Press, 1987), 211. Harris: 'G.C. Storr was certainly the most notable and the most influential of all Hegel's teachers at Tübigen and his influence on Hegel was in fact considerable, though almost entirely negative' *Hegel's Development*, 1: 91). I hope to temper this opinion, which seems to reflect Schelling's opinion far more than Hegel's.

7 Some of Hegel's fellow students also refer to his interest in Kant. Strauss writes that Hegel and Maerklin threw themselves into Kantian philosophy, 'with remarkable enthusiasm.' (Nicolin, *Hegel in Berichten*, 9). Schwegler mentions Hegel's laziness at the beginning of his Tübingen studies, with the exception of his study of Kant (ibid., 13).

8 It is tempting to interpret the writings on the positivity of religion, against the authority of faith, as a polemic against Storr and the authority of revelation (e.g., Harris, *Hegel's Development*, 1: 224–6). However, what Hegel challenges in Christian positivity, in his essay on that subject, is not the authority of revelation but that of the Church. Hegel's reaction against the positivity of religion is also generally seen as an opposition to the doctrine of miracles as instances of divine revelation, as we find in Storr. However, Hegel seems to interpret miracles through his reading of Lessing's *Education of Humanity*, which Hegel had read and appreciated, where miracles are presented as a pedagogical necessity.

9 Harris, *Hegel's Development*, 1: 83n1. Harris cites Karl Rosenkranz, *Georg Wilhelm Friedrich Hegels Leben* (Darmstadt: Wissenschaftlische Buchgesellschaft, 1963), 14.

10 Harris, *Hegel's Development*, 1: 84 n1. Harris cites Dieter Henrich, 'Carl Immanuel Diez. Zur Enstehungsgeschichte des deutschen Idealismus,' *Hegel-Studien*, 111 (1965), 70–1n, and Carmelo Lacorte, *Il Primo Hegel* (Florence: Sansoni, 1959), 301–2. Cf. Johannes Hoffmeister, ed., *Dokumente zu Hegels Entwicklung* (Stuttgart: Frommann, 1974 [1936]), 195–217, for the manuscript on psychology, with Hoffmeister's commentaries, 448–53.

11 Hoffmeister, *Dokumente*, 115–36.

12 Hoffmeister notes that the attribution of the power of abstraction to reason is also something Hegel adds to Garve's text (ibid., 122n3): cf. Harris, *Hegel's Development*, 1:36.

13 Hoffmeister, *Dokumente*, 122.

14 Kant, *Critique of Pure Reason*, trans. Werner S. Pluhar (Indianapolis: Hackett, 1996), 122–3.

15 Hoffmeister, *Dokumente*, 454.

16 Harris, *Hegel's Development*, 1:87 and 85n4. Harris evokes the possibility that the lost essay, whose title is known, may come from something Hegel wrote for Flatt's course, in 1789.

17 Harris comments on the 1794 manuscript *Hegel's Development*, 1: 175–7. According to Harris, the Hegelian determination of *Vernunft* is missing in the text, other than as a brief subsection of the *Reflectierende Urteilskraft*. However, Harris does not mention the subsection on *Kosmologie*, and this is precisely where we find what actually defines reason for Kant and Hegel, namely, its dialectical activity. Cf. Hoffmeister, *Dokumente*, 210–17 and 448–54.

18 Hoffmeister, *Dokumente*, 213.

19 Ibid., 214.

20 Ibid., 215.

21 Ibid., 216.

22 Ibid., 217.

23 Hegel, *The Difference between the Systems of Fichte and Schelling* (*Werke* 2: 39; my emphasis).

24 'A = A includes the difference between A as subject and A as object, as well as their identity: A = B includes the identity on A and B, as well as the difference between the two' (ibid.).

25 Ibid.

26 Hegel, *Faith and Knowledge* (*Werke* 2: 304).

27 Ibid.

28 In his *Leçons de métaphysique allemande*, vol. 1, 191–3 (Paris: Grasset, 1990), Jacques Rivelaygue discovers the idea of original judgment (*Ur-teilung*), which presupposes the totalizing union of subject and object, in Hölderlin's short text 'Being and Judgment' (*Hyperion* period 1794–8).

29 Hegel, *Faith and Knowledge* (*Werke* 2: 306).

30 Ibid., 305.

31 Ibid., 306.

32 Ibid.

33 '*Schluss*' is generally translated here as 'conclusion' (ibid., 307).

34 Ibid. The theory of the syllogism, as found in the *Logics*, develops the copula into the middle term, i.e., into the moment of the particular, between the universal and the singular.

35 Alexis Philonenko, Introduction to his translation of *Foi et Savoir* (Paris: Vrin, 1988), 28.

36 On G.C. Storr: M. Brecht and J. Sandberger, 'Hegels Begegnung mit der Theologie im Tübinger Stift,' *Hegel-Studien* 5 (1969): 47–81; Beiser, *Fate of Reason*, 212; Pinkard, *Hegel*, 35; Harris, *Hegel's Development*, 1: xxiii, 91–6;

Lacorte, *Il Primo Hegel*, 139–41, 154–61, 166–72; Klaus Düsing, 'Die Rezeption der Kantischen Postulatenlehre,' *Hegel-Studien* 9 (1973): 53–90; Otto Pfeiderer, *The Development of Theology in Germany since Kant*, trans. Smith, 2nd ed. (London: Sonnenschein, 1893), 85–7.

37 On I.C. Diez: *Immanuel Carl Diez, Briefwechsel und Kantische Schriften*, ed. Dieter Henrich, (Stuttgart: Klett-Cotta, 1997); Pinkard, *Hegel*, 34, 36; Harris, *Hegel's Development*, 1: 107n1; 98n3; D. Henrich and Doderlein, *Hegel-Studien* 3, 276–87 (cited by Harris).

38 Years later, in 1829, in his Berlin lectures on religion, Hegel writes: 'It is in God's nature ... to exist for the human mind, to communicate to him ... God *exists* (*ist*) and puts Himself in relation to man' (*Werke* 17: 382–3).

39 From a 1787 essay. Hoffmeister, *Dokumente*, 172.

4. The Fiery Crucible, Yorick's Skull, and Leprosy in the Sky: The Language of Nature

1 Speculative or scientific truth in the Hegelian sense is the identity of identity and difference. It may be presented either intuitively, 'in a common form, brought close to the representation, imagination or the heart; for example, about nature, we speak of ... God's son abandoned into temporality, the world etc.,' or scientifically, 'in the form of the concept.' Letter-report to Niethammer (*Werke* 4: 415). See also Hegel's reference to Jakob Böhme in the Preface to the 2nd ed. of the *EPS* (*Werke* 8: 28).

2 The problematic nature of this relationship and its polemical interpretations are evident in the recent issue of *OM* 34, 1 (2003) dedicated to the topic. In other words: 'Resistance of contingent nature to the demands of rational thought continues to bedevil students of Hegel's philosophy of nature.' Michael Hoffheimer, 'Law, Fossils, and the Configuring of Hegel's Philosophy of Nature,' *Idealistic Studies* 25, 3 (1995): 166. Hoffheimer sees thought's resistance to natural contingency as an enduring tension in Hegel's system, reflected in the quadratic form of certain sections of the philosophy of nature.

3 On the completeness of the system, see *Encyclopedia Logic* (*EL*), §§14, 15. Edward Halper puts the problem this way: '[A] comprehensive system seems to undermine itself: either it includes everything and there is nothing beyond it to explain, or it explains everything and there *is*, thus, something beyond that it does not include.' 'The Idealism of Hegel's System,' *OM* 34, 1 (2003): 20.

4 Heinrich Heine, *Sämmtliche Werke*, vol. 14 (1862), 275–82. Quoted in Walter Kaufmann, *Hegel: A Reinterpretation* (New York: Doubleday / Anchor Books,

1966), 366–7. I realize that this account does not enjoy the same textual status as something Hegel actually wrote or a comment he made in the lecture
hall. The Hegelian attitude towards nature which I believe it reveals will be
further witnessed in other, more academic, although less evocative references.

5 Writers and editors on the question often begin with this type of disclaimer,
 e.g., Stephen Houlgate, editor of the collection of essays, *Hegel and the Philosophy of Nature* (Albany: SUNY Press, 1998) begins his Introduction by
 stating: 'G.W.F. Hegel's Philosophy of Nature ... has long been the object of
 ridicule and disdain' (xi).

6 I mean 'theory' as we might find it defined in contemporary philosophy of
 science: a series of axioms and propositions that are tested (falsified), by
 experiment, as hypotheses.

7 Alain Lacroix points out how Hegel's reservations regarding Newton are
 partly based on his 'mathematical formalism' which Hegel saw as adding
 nothing new to the discoveries of Galileo and Kepler. *Hegel: La philosophie de
 la nature* (Paris: Presses Universitaire de France, 1997), 79–99.

8 William Maker gives a number of examples of this line of interpretation in
 his important article, 'The Very Idea of the Idea of Nature,' in Houlgate,
 Hegel and the Philosophy of Nature, 21n3. His examples are drawn from
 Charles Taylor, Errol Harris, Michael Rosen, and R.G. Collingwood. In fact,
 Hegel explicitly rejects the idea of nature itself progressing logically, in an
 evolutionary way. 'It was a clumsy representation of the ancient and even
 the new philosophy of nature to consider the development and the passage
 from one natural form and sphere to a superior form and sphere as a real,
 exterior product.' *Encyclopedia,* Philosophy of Nature, §247 Remark (*EPS*
 §247R). In his later article 'Idealism and Autonomy,' *OM* 34, 1 (2003): 60,
 Maker describes the processional view as claiming, 'nature and spirit *are*
 the Idea.' He opposes this view to an equally erroneous Kantian approach,
 where, 'logical categories are applied to an independent given reality as
 form to content' (ibid.). Maker claims that Hegel's position is an *Aufhebung*
 of these two extremes, a position he calls 'methodological idealism,' where
 the system acknowledges 'the existence of a domain which is ontologically
 distinct from the system as a system of thought' (ibid., 61).

9 In the words of Louis Althusser, 'Jean Hyppolite decisively proved that
 Hegel's conception of history had nothing to do with any anthropology.'
 'Lenin before Hegel,' in *Lenin and Philosophy and other Essays*, trans. Ben
 Brewster (New York: Monthly Review Press, 2001), 81.

10 Friedrich Engels, *Dialectics of Nature*, trans. Clemens Dutt (New York: International Publishers, 1963).

11 Maker puts it this way: 'How can a philosophy that ... claims to generate its
    own determinations from within nonetheless attend to the worlds of nature
    and spirit as found beyond the system?' 'Idealism and Autonomy,' 60. Cf
    Halper's formulation of the question, above, 'Idealism,' 20. The problem of
    the relation between thought and nature is sometimes explicit but it is also
    implicit in the two 'other' main currents of interpretation, which are also
    relevant to my argument: how the empirical sciences of Hegel's day are
    related to his philosophy of nature and, more rarely, how to understand the
    transition from the Absolute Idea, at the end of the *Logics*, to natural being,
    with which the *Philosophy of Nature* begins. In his review of the book, Jere
    Surber summarizes these different directions as they are represented in
    Houlgate's 'Hegel and the Philosophy of Nature,' *OM* 33, 1 (2002): 119–24.
12 Here, scholarly activity often takes the form of 'discoveries,' within the
    Philosophy of Nature, of various forms and articulations that can also be
    identified in the *Logics*. A good example is Alison Stone's article, 'Hegel's
    Philosophy of Nature: Overcoming the Division Between Thought and
    Matter,' where we find: 'A few scholars have attempted to reconstruct
    Hegel's overall view of natural development, but without recognizing his
    basic account of nature's progressive unification of thought and matter.'
    Dialogue 29, 4 (2000): 741 n2.
13 Hegel explicitly rejects this conception in *EPS*, §247R, and in texts where he
    distinguishes his own views from those of Schelling, e.g., in *EL*, §23Add.
    (*EL*, §23Z).
14 Some commentators do this. Natural contingency simply falls outside the
    province of the philosophy of nature, which deals only with that part of
    nature that adheres to the concept. Stephen Houlgate claims there is a 'dis-
    tinctive logic of nature' by which 'certain natural processes are made neces-
    sary' as opposed to 'contingencies in nature that only empirical science can
    discover.' 'Logic and Nature in Hegel's Philosophy: A Response to John W.
    Burbidge,' *OM* 34, 1 (2003): 107. In the same issue, Will Dudley writes: 'The
    necessary contingency of natural beings and the intrinsic limits to system-
    atic conceptual determinacy, mean that the correspondence between expe-
    rience and philosophy will always be imperfect.' 'Systematic Philosophy
    and Idealism' (ibid. 99). I am arguing for a more dynamic relation between
    natural contingency and the philosophy of nature, one that is mediated by
    the natural sciences.
15 That Hegel recognizes that nature is contingent does not, in itself, refute the
    processional view. One can remain a processionalist while arguing that
    Hegel recognizes the double aspect of nature, as both logical and chaotic,
    when he writes of nature's impotence, the fact that it is incapable of adher-

ing to the concept and is always lapsing into contingency (*EN*, §250). However, the fact that Hegel himself would here have to decide what is contingent and what is necessary would refer back to the arbitrary nature of the whole construction, again jeopardizing any claim to objectivity.

16 *SL* (*Werke* 6, 202–7).

17 As Hegel writes in *EPS*, §248: 'In nature, not only does the play of forms manifest an unruly, unbridled capriciousness, but as well, each form in itself is devoid of its own concept.' In *EL*, §145add., he writes: 'This richness [of nature] as such ... is of no higher rational interest and it only gives rise in us, in the great variegated diversity of its inorganic and organic formations, to an intuition of contingency, losing itself in indeterminacy.' In *EL* §21add., Hegel refers specifically to the stars: 'We see the stars, today here, tomorrow there; this disorder is something inappropriate [*ein Unangemessenes*] to spirit, something not to be trusted.' Hegel's feeling, or lack thereof, for natural wonders is starkly captured in the diary of his trip through the Alps, where he describes the glaciers as 'filthy' and the mountains themselves as 'eternally dead masses [that] gave me nothing but the monotonous and at length boring notion: this is how it is [*es ist so*].' In Kaufmann, *Hegel*, 307–9. Hegel's feeling for nature is perhaps akin to the protagonist's epiphany, in Sartre's *Nausea*, when the character experiences the nauseating presence of the tree root under his park bench.

18 On the other end of the spectrum from the processional view, William Maker sees nature, in Hegel, as having 'nothing in common' with thought ('The Very Idea of the Idea,' 4). In his article 'Chemism and Chemistry,' John Burbidge presents the sides of the debate in a similar fashion, grouping Halper, Winfield, and Wandschneider together at one pole, as those for whom 'philosophy of nature and philosophy of spirit are simply extensions of logic,' as opposed to Maker, for whom 'nature is a domain that is radically other than systematic thought,' 'The Very Idea,' 4. Between these two poles, we might place the intermediary positions of John Burbidge and, in a different way, myself.

19 In *EL*, §23add. Hegel distinguishes his own conception of the relation between thought and nature from Schelling's. For Schelling, thought is immediately 'petrified' in nature, while for Hegel, in dealing with nature, we are dealing with 'thought-determinations,' a kind of second nature that has been determined by human thinking. Although they overcome the 'antithesis between subjective and objective (in their usual sense [i.e., in the sense we witness in the *Phenomenology*]),' thought-determinations are the objective content of speculative (Hegelian) thought.

20 Hegel may have adopted this vocabulary from Schiller, who refers to each

one-sided aspect of the holistic truth (either through intuition or through understanding) as barbarous or savage, in his *Letters on the Esthetic Education of Mankind*. See Letter 4, where Schiller uses the synonym *Wilder* to describe a state where feeling dominates principles, and *Barbar* where reasoning is dominant. Hegel seems to use 'barbarian' terms for either unilateral position. Thus, Hegel writes in another Jena aphorism (#46): 'Remaining in intuition is barbarous, e.g., Jakob Böhme' (*Werke* 2: 551). On the other hand, remaining fixed in the unilateral use of the understanding's principles is equally barbarous, as we see in Hegel's essay on scepticism, where he refers to 'that barbarity that consists in attributing an irrefutable certitude and truth to facts of consciousness,' where 'the understanding is raised to absolute status' (*Werke* 2: 250). Michael Hoffheimer shows how Hegel's early attempts to configure his philosophy of nature in terms of geometrical symbols reflecting the triadic and quadratic structure of crystals stems from Böhme and Baader. Hoffheimer, 'Law, Fossils and Configuring,' 156. See also his introduction in 'Fragment on the Life-course of God,' *Clio* 12, 4 (1983): 401–9, including an English translation of the fragment we are discussing.

21 *Werke* 2: 552.

22 *EL*, §244. 'The absolute freedom of the Idea is, however, that it ... decides in the absolute truth of itself ... to freely let itself go out of itself as nature.' We find a similar articulation at the end of the *Science of Logic* (*SL*) where the Idea's punctuality is expressed as 'the absolutely unique' (*Werke* 6: 573). In the Jena aphorism we are discussing, 'frei entlassen' is expressed as 'Gott, zur Natur geworden, hat sich ausgebreitet.'

23 *EPS*, §247add. This addition goes on to describe the Idea's self-othering as (*als*) nature, using some of the mythical or religious images we find in Böhme: e.g., nature is described as the Son of God, let go into the world and then taken up again. In his remark to the following section, Hegel describes nature as the 'fall' from the Idea.

24 In our aphorism, Hegel uses the term *Lebenslauf Gottes*, the life-course of God. In the *Lessons on the Philosophy of Religion*, we find: 'It is the absolute freedom of the Idea that, in its determining and judgment, lets go of the other as something free and independent. This other, let go and independent, is nothing less than the world' (*Werke* 17: 243). Cf. *Encyclopedia*, Philosophy of Spirit §577, where the self-dividing or judgment of the Idea produces nature and spirit.

25 Having inter-penetrated and recognized each other at the end of the *Logic*, Nature and Spirit let each other go. Hermann Braun, 'Zur Interpretation der Hegelschen Wendung: frei entlassen' in *Hegel: L'esprit objectif, l'unité de*

l'histoire, actes du 2e congrès de l'association internationale pour l'étude de la philosophie de Hegel, 1968, 51–64.

26 *SL*, 573. As well, the *frei entlassen* Braun refers to is, in fact, in *EL*, §244, a *'sich frei aus sich entlassen'* (freely letting itself go out of itself), where the reflexive pronoun appears twice.

27 Dieter Wandschneider, 'Das Problem der Entäusserung der Idee zur Natur bei Hegel,' *Hegel-Jahrbuch* (1990): 25–33.

28 Richard Dien Winfield, 'Objectivity in Logic and Nature,' *OM* 34, 1 (2003): 77–90. William Maker also seeks to establish the freedom of thought as self-determining and therefore free of natural determination. However, he goes further than Winfield by acknowledging this also grants nature its own status as self-determining and autonomous of thought. Maker, 'Idealism and Autonomy,' 66.

29 Wandschneider, 'Das Problem,' 30.

30 *Philosophy of Religion* (*Werke* 17: 243).

31 *EN*, §250.

32 Wandschneider, 'Das Problem,' 31. Another version of this view, that solves the problem of natural otherness by refusing the *otherness* of nature, by partitioning the contingency of nature from what is logically immanent in it, can be found in Louk Fleischhacker's 'Gibt es etwas Ausser der Ausserlichkeit? Über die Bedeutung der Veräusserlichung der Idee,' *Hegel-Jahrbuch* (1990): 35–41. See also Houlgate's account, where 'there are contingencies in nature that only empirical science can discover' and which have no influence on 'the distinctive logic of nature.' Houlgate, 'Logic,' 107. For Will Dudley, as well, 'the system ... excludes those contingencies that exceed the determinacy of the concept.' 'Systematic Philosophy and Idealism,' *OM* 34, 1 (2003): 101. I am arguing that while there is always contingency outside the system, rather than excluding it, thought seeks relentlessly to negate and incorporate it, at first through the natural sciences.

33 Already in Hegel's *Differenzschrift*, e.g., we find that in Fichte, 'the viewpoint which posits nature as living disappears; for its essence, its in-itself, are said to be nothing but a limit, a negation' (*Werke* 2, 79).

34 *EL*, §244. T.F. Geraets, W.A. Suchting, and H.S. Harris translate 'sich entschliesst' as 'resolves.' I think 'decides' is better, in that at least it captures the idea of breaking or cutting off, as in 'de-cision.' Another possibility, given Suchting's dissenting (and fitting) translation of 'Zusammenschliessen' as 'to close with itself,' would be to translate 'sich entschliessen' as 'to disclose itself.' The syllogistic meaning of 'Schluss' is lost in any case. *EL*, xlvii–xlviii.

35 *WL*, 573.

36 'Unangemessenheit' (*EN*, §248R).
37 Böhme refers to Lucifer in his cosmogony in *Von der Menschwerdung Jesu Christi*, vol. 1, chapter 5, §11.
38 Hegel plays on the words 'zufällig' (contingent) and 'ein Fallendes' (the fallen) referring to the purely natural world, in his remark to *EL*, §50. Hegel refers to nature in terms of the fall in *EPS*, §248R. The hybrid quality of nature is also reflected in Hegel's reference to it as the 'son of God,' as I mentioned above (*EPS*, §247add.). This hybrid aspect also reflects nature's impotence, the fact that if follows some 'laws' but always falls into contingency. Briefly, insofar as nature represents the possibility of being 'crucified' and reborn as spirit, it can be seen as Jesus Christ. However, in its recalcitrant and scandalous otherness, it is Lucifer. Hegel points out that Böhme himself represents nature as both (*Werke* 17: 244–51).
39 *Werke*, 2: 552 (#49).
40 Ibid. Hegel also refers to the negativity of thought as purifying immediate worldly content and raising it to the universal, in *EL*, §50.
41 '[A]ls den Prozess der *subjektiven* Tätigkeit der Idee' (*EPS*, §577).
42 See Adriaan Peperzak's 'Second Nature: Place and Significance of Objective Spirit in Hegel's Encyclopedia,' *OM*, 27, 1 (1995): 51–66.
43 *EPS*, §246R. This insistence on content derived from the positive sciences is particularly evident in Hegel's writings on education. In his letter report to Niethammer, Hegel writes that 'philosophy is nonetheless a systematic complex of content-rich sciences [*Szientien*]' (*Werke* 4: 411). In his letter to von Raumer, on philosophy in the universities, Hegel complains that 'the contents of the particular sciences have ... not yet received their reworking and adoption into the new idea' (ibid., 419). A few pages further on, Hegel writes of the 'concrete content' supplied by the 'positive sciences' and how 'the study of these sciences shows itself as necessary for the fundamental insight of philosophy' (ibid., 423). These pedagogical texts are particularly pertinent since one too often forgets that the ultimate articulation of Hegel's system, the *Encyclopedia*, was conceived as a teaching manual. They also show how, for Hegel, the practice of philosophy, in the university, first requires the painstaking acquisition of representational content, e.g., history, law, religious studies, ancient literature, and *then* subjecting this content to dialectical thought.
44 For example, '[W]e must then attempt to ascertain the extent to which various empirical phenomena correspond to the determinations that have been articulated.' Dudley, 'Systematic Philosophy,' 99.
45 This idea of human agency is expressed succinctly in the *Philosophy of Religion*: 'Nature only comes forward in the relation to man, not *for itself* in the

relation to God, for nature is not a knowing thing. God is Spirit; nature knows nothing of Spirit. Nature is created by God but it does not come out of itself in its relation to God, in the sense that it is not knowing. It only is in relation to Man' (*Werke* 17: 248).

46 *Werke* 3: 251; cf. *PS*, §333.

47 Cf. Alasdair MacIntyre, 'Hegel on Faces and Skulls,' in *Hegel: A Collection of Critical Essays*, ed. Alasdair MacIntyre (New York: Anchor Books, 1972), 119–236.

48 *Werke*, 3: 251. We can apply Hegel's critique of phrenology to the materialistic flavor of contemporary neuroscience, where scientists are continually finding the 'seat' of some faculty in the brain, believing that they are thus explaining the thing seated there, e.g., language, love, crime.

49 *EL*, §21 and Add. 52–3.

50 I.e., in the *Encyclopedia*'s discussion of language (§§ 451–64). This section is insightfully commented by John McCumber in *The Company of Words, Hegel, Language and Systematic Philosophy* (Evanston, IL: Northwestern University Press, 1993), 220–38.

51 *EPS*, §459 (*Werke* 10: 274).

52 *PS* (*Werke* 3: 251). Empty words, pure signifiers or 'names' are no more than 'stones and coals,' writes Hegel, in his letter report to Niethammer (*Werke*, vol. 4: 415).

53 McCumber, *Company of Words*, 233.

54 'The word gives to thoughts their most worthy and true existence' (*EPS*, §462add.). Or, 'With this, we again see language as the existence of Spirit' (*PS*, *Werke* 3: 478). Regarding language as the negation and rebirth of nature: 'Language is the murder of the sensible world in its immediate presence, its becoming-subsumed in a presence that is a resonating call in all thinking (representing) beings.' From the Jena Science of Spirit, par. 158, quoted by Yvon Gauthier, *L'Arc et le Cercle* (Montreal: Bellarmin, 1969), 51.

55 I believe Derrida, in his desire to establish a Hegelian semiology, misunderstands the point of Hegel's pyramid analogy: when sign and signified remain separate or linked arbitrarily, then meaning is dead, like the dead mummy entombed in the stone. This relationship is symbolic and ultimately arbitrary and 'romantic' and/or primitive. In scientific (speculative) discourse, the signifier *is* the signified, i.e., the meaningful word, which is rather like Derrida's own conception of 'différance.' 'The Pit and the Pyramid: Introduction to Hegel's Semiology,' *Margins of Philosophy* (Brighton: Harvester Press, 1982).

56 John Burbidge, 'Hegel on Galvanism,' in *Hegel on the Modern World*, ed. A.

Collins (Albany: SUNY Press, 1995), 11–124. Burbidge shows how Hegel chooses Pohl over Berzelius (in *EN*, §330Z), on galvanism. He shows how Hegel was up to date on his readings since we see an evolution in the same reference between the 1817 edition (§249) and the 1830 edition. Hegel chooses Pohl because he 'grasps the empirical in its synthesis ... the speculative concept.' (118). The role of representative thought, the activity of the natural sciences, is described very clearly in the addition to *EPS*, §246. 'The more thinking there is in the representations, the more things lose their naturalness, their individuality and immediacy: through the penetrating action of thought, the wealth of infinite many-shaped nature is impoverished, its springtimes die out, its play of colors is drained.' It is in this pre-digested form that the philosophy of nature encounters nature. It is thought thinking thought. This is, again, what Hegel means when he writes, in the body of the same section: '[P]hilosophical science has as a presupposition and a condition, empirical physics,' but only if we take empirical physics for what they are, not animallike, sensual perceptions of reality, but thought thinking raw nature.

57 I believe this is how the important addition to *EPS*, §254 should be read, why Hegel maintains it is necessary to 'test whether space is appropriate to our thought,' by comparing 'the *representation* of space with the determination of our concept.' In this encounter, which must take place if 'our representation' of space is to be proven 'necessary,' speculative thought risks nothing. It is indeed conceptual, dialectic and 'true,' regardless of the representations it encounters.

58 *EPS*, §254add.

59 Ibid.

60 Although the latest data strongly support the ever-expanding scenario, I will do what Hegel does and consider the account that is more amenable to speculative thought.

61 This is already implicit in the fact that the Big Bang theory takes the singularity as an axiom; as such it is both a reason and a thing.

62 A helpful physicist reader of this paper commented that most cosmologists are 'pinning their hopes on something non-anthropic, such as string theory.' Again, I am exercising my Hegelian prerogative in choosing the scientific accounts I want to speculate on.

5. Presenting the Past: Hegel's Epistemological Historiography

1 For example Beiser writes, 'Once we recognize that Hegel's method is phenomenological, we can quickly see what is wrong with those who accuse

Hegel of following a "speculative" or a priori method. The very opposite is the case, given that it was precisely Hegel's aim to avoid the problems of such methods. His own phenomenological method is more akin to the empirical method of the historian, who immerses himself into his subject matter.' 'Hegel's Historicism,' in Frederick C. Beiser, ed., *The Cambridge Companion to Hegel* (Cambridge University Press, 1993), 287. Already more than thirty years ago George Dennis O'Brien wrote: 'Hegel is universally regarded as a speculative philosopher of history, but it seems that from the standpoint of his own system no such philosophical enterprise can be derived.' *Hegel on Reason and History* (Chicago and London: University of Chicago Press, 1975), 13.

2 I will refer to Robert S. Hartman's translation of *Reason in History* (with occasional alterations) which is taken from the second German edition, edited by Hegel's son Karl and published in 1840. For the German text, I refer to *Werke* 12, which is based on the Karl Hegel edition. I subscribe to Moldenhauer and Michel's affirmation that the Karl Hegel text is more 'authentic' than either Lasson's (1917–23) or Hoffmeister's (1955). This preference is particularly justified where the opening pages of the Introduction, dealing with the different forms of historiography, are concerned. For an explanation of this preference, see *Werke* 12: 566–8.

3 Ultimately, this means, how can historical discourse take place in the *Encyclopedia of Philosophical Sciences*.

4 I am certainly not saying Hegel's thought is not metaphysical. However, for Hegel, what is truly metaphysical cannot be what is commonly meant by the term: an abstract, transcendent, a priori ideal.

5 §235 (*Werke* 3, etc.).

6 Andrew Buchwalter associates the self-recognition through reflection on the past, implied by Hegel's historiography, with his political theory of constitutionalism, in 'Historiography and Constitutionalism in Hegel,' *Hegel-Jahrbuch* (1998): 175. Buchwalter rightly sees Hegel's historiography, in terms Buchwalter takes from the *Lectures on the History of Philosophy*, as not just 'the becoming of things foreign to us, but the becoming of ourselves and of our own knowledge' (175). Cf. *Lectures on the History of Philosophy*, trans. E.S. Haldane and F.H. Simson (London, New York: Routledge and Kegan Paul, the Humanities Press, 1955, 4). Buchwalter does not develop the true nature of the symmetry he notices between Hegel's historiography and his constitutionalism: their shared linguistic content. The original historiography of the history of constitutional law (which is integral to the history of states and therefore to world history) recounts or represents past constitutions, just as it recounts or represents past events.

In other words, as laws and constitutions are linguistic or narrative contents of original historiography, they may also become part of reflective
and philosophical historiography.

7 We can certainly view Reason and Spirit from the point of view of the
Absolute or God or the Idea. We may say, e.g., that Spirit is the historical
realization of the self-consciousness of God or the Idea. However, this view
is one more suited to the perspective of the Logics or the Absolute Idea.
Philosophical historiography sees Reason in terms of a relationship
between human consciousness and historical objectivity. Thus Hegel writes
that Reason, in the philosophy of history, 'may be accepted here without
closer examination of its relation to God' and that its relation to 'the True,
the Eternal, the Absolute Power ... is being presupposed here as proved'
(*Reason in History* [*RH*], 11; *Werke* 12: 20–1).

8 *Lectures on the Philosophy of World History, Introduction: Reason in History,*
trans. H.B. Nisbet, from the Hoffmeister edition (Cambridge: Cambridge
University Press, 1980).

9 Paul Redding sees this historical recognition (*Anerkennen*) 'in the type of
reflective history which treats the historical world as a spectacle of passions
... structurally analogous to that operative in civil society.' Redding con-
trasts this 'abstract recognition' with a more concrete recognition of one's
actual personal identity as historical and constituted by other societies.
'Absorbed in the Spectacle of the World: Hegel's Criticism of Romantic Historiography,' *Clio* 16, 4 (1987), 306. For Redding, the recognition involved in
reflective history is related to a devalued, Debordian world of the spectacle,
opposed to a more authentic intersubjectivity, à la Charles Taylor, engendered through philosophical history. I am not sure this distinction is justified. In any case, I want to show how original and reflective narratives are
integral to the ultimate philosophical recognition (Reason) between self
and world and hence Scientific.

10 *RH*, 4 (*Werke* 12: 12).

11 In fact, these questions stretch back (at least) to Hegel's time. Historical
realism, as an epistemological position, can be traced back to the classical
historicism of Ranke (who was already critical of the speculative, perhaps
overly narrative quality of Hegel's philosophy of history) and continues
through the twentieth century with the *Annales* and Social Science schools.
The constructivist or narrative trend is perhaps best represented by Hayden
White.

12 *RH*, 4 (*Werke* 12: 11).

13 *EPS*, §§455–60.

14 *RH*, 4 (*Werke* 12: 11). 'Conditions' may include laws and constitutions,

founding the possibility of history of law – an essential aspect of history of States and therefore of world history.

15 In the Introduction to his *Lectures*, Hegel refers to the poet's representations as based on emotion (*Empfindung*). The reference to emotion is dropped from the *RH* text (*Werke* 12: 11).

16 Hegel's exclusion of 'myths, folk songs, traditions' from original history and his affirmation: 'The base of intuited or intuitive (*angeschauter oder anschaubarer*) reality provides a more solid foundation for history than those growing out of myths and epics' (*Werke* 12: 12) reflects his criticism of B.G. Niebuhr's hypothesis, presented in his *History of Rome*, that Livy's accounts of early Rome are based on folk tales and traditional songs. Indeed for Niebuhr there is an unbridgeable gulf between the marvelous in myth and the dryness of historical fact. It is an error to attempt to derive the latter from the former. See also Hegel's review of Solger's work, where Hegel aligns himself with A.W. Schlegel and Solger in their condemnation of Niebuhr's hypothesis (*Werke* 11: 222).

17 Hegel's term 'anschaulich' may also be translated as 'lively' (the French translation of the text gives 'vivant' – see *Leçons sur la philosophie de l'histoire*, trans. by J. Gibelin (Paris: Vrin, 1987), 19 – or, apparently by 'plastic,' which is found in *RH*, 6. Hegel uses the term to describe the immediate sensible intuitions experienced by the original historiographer (*Werke* 12: 12) but also to describe the best sort of reflective historiography, i.e., the one that reproduces in writing what is successful in original historiography. In both cases, the historiography represents the immediate knowing relationship between the original historiographer and his epoch, a knowing relationship which is not yet truly reflective or determined by understanding.

18 *Werke* 12: 13. 'Reden aber sind Hundlungen unter Menschen, und zwar sehr wesentlish wirksame Handlungen.'

19 Ibid. (*RH*, 4–5).

20 *Werke* 12: 14 (*RH*, 5).

21 Jere Surber puts the strong version as including 'the "end" of "universal history" as a temporal sequence capable of "rational comprehension."' 'The 'End of History' Revisited,' in *Hegel's History of Philosophy: New Interpretations*, ed. David A. Duquette (Albany: SUNY Press, 2003), 212. The continued production of original historiography as the foundation of further reflective philosophical historiography would seem to contradict the idea of 'the end of universal history as a temporal sequence.'

22 *Werke* 12: 14 (*RH*, 5).

23 *Werke* 12: 15 (*RH*, 6).

24 *Werke* 12: 16 (*RH*, 7).

25 *Werke* 12: 18 (*RH,* 9).
26 *Werke* 12: 18 (*RH,* 8).
27 *Werke* 12: 18–19 (*RH,* 9). Terms such as 'höher Kritik' as well as forms of 'Eitelkeit,' 'Kühnheit,' and 'Vortrefflichkeit,' all found in this passage on critical historiography, are typical of Hegel's references to F. Schlegel. In Hegel's *Lectures on Esthetics, Werke* 13: 93–4, e.g., in his review of Solger's work (*Werke* 11: 233–4). In the present passage on critical historiography, Hegel refers to critical philology and history of literature, exactly the same areas he criticizes in his review of Solger's work (par. 23). Hegel seems to be referring to Fr. Schlegel's early philological writings and his later work *On the Language and Wisdom of the Indians* (1808). Hegel is not referring to Fr. Schlegel's *Philosophy of History,* taken from his lectures in Vienna, published in 1828, which Hegel almost certainly hadn't read when he wrote the first part of *Reason in History* (1822 and 1828).
28 It is, therefore, probably not by accident that Niebuhr is generally considered the first critical historian and that the Hoffmeister edition refers to him.
29 'Pure self-recognition in absolute otherness … is the ground and soil of Science or knowledge in general' (*PS,* §26).
30 Hegel is explicit about this here. 'The last kind of reflective history … forms a transition [*Übergang*] to philosophical world history' (*Werke* 12: 19; *RH,* 9).
31 This is the name Hartman gives to the section, in his translation of '*Teilweise.*' Nisbet chooses 'specialized history.'
32 *Philosophy of Right,* §344.
33 *Lectures on the History of Philosophy,* vol. 1, trans. E.S. Haldane, 2 (*Werke* 18: 21).
34 'The Origins of Postmodern Historiography,' in *Historiography between Modernism and Postmodernism,* ed. Jerzy Topolski (Amsterdam, Atlanta: Rodopi, 1994), 110.
35 *Werke* 12: 18 (*RH,* 9).
36 *Werke* 12: 12 (*RH,* 4). Georg G. Iggers sees the newly created University of Berlin as the 'embodied fusion of *Wissenschaft* and *Bildung.*' Within this context, 'History was to be both a scientific discipline and a source of culture.' Leopold von Ranke, who began teaching there in 1825 was motivated by this ideal, which he shared with Hegel, in spite of their different conceptions of science. Ranke wrote his thesis on Thucydides. *Historiography in the Twentieth Century: From Scientific Objectivity to the Postmodern Challenge* (Hanover, NH, and London: University Press of New England, 1997), 24–5. On historical thought at the University of Berlin, see also T. Ziowlkowski, *Clio, the Romantic Muse: Historicizing the Faculties* (Ithaca and London: Cor-

nell University Press, 2004) and my review of the book in *Clio* 34, 1–2 (2005):
199–206.

6. The State University: The University of Berlin and Its Founding Contradictions

1 Contrary to what one might think, the first state universities were not French. Revolutionary France dismantled the existing 'system' in order to develop a network of 'Grandes écoles.' Today, these institutions still enjoy state privileges over the universities, which were only resurrected subsequently.

2 In fact, Hegel had already participated in the early definition of the University of Berlin through his correspondence with von Raumer in 1816. See *Werke* 4: 418–25.

3 Humboldt was the university's founder; Fichte was the first Rector, and Schleiermacher taught theology there from 1810.

4 The notion of the monad represents an interpretive extension of the scholastic and Aristotelian definitions of the soul. This is both an 'animus,' that which animates and provides movement (the monad's appetite) and a passive, feeling substance (the monad's perception). With the *Aufklärung* thinkers, rational thinking is not a creative act; the purpose of reason's appetite is to gain an adequate perception of the truth, which is already *there*.

5 Both artistic creation and its appreciation involve genius, since both are grounded in true feeling.

6 Cf. Bernard Bourgeois, 'La pédagogie de Hegel,' the introduction to his translation of Hegel's main pedagogical writings, *La pédagogie de Hegel* (Paris: Vrin, 1990), 25.

7 Fichte, 'On the Only Possible Disruption of Academic Freedom,' *Sämmtliche Werke*, ed. J.H. Fichte, vol. 6 (Berlin, 1845–56), 454.

8 Ibid.

9 In 1830, 19% of the University of Berlin's students were enrolled in philosophy (which included the natural sciences), a figure which grew to 31% by 1860. T. Nipperdey, *Deutsche Geschichte, 1800–1866* (Munich: C.H. Beck, 1984), 476.

10 For an elaboration of this view of nature in Hegel, see Essay 4 of this book.

11 Cf. *Philosophy of Right*, §173 sq.

12 Ibid., §239.

13 School must bring about this passage between family life and 'the higher interest and earnestness of public life.' Gymnasium speech from 2 Septem-

ber 1811 (*Werke* 4: 352). Or, in the same speech: 'School is the intermediary sphere that moves man from the family circle into the world' (349).

14 Schultze was Hegel's neighbour; von Raumer received Hegel's report on teaching philosophy at university, written in 1816 while he was still in Nuremberg, two years before he was called to Berlin. Cf. *Werke* 4: 418.

15 In the words of Walter Kaufmann: 'Anyone who seriously compares Hegel before the age of forty with the Professor Hegel of the last fifteen years of his life is bound to ask: Whatever happened to him? We can now answer that question in a single sentence: for eight long years the poor man was headmaster of a German secondary school.' *Hegel: A Reinterpretation* (New York: Anchor Books, 1966), 174.

16 Cf. Bourgeois, 'La pédagogie,' 17.

17 Report to Niethammer (*Werke* 4: 412).

18 Cf. Kant's 'Architectonic of Pure Reason' in the first *Critique*.

19 Cf. Report to Niethammer, *Werke* 4: 412.

20 For Hegel, this teaching could be confined to two hours a day for the last two or three years at the Gymnasium. Cf. Bourgeois, 'La pédagogie,' 65.

21 Report to Niethammer (*Werke* 4: 411).

22 Ibid., 414.

23 Ibid., 415.

24 Report to von Raumer (*Werke* 4: 418).

25 Ibid.

26 Ibid., 421.

27 Ibid., 419.

28 Ibid., 421.

29 Ibid., 419.

30 Ibid., 411. Thus the three parts of the *Encyclopedia* (the sciences of logic, nature, and the philosophy of spirit) correspond to the three main university faculties: theology, medicine, and law. As with Fichte, but in a completely different manner, Hegel's philosophy can be seen as the expression of the university project.

31 Report to von Raumer (*Werke* 4: 423).

32 Ibid.

33 Ibid., 421.

34 Ibid., 420.

35 *Selbstdenken* (ibid., 422). The term is taken from Kant's third *Critique*.

36 Report to von Raumer (*Werke* 4: 422–3).

37 Ibid., 424.

38 Ibid., 420.

39 These measures, known as the Carlsbad Resolutions, included, besides

explicit recognition of the principle of monarchy, censorship and surveillance of university professors.

40 Hoffmeister's note 10 to *Briefe von und an Hegel*, Letter 359, 30 October 1819.

7. Music and Monosyllables: The Language of Pleasure and Necessity

1 *Phenomenology of Spirit (PS)*, trans. by A.V. Miller (Oxford: Oxford University Press, 1977) par. 230; *Werke* 3: 177.

2 This original version of Goethe's *Faust* project, which spanned some sixty years, was written in 1775 and published in 1790. It is the only version Hegel could have known.

3 H.S. Harris, *Hegel's Ladder*, vol. 2, 'The Odyssey of Spirit' (Indianapolis and Cambridge: Hackett, 1997), 24–5. In an earlier commentary, Judith Shklar finds the same natural and societal aspects involved in necessity. The pleasure seeker's individualism runs up against 'a unit, a society that is a new trans-individual situation.' As well, as a subject immersed in natural life, he discovers he has no purpose beyond his part 'in the natural order,' 'in death and extinction.' *Freedom and Independence: A Study of the Political Ideas in Hegel's Phenomenology* (Cambridge: Cambridge University Press, 1976), 103–4. John Russon also finds this societal character in necessity. The lover (not the erotic pleasure seeker) finds himself defeated by the 'great mass of society' which claims actualized love through its own institutions of marriage and family. *The Self and Its Body in Hegel's Phenomenology of Spirit* (Toronto: University of Toronto Press, 1997), 41. Terry Pinkard also sees the necessity arising from hedonism (not the erotic pleasure seeker) as the compulsive character of hedonism, where one is a 'mere slave to desire.' *Hegel's Phenomenology: The Sociality of Reason* (New York: Cambridge University Press, 1994), 96.

4 Robert C. Solomon is the only other commentator I have read who refers to Don Juan and Kierkegaard as a key to understanding this section. Regarding 'the conversion of the pursuit of pleasure into necessity ... Faust is explicitly quoted but Don Juan will do as well.' *In the Spirit of Hegel* (Oxford: Oxford University Press, 1983), 505. For Solomon, necessity refers to the inevitably compulsive character of pleasure seeking: 'what starts as positive pleasure becomes the elimination of pain. Thus Don Juan initially enjoys his liaisons; later he needs them' (ibid.). Solomon's willingness to consider Don Juan is reinforced by his tentative recognition that Hegel is actually talking about sex. 'It is not far-fetched or a matter of scholarly licentiousness to suggest [Hegel] is talking about sex' (503). Charles Taylor is also a rare commentator of the passage who refers to sex, although not to

Don Juan. Taylor sees necessity as primarily natural, a result of the fact that his pleasure never raises itself beyond a point where 'death is an abrupt and total ending.' *Hegel* (Cambridge: Cambridge University Press, 1975).

5 See Hegel's letter to Nanette Endel, 22 March 1797. He saw the opera at least one other time, in Berlin, in the fall of 1820. See Terry Pinkard, *Hegel: A Biography* (Cambridge: Cambridge University Press, 2000), 462.

6 *PS*, §233 (*Werke* 3: 179).

7 *PS*, §230 (*Werke* 3: 177).

8 '[W]elchem Zwecke denn alles Übrige dient' (*Werke* 1: 244–50).

9 *PS*, §§364–5 (*Werke* 3: 273–4).

10 *PS*, §80 (*Werke* 3: 74). None of the commentators mentioned in this chapter appears to notice the centrality of feeling underlying this dialectic, the fact that this is what Hegel means by an immediate form of knowing. Only through feeling can we understand how death is relevant to carnal knowledge and its perfectly consistent transition into the subsequent form, the Law of the Heart.

11 *Werke* 1: 248. The original version of the fragment, which I am referring to, is found in the note at the bottom of the page.

12 In the fragment, the renewed feeling of the other as a natural object (of desire) is brought about through the awareness of the other's mortality.

13 Written in 1803. See Hegel, *Schriften zur Politik und Rechtsphilosophie*, ed. Georg Lasson (Hamburg: Meiner, 1922), 425–6.

14 *PS*, §175 (*Werke* 3: 143). This compulsive aspect of necessity is emphasized by Solomon (supra n4), and although neither Hegel nor Harris mentions it, it is clearly stated in the *Faust-Fragment*: 'So tauml ich von Begierde zu Gnuss / Und im Genuss verschmacht ich nach Begierde' (ll. 1922–4). Goethe, *Berliner Ausgabe*, vol. 8 (Berlin and Weimar: Aufbau-Verlag, 1978), 136. The most convincing presentation of this type of necessity and of the whole section under discussion is still that of Jean Hyppolite, *Genèse et structure de la Phénoménologie de l'esprit*, vol. 1 (Paris: Aubier, 1941), 272–3.

15 Solomon (*In the Spirit*) does not distinguish between the singular or individual and the particular moments. This causes him to explain the failure of hedonism in terms of the inability of the particular pleasures to attain the universal. I would express this as the failure of individual pleasures to attain mediating particularity and, therefore, to constitute a substantial universal.

16 *PS*, §364 (*Werke* 3: 274).

17 Kierkegaard writes that the number has a 'reckless, lyrical quality,' that it 'becomes comic,' that it is 'uneven and accidental, which is by no means unimportant.' *Either/Or*, Part I, *Kierkegaard's Writings*, vol. 3, ed. and trans.

with introduction and notes by Howard V. Hong and Edna H. Hong (Princeton: Princeton University Press, 1987), 91–3.

18 Kierkegaard compares the story of Don Juan to that of Faust. The latter is based on a written 'folk book,' whereas the legend of Don Juan is unwritten. Thus, according to Kierkegaard, Faust lends itself to many presentations, and 'every would-be assistant professor or professor thinks he will be accredited as intellectually mature by the reading public through the publication of a book about Faust, in which he faithfully repeats what all the other graduates and scholarly confirmands have already said' (ibid., 91).

19 *Werke* 13: 121. Although I won't discuss it here, there is a temporal dimension to Hegel's idea of natural necessity. As an expression of natural necessity, time is as an endless series of identical instants, a notion of time opposed to its concept as the progression of Spirit. Erotic love encounters purely punctual time, whether in the form of the day-in/day-out rhythm of social convention or natural time, where our lives are counted out. This temporal dimension of necessity is perhaps best expressed in the opera, since 'in music, time is what is dominant' (*Werke* 15: 163).

20 'Zerstäubt.' *PS*, §364 (*Werke* 3: 273).

21 Ibid., 274. Beyond their purely destructive impact, the terms 'pulverized' and 'smashed to bits' express the breaking down of unique sexual pleasure into a dust of similar points, forming an empty universal.

22 The libretto also evokes the temporal necessity in punctual terms: 'Your hour of doom is near,' 'Now, your time has come,' the statue tells Don Giovanni. The excerpt is from the score, Edition Peters, Leipzig, ed. by Georg Schünemann with the collaboration of Kurt Soldan.

23 *PS*, §590 (*Werke* 3: 436).

24 *PS*, §591 (*Werke* 3: 436).

25 *PS*, §590 (*Werke* 3: 436).

26 *PS*, §364 (*Werke* 3: 273).

27 *PS*, §588 (*Werke* 3: 434).

28 *PS*, §742 (*Werke* 3: 541).

29 In 'Pleasure and Necessity,' Hegel writes, 'The transition is made from the form of the one or unit into that of universality, from one absolute abstraction into the other' (*PS*, §364; *Werke* 3: 273).

30 *PS*, §363 (*Werke* 3: 273).

31 Don Giovanni's last words are 'What terror!'

32 Comedy and terror are also present in Goethe's *Faust-Fragment*, which is perhaps why it is such a powerful representation of the pleasure-seeker and his fate. This does not, however, mean it is the only way to approach Hegel's text.

8. Hegel's Critique of Solger: The Problem of Scientific Communication

1 'Solgers nachgelassene Schriften und Briefwechsel,' in *Jahrbücher für wissenschaftliche Kritik*. The writings were edited by Solger's friends Ludwig Tieck and Friedrich von Raumer and published in 1826. Hegel's review is found in *Werke* 11: 205–74. My French translation and lengthy commentary is in *Hegel: L'ironie romantique* (Paris: Vrin, 1997). For an English translation, see Diana Behler, trans.; 'Solger's Posthumous Writings and Correspondence,' in *Encyclopedia of the Philosophical Sciences in Outline and Critical Writings*, ed. Ernst Behler (New York: Continuum, 1990), 265–319. The translations in this essay are my own.

2 Cf. M. Boucher's article 'Solger, théoricien de l'ironie romantique,' *Cahiers du sud* (May 1937).

3 On Solger: J. Heller, *Solgers Philosophie der ironischen Dialektik* (Berlin: Reuther & Reichard, 1928); M. Boucher, *K.W.F. Solger, esthétique et philosophie de la présence* (Paris, 1934); B. Allemann, *Ironie und Dichtung* (Pfullingen, 1956), 83–99; P. Matenko, ed., *Tieck and Solger: The Complete Correspondence* (New York, 1932). On Hegel and Solger: S. Kierkegaard, 'The Concept of Irony,' ed. and trans. H. Hong and E. Hong (Princeton: Princeton University Press, 1992); R. Bodei, 'Il primo romanticismo come fenomeno storico e la filosofia di Solger nell'analisi di Hegel,' *Aut Aut* 101 (Dec. 1967): 68–80; Otto Pöggeler, *Hegels Kritik der Romantik* (Bonn: 1956), 263–97; W. Linden, *Solger und Hegel, Bemerken aus Anlass eines Vergleiches ihrer aesthetischen Schriften* (Hamburg, 1938); G. Müller, 'Solger's Aesthetics: A Key to Hegel,' in A. Schirokauer and W. Paulsen, eds., *Corona, Studies in Celebration of the 80th Birthday of Samuel Singer* (Freeport, NY: Books for Libraries Press, 1968, 1st ed. c. 1941).

4 Cf. Pöggeler, *Hegels Kritik*, 264 where he mentions a letter to Tieck from 26 April 1818, where Solger expresses his desire to see Hegel in Berlin: 'I have the greatest respect for Hegel and agree with him on a great number of points. In the dialectic, we have both, independently from one another, taken the same path.' Six months later, in a letter to von Raumer, Solger writes that he is pleased with Hegel and hopes to get to know him better (ibid.). This desire doesn't appear to have been satisfied. There is no letter to Solger, nor mention of him, in Hegel's correspondence, other than a reference to his burial: 'Before yesterday, I accompanied Solger to his final resting place. His tomb is not far from Fichte's and therefore close to where mine will be, beside my colleagues. Philosophers, judging by these ones, do not grow old here.' J. Hoffmeister, *Briefe von und an Hegel*, Letter from 30 October 1818.

5 There are few commentaries of Hegel's review, other than the one preceding my French translation.
6 The literary, philosophical review was edited by the Schlegel brothers and published between 1798 and 1800.
7 *Werke* 11: 240, in Hegel's footnote.
8 Ibid., 224.
9 Ibid., 235.
10 The qualifier 'serious' is repeated several times in the review. It is, in part, his serious personality that favours Solger over the other theoreticians of irony, such as Schlegel and Tieck. However, one cannot help feeling that Hegel found Solger a little too serious, particularly regarding his relationship with the public.
11 Ibid., 266.
12 Ibid., 268. The reference is to *Erwin, Vier Gespräche über das Schöne und die Kunst*, 2 vol. (Berlin, 1815). Müller's article provides a summary of this text. During his lifetime, besides his *Erwin*, Solger also published *Philosophische Gespräche* (1817). His other (posthumous) writings are *Vorlesungen über Aesthetik* (1829) and *Posthumous Writings and Correspondence* (1826).
13 *Werke* 11: 241–2.
14 Ibid., 233.
15 Fr. Schlegel, *Über Sprache und Weisheit der Indier* (Heidelberg: Mohr and Zimmer, 1808).
16 *Werke* 11: 232–3.
17 Ibid., 233.
18 Ibid. Hegel once again adopts Solger's expression.
19 I have capitalized Thing (*Sache*) to distinguish it from the thing (*Ding*). Oddly, the vernacular 1960s American use of the word 'thing' ('What's your thing?' 'Discipline is not my thing.') may be one way to think of 'thing' as a translation for the word *Sache*.
20 In the Hegelian system, as presented in the *EPS*, the Thing is almost always defined in terms of language; see the *PS*, §§462 Add., 464, 486, 487, 491.
21 'The form of the proposition, or more precisely, of judgment, is unfit to express that which is concrete – the truth is concrete – and speculative.' *Encyclopedia Logic* (*EL*), §31.
22 *Werke* 11: 233.
23 Ibid.
24 *EPS*, §462add.
25 *Werke* 11: 233.
26 Ibid., 242.
27 *Science of Logic* (*SL*), Doctrine of Essence (*Werke* 6: 36).

28 *Werke* 11: 262.

29 Ibid.

30 Ibid., 266. Hegel is quoting Solger.

31 Ibid. Hegel is quoting Solger.

32 See Hegel's reference to the pyramid and its dead soul, a metaphor for the alienated relationship between the symbol and what is symbolized. *EPS*, Philosophy of Spirit §458.

33 Heller stresses the difference between symbol and sign in Solger; the symbol is a sign inhabited by the Idea. In this sense, 'all art is symbolic,' a proposition that Hegel might translate as 'all art is romantic.' Heller, *Solgers Philosophie*, 141. Cf. Matenko, *Tieck and Solger*, 51–2.

34 Hegel uses the expression 'empirische Menge' (*Werke* 11: 262).

35 See Hegel's Repport to Niethammer (*Werke* 4: 403–17).

36 In his article 'Komödie des Lebens: Theorie der Komödie,' in *Hegel in Berlin* (Berlin: Staatsbibliothek Preussischer Kulturbesitz in Verbindung mit dem Hegel-Archiv, 1982), Pöggeler fills us in on Hegel's social life, particularly on his frequenting of the theatrical demimonde of that city.

37 *Werke* 11: 265.

38 Ibid.

9. On Schleiermacher and Postmodernity

1 See, e.g., Jeffrey Hoover, 'The Origin of the Conflict between Hegel and Schleiermacher at Berlin,' *OM*, 20, 1 (1988): 69–79.

2 Cf. *Philosophy of Right*, §164add.

3 *Philosophy of Right*, §140add.

4 I mean Hegel's notion of science, as represented in the system of his *Encyclopedia*.

5 The first edition appeared in 1799; the second appeared in 1806.

6 *Werke* 11: 42–67; English translation by Eric Von Der Luft, *Hegel, Hinrichs and Schleiermacher on Feeling and Religion* (Lewiston, NY: Mellen Press, 1987).

7 See Brecht and Sandberger, 'Hegels Begegnung mit der Theologie im Tübinger Stift,' *Hegel-Studien* 5 (1969): 47–81. Carl Immanuel Diez, *Briefwechsel und Kantische Schriften: Wissensbegründung in der Glaubenskrise Tübingen-Jena (1790–1792)*, ed. D. Henrich (Stuttgart: Klett-Cotta, 1997).

8 *Werke* 2: 13.

9 In the first edition of his *Speeches on Religion*, Schleiermacher refers almost exclusively to the 'universe' rather than to 'God.'

10 Hegel uses the expression in his preface to Hinrichs's work on religion. In

this preface, Hegel refers primarily to Schleiermacher's *Dogmatics* (*Der christliche Glaube nach den Grundsätzen der evangelischen Kirche im Zusammenhange dargestellt*), where he further develops his theory of religious feeling.

11 *Glauben und Wissen* (*Werke* 2: 391).

12 *Werke* 11: 46.

13 Ibid., 48.

14 Ibid. It should be noted that these same words, grasped differently, i.e., speculatively, will form the objective truth of religious content within science. The linguistic dimension of objectivity will resurface in our discussion of various postmodern accounts, e.g., in Lyotard and Baudrillard.

15 Ibid.

16 This is the 'thoroughgoing scepticism' that Hegel refers to in the introduction to the *Phenomenology of Spirit*.

17 'Thus appearance is the phenomenon of skepticism, or again, the phenomenon of [subjective] idealism, an immediateness that is not something or a thing, absolutely not an independent being that would be outside its determination and its relation to the subject' (*SL*, Doctrine of Essence, *Werke* 6, 19).

18 *Werke* 11: 50

19 Ibid., 49.

20 Ibid., 51.

21 Ibid.

22 Ibid.

23 Ibid., 52.

24 Ibid.

25 Ibid., 54.

26 Ibid., 56.

27 Jean-François Lyotard, *La condition postmoderne* (Paris: Editions de Minuit, 1979), 63–8.

28 Ibid., 13.

29 An example can be found in the chapter on 'Sense-certainty' of the *Phenomenology*, where Hegel describes the 'wisdom' of animals regarding the essential nothingness of finite things of the senses. 'Completely convinced of their nothingness, they simply gobble them up' (*Werke* 3: 61; *PS*, §109).

30 Jean Baudrillard, *La société de consommation* (Paris: Denoël/Folio, 1970), 309.

31 Gilles Lipovetsky, *L'ère du vide* (Paris: Gallimard, 1983), 16.

32 Ibid.

33 Hannah Arendt, *The Human Condition* (Chicago: University of Chicago Press, 1958), 133.

34 Michel Foucault, *The Order of Things*, trans. anon. (New York: Vintage Books, 1994), 317.

35 As I showed in the opening essay, this is how Hegel defines romantic irony: an evacuation (*Vereitelung*, rendering vain) of true objectivity; see Hegel's *Review* of Solger's works (*Werke* 11: 233). This postmodern assault on objectivity, through romantic irony is reflected in Carl Rapp's *Fleeing the Universal: The Critique of Post-Rational Criticism* (Albany, SUNY Press, 1998). The view that Hegel's critique of Early German Romanticism can be understood as a critique of postmodernity should be distinguished from views that see Hegel's political philosophy as a critique of *modernity*, i.e., of the pure Enlightenment view of the state and freedom. Cf. David Kolb, *The Critique of Pure Modernity: Hegel, Heidegger and After* (Chicago: University of Chicago Press, 1986) and Richard Dien Winfield, 'Hegel, Romanticism and Modernity,' *OM* 27, 1 (1995): 3–18.

36 This is the theme of Charles Taylor's essay, *The Malaise of Modernity* (Concord, ON: Anansi Press, 1991). In his magisterial *Sources of the Self*, Taylor refers to 'two big constellations of ideas' that define our present condition: '[O]ne joins a lively sense of our powers of disengaged reason to an instrumental reading of nature; the other focuses on our powers of creative imagination and links these to a sense of nature as an inner moral source.' (Cambridge, MA: Harvard University Press, 1989), 319.

Bibliography

Cited Works by Hegel

Gesammelte Werke, vol. 7. Ed. R.P. Horstmann and J.H. Trede. Hamburg: Felix
Meiner, 1968.
Hegels theologische Jugendschriften. Ed. Heman Nohl. Tubingen: Mohr 1907.
Schriften zur Politik und Rechtsphilosophie. Ed. Georg Lasson. Hamburg: Felix
Meiner, 1922.
Werke in 20 Bänden. Ed. Eva Moldenhauer and Karl Markus Michel. Frankfurt
am Main: Suhrkamp, 1970.
Wissenschaft der Logik, Die Lehre von Sein (1812). Ed. Hans Jürgen Gawoll.
Hamburg: Felix Meiner, 1986.
Wissenschaft der Logik, Die Lehre von Sein (1832). Ed. Hans Jürgen Gawoll.
Hamburg: Felix Meiner, 1990.

Cited Works by Hegel, in Translation

The Encyclopedia Logic. Trans. T.F. Geraets, W.A. Suchting, and H.S. Harris
Indianapolis: Hackett, 1991.
Leçons sur la philosophie de l'histoire. Trans. J. Gibelin. Paris: Vrin, 1987.
Lectures on the History of Philosophy. Trans. E.S. Haldane and F.H. Simson. London, New York: Routledge and Kegan Paul, the Humanities Press, 1955.
Lectures on the Philosophy of World History. Introduction: Reason in History. Trans.
H.B. Nisbet [from the Hoffmeister ed.] Cambridge: Cambridge University
Press, 1980.
La pédagogie de Hegel. Trans. B. Bourgeois. Paris: Vrin, 1990.
Phenomenology of Spirit. Trans. A.V. Miller. Oxford: Oxford University Press,
1977.

Reason in History. Trans. Robert S. Hartman. Indianapolis, New York: Bobbs-Merrill, the Humanities Press, 1953.

Selected Writings on Language Issues

Bayer, Oswald. *Vernunft ist Sprache: Hammans Metakritik Kants.* Stuttgart: Frommann-Holzboog, 2002.

Bodammer, Theodor. *Hegels Deutung der Sprache.* Hamburg: Felix Meiner, 1969.

Burns, Tony. 'The Purloined Hegel: Semiology in the Thought of Saussure and Derrida.' *History of the Social Sciences* 13, 4 (2000): 1–24.

Colliot-Thélène, Catherine. 'Logique et langage, L'idéalisme spéculatif.' *Archives de Philosophie* 62 (1999): 17–45.

Coltman, Rodney. 'Gadamer, Hegel and the Middle of Language.' *Philosophy Today* (Spring 1996): 151–59.

– 'Hegel, Marx and Wittgenstein.' *Philosophy and Social Criticism* 10 (Fall 1984): 50–74.

Cook, Daniel J. *Language in the Philosophy of Hegel.* The Hague, Paris: Mouton, 1973.

Derrida, Jacques. 'The Pit and the Pyramid: Introduction to Hegel's Semiology.' In *Margins of Philosophy,* trans. A. Bass, 30–69. Brighton: Harvester Press, 1982.

Donougho, Martin. 'The Semiotics of Hegel.' *Clio* 11, 4 (1982) 415–30.

Dulckeit, Katharina. 'Can Hegel Refer to Particulars?' *Owl of Minerva* 17, 2 (1986): 181–94.

Garrison, Jim. 'Dewey's Philosophy and the Experience of Working: Labor, Tools and Language.' *Synthese* 105 (1995): 87–114.

Gauthier, Yvon. *L'Arc et le Cercle.* Montreal: Bellarmin, 1969.

Graeser, Andreas. 'Hegel über die Rede vom Absoluten. Teil 1: Urteil, Satz und spekulativer Gehalt.' *Zeitschrift für philosophische Forschung* 44 (1990): 175–93.

– 'Hölderlin über Urteil und Sein.' *Freiburger Zeitschrift für Philosophie und Theologie* 38 (1991): 111–28.

Harvey, Irene E. 'The Linguistic Basis for Truth for Hegel.' *Man and His World* 15 (1982): 285–97.

Hoffman, Thomas Sören. 'Hegels Sprachphilosophie.' In *Klassiker der Sprachphilosophie,* ed. Tilman Borsche. Munich: C.H. Beck, 1995.

Lamb, David. 'Hegel and Wittgenstein on Language and Sense-Certainty.' *Clio* 7, 2 (1978): 285–301.

– *Language and Perception in Hegel and Wittgenstein.* New York: St Martins Press, 1979.

Lütterfelds, Wilhelm. 'Die Einsamkeit der Privaten Sprache: Hegels Dialek-

tische Konzeption von Wittgensteins These über Innen und Aussen.'
Deutsche Zeitschrift für Philosophie 50, 5 (2002): 715–31.

Marx, Werner. *Absolute Reflexion und Sprache*. Frankfurt am Main: Klostermann,
1967.

McCumber, John. *The Company of Words: Hegel, Language, and Systematic Philosophy*. Evanston, IL: Northwestern University Press, 1993.

Omotoso, Kole. 'Expressing One Culture in the Language of Another.' *Quest*
12, 1 (1998): 77–94.

Schalow, Frank. 'The Question of Being and the Recovery of Language within
Hegelian Thought.' *Owl of Minerva* 24, 2 (1993): 163–80.

Scheer, Brigitte, and Günter Wolfart, eds. *Dimensionen der Sprache in der Philosophie des Deutschen Idealism*. Würzburg: Königshausen und Newmann, 1982.

Sikka, Sonia. 'Herder on the Relation between Language and the World.' *History of Philosophy Quarterly* 21, 2 (2004): 183–200.

Simon, Joseph. *Das Problem der Sprache bei Hegel*. Stuttgart, Berlin: Kohlhammer, 1966.

Surber, Jere Paul. 'Hegel's Speculative Sentence.' *Hegel-Studien* 10 (1975): 211–
30.

– 'The Problems of Language in German Idealism: An Historical and Conceptual Overview.' In *Phenomenology on Kant, German Idealism, Hermeneutics and
Logic*, ed. O.K. Wiegand et al., 305–36. The Hague: Kluwer, 2000.

– 'Satz and Urteil in Kant and Fichte.' In *New Essays in Fichte's Foundation of the
Entire Doctrine of Scientific Knowledge*, ed. D. Breazeale and T. Rockmore.
Amherst, NY: Humanities Press, 2001.

Wohlfahrt, Günter. *Der speculative Satz*. Berlin and New York: de Gruyter, 1981.

Selected Writings on Hegel and Kant

Ameriks, Karl. *Kant and the Fate of Autonomy: Problems in the Appropriation of the
Critical Philosophy*. Cambridge: Cambridge University Press, 2000.

Beiser, Frederick C. *The Fate of Reason: German Philosophy from Kant to Fichte*.
Cambridge, MA: Harvard University Press, 1987.

Brecht, M., and J. Sandberger. 'Hegels Begegnung mit der Theologie im Tübinger Stift.' *Hegel-Studien* 5 (1969): 47–81.

Diez, Immanuel Carl. *Briefwechsel und Kantische Schriften: Wissensbegründung in
der Glaubenskrise Tübingen-Jena (1790–1792)*, ed. Dieter Henrich. Stuttgart:
Klett-Cotta, 1997.

Di Giovanni, George. 'The First 20 Years of Critique.' In *The Cambridge Companion to Kant*, ed. Paul Guyer, 417–47. Cambridge: Cambridge University Press,
1992.

Di Giovanni, G., and H.S. Harris. *Between Kant and Hegel: Texts in the Development of Post-Kantian Idealism*. Indianapolis: Hackett, 2000 [Albany: SUNY Press, 1985].

Düsing, Klaus. 'Die Rezeption der Kantischen Postulatenlehre.' *Hegel-Studien* 9 (1973): 53–90.

Görland, Ingtraud. *Die Kantkritik des jungen Hegels*. Frankfurt: Klostermann, 1966.

Harris, H.S. *Hegel's Development*. Vol. 1. *Toward the Sunlight*. Oxford: Oxford University Press, 1972.

Henrich, Dieter. 'Carl Immanuel Diez. Zur Entstehungsgeschichte des deutschen Idealismus,' *Hegel-Studien* 111 (1965): 276–82.

– 'Historische Voraussetzungen von Hegels System.' In *Hegel im Kontext*, 51–61. Frankfurt am Main: Suhrkamp, 1971.

– *Konstellationen: Probleme und Debatten am Ursprung der idealistischen Philosophie (1789–1795)*. Stuttgart: Klett-Cotta, 1991.

– 'Some Presuppositions of Hegel's System.' In *Hegel and the Philosophy of Religion*, ed. D. Christensen, 25–44. The Hague: Nijhoff, 1970.

Hoffmeister, Johannes, ed. *Dokumente zu Hegels Entwicklung*. Stuttgart/Bad Cannestatt: Friedrich-Frommann, 1974 [1936].

Kroner, Richard. *Von Kant bis Hegel*. Tübingen: Mohr, 1961.

Lacorte, Carmelo. *Il Primo Hegel*. Florence: Sansoni, 1959.

Nicolin, Günther, ed. *Hegel in Berichten seiner Zeitgenossen*. Hamburg: Felix Meiner, 1970.

Nohl, Herman, ed. *Hegels Theologische Jugendschriften*. Frankfurt am Main: Minerva, 1966 [Tübingen: Mohr, 1907].

Pfeiderer, Otto. *The Development of Theology in Germany since Kant*, 2nd ed. Trans. J.F. Smith. London: Sonnenschein, 1893.

Philonenko, Alexis. Introduction to *Foi et Savoir*, 8–82. Paris: Vrin, 1988.

Pinkard, Terry. *Hegel: A Biography*. Cambridge: Cambridge University Press, 2000.

Pippin, Robert. *Hegel's Idealism: The Satisfactions of Self-Consciousness*. Cambridge: Cambridge University Press, 1989.

Priest, Stephen, ed. *Hegel's Critique of Kant*. Oxford: Oxford University Press: 1987 [Gregg Revivals, 1992].

Rivelaygue, Jacques. *Leçons de métaphysique allemande*, vol. 1. Paris: Grasset, 1990.

Rockmore, Tom. *Before and After Hegel*. Berkeley: University of California Press, 1993.

Rosenkranz, Karl. *Georg Wilhelm Friedrich Hegels Leben*. Darmstadt: Wissenschaftliche Buchgesellschaft, 1963.

Sedgwick, Sally, ed. *The Reception of Kant's Critical Philosophy: Fichte, Schelling and Hegel*. Cambridge: Cambridge University Press, 2000.

Smith, John. 'Hegel's Critique of Kant.' *Review of Metaphysics* 26 (1973): 438–60.

Storr, Gottlob Christian. *Bemerkungen über Kants philosophische Religionslehre.* Brussels: Série Aetas Kantiana, Culture et Civilisation, 1968 [Tübingen: Cotta, 1794].

Selected Writings on Hegel and Nature

Bonsiepen, W. 'Hegels Vorlesungen über Naturphilosophie.' *Hegel-Studien* 26 (1985): 40–54.

Braun, H. 'Zur Interpretation der hegelschen Wendung: Frei entlassen.' In *Hegel, l'esprit objectif, l'unité de l'histoire*. Actes du IIe congrès international de l'association pour l'étude de la philosophie de Hegel, 51–64. Lille: Presses universitaires de Lille, 1968.

Breidbach, O. 'Hegels Evolutionskritik.' *Hegel-Studien* 22 (1983): 165–72.

Burbidge, John. 'Chemism and Chemistry.' *Owl of Minerva* 34, 1 (2003): 3–17.

– 'The Necessity of Contingency: An Analysis of Hegel's Chapter on "Actuality" in the Science of Logic.' In *Selected Essays on G.W.F. Hegel*, ed. Lawrence S. Stepelevich, 60–73. Atlantic Highlands, N.J.: Humanities Press, 1993.

– *Real Process: How Logic and Chemistry Combine in Hegel's Philosophy of Nature*. Toronto: University of Toronto Press, 1996.

Cohen, R.S., and M.W. Wartofsky, eds. *Hegel and the Sciences*. Dordrecht: Reidel, 1984.

Collins, Ardis. 'Hegel's Unresolved Contradiction: Experience, Philosophy and the Irrationality of Nature.' *Dialogue* 39, 4 (2000): 771–96.

Doull, J.A. 'Hegel's Philosophy of Nature.' *Dialogue* 11, 3 (1972): 379–99.

Dudley, Will. 'Systematic Philosophy and Idealism.' *Owl of Minerva* 34, 1 (2003): 91–106.

Engels, F. *Dialectics of Nature*. Trans Clemens Dutt. New York: International Publishers, 1963.

Fleischhacker, Louk. 'Gibt es etwas ausser der Äusserlichkeit? Über die Bedeutung der Veräusserlichung der Idee.' *Hegel-Jahrbuch* (1990): 35–41.

Halper, Edward. 'The Idealism of Hegel's System.' *Owl of Minerva* 34, 1 (2003): 19–58.

Hoffheimer, Michael. 'Law, Fossils, and the Configuring of Hegel's Philosophy of Nature.' *Idealistic Studies* 25, 3 (1995): 155–73.

Horstmann, R.-P., and M.J. Petry, eds. *Hegels Philosophie der Natur: Beziehungen zwischen empirischer und speculativer Naturkenntnis*. Stuttgart: Klett-Cotta, 1986.

Houlgate, Stephen, ed. *Hegel and the Philosophy of Nature*. Albany: SUNY Press, 2003.

– 'Logic and Nature in Hegel's Philosophy: A Response to John W. Burbidge.' *Owl of Minerva* 34, 1 (2003): 107–25.

Lacroix, Alain. *Hegel: La Philosophie de la Nature*. Paris: Presses Universitaire de France, 1997.

Maker, William. 'Idealism and Autonomy.' *Owl of Minerva* 34, 1 (2003): 59–76.

– 'The Very Idea of the Idea of Nature or Why Hegel Is Not an Idealist.' In *Hegel and the Philosophy of Nature*, ed. Stephen Houlgate, 1–27. Albany: SUNY Press, 1998.

Peperzak, Adriaan. 'Second Nature: Place and Significance of Objective Spirit in Hegel's Encyclopedia.' *Owl of Minerva* 27, 1 (1995): 51–66.

Petry, M.J., ed. *Hegel und die Naturwissenschaften*. Stuttgart: Frommann-Holzboog, 1987.

Petry, M.J., ed. *Hegel and Newtonianism*. Dordrecht: Kluwer, 1993.

Renault, Emmanuel. *Hegel: La naturalisation de la dialectique*. Paris: Vrin, 2001.

Schipperges, Dieter. 'Hegel und die Naturwissenschaften.' *Hegel-Studien* 11 (1974): 105–10. This volume contains several other articles on Hegel and specific sciences of nature, fruits of the 1970 *Hegel-Tage* colloquium, in Stuttgart, celebrating the 200th anniversary of the philosopher's birth.

Stone, Alison. 'Hegel's Philosophy of Nature: Overcoming the Division between Matter and Thought.' *Dialogue* 39, 4 (2000): 725–43.

Wandschneider, Dieter. 'Nature and the Dialectic of Nature in Hegel's Objective Idealism.' *Bulletin of the Hegel Society of Great Britain* 26 (1992): 30–51.

Wandschneider, Dieter, and Vittorio Hösle. 'Die Entäusserung der Idee zur Natur und ihre Zeitliche Entfaltung als Geist bei Hegel.' *Hegel-Studien* 18 (1979): 173–6.

Winfield, Richard Dien. 'Objectivity in Logic and Nature.' *Owl of Minerva* 34, 1 (2003): 77–90.

Other Writings

Allemann, B. *Ironie und Dichtung*. Pfullingen: Neske, 1956.

Althusser, Louis. 'Lenin before Hegel.' In *Lenin and Philosophy and other Essays*. Trans. Ben Brewster, 71–83. New York: Monthly Review Press, 2001.

Ankersmit, Frank R. 'The Origins of Postmodern Historiography.' In *Historiography between Modernism and Postmodernism*, ed. Jerzy Topolski, 87–117. Amsterdam, Atlanta, GA: Rodopi, 1994.

Arendt, Hannah. *The Human Condition*. Chicago: University of Chicago Press, 1958.

Aubenque, Pierre. *Le problème de l'être chez Aristote*. Paris: Presses Universitaires de France, 1962.

Baudrillard, Jean. *La société de consommation*. Paris: Denoël/Folio, 1970.

Beiser, Frederick C. 'Hegel's Historicism.' In *The Cambridge Companion to Hegel*, ed. Frederick C. Beiser, 270–300. Cambridge: Cambridge University Press, 1993.

Bodei, R. 'Il primo romanticismo come fenomeno storico e la filosofia di Solger nell'analisi di Hegel.' *Aut Aut* 101 (Dec. 1967): 68–80.

Boucher, M. *K.W.F. Solger, esthétique et philosophie de la présence*. Paris: Presses Universitaires de France, 1934.

Bourgeois, Bernard. 'La pédagogie de Hegel.' Introduction to *La pédagogie de Hegel*, 7–72. Paris: Vrin, 1990.

Buchwalter, Andrew. 'Historiography and Constitutionalism in Hegel.' *Hegel-Jahrbuch* (1998): 175–9.

Burbidge, John. 'Hegel in Canada.' *Owl of Minerva* 25, 2 (1994): 215–19.

Butler, Judith. *Antigone's Claim: Kinship between Life and Death*. New York: Columbia University Press, 2000.

Denker, Alfred, and Michael Vater, eds. *Hegel's Phenomenology of Spirit: New Critical Essays*. Atlantic Highlands, NJ: Humanities Press, 2002.

Desmond, William. *Art and the Absolute*. Albany: SUNY Press, 1986.

Fetscher, I. *Hegels Lehre vom Menschen*. Stuttgart: Friedrich Frommann Verlag, 1970.

Fichte, Johann Gottlieb. *Werke*, ed. J.H. Fichte. Berlin: de Gruyter, 1971.

Forster, Michael. *Hegel's Idea of a Phenomenology of Spirit*. Chicago: University of Chicago Press, 1998.

Foucault, Michel. *The Order of Things*, trans. anon. New York: Vintage Books, 1994.

Goethe, Wolfgang von. *Berliner Ausgabe*. Berlin and Weimar: Aufbau-Verlag, 1978.

Greene, Murray. *Hegel on the Soul*. The Hague: Martinus Nijhoff, 1972.

Harris, H.S. *Hegel's Ladder*, vols. 1 and 2. Indianapolis and Cambridge: Hackett, 1997.

– *Phenomenology and System*. Indianapolis: Hackett, 1995.

Heller, J. *Solgers Philosophie der ironischen Dialektik*. Berlin: Reuther & Reichard, 1928.

Henrich, Dieter, ed. *Hegels Philosophische Psychologie*. Special issue of *Hegel-Studien* 19 (1979).

Hölderlin, *Sämtliche Werke*. Ed. F. Beissner. Stuttgart: W. Kohlhammer, 1962.

Hoover, Jeffrey. 'The Origin of the Conflict between Hegel and Schleiermacher at Berlin.' *Owl of Minerva* 20, 1 (1988): 69–79.

Hyppolite, Jean. *Genèse et structure de la Phénoménologie de l'esprit*. Paris: Aubier, 1941.

Iggers, George. *Historiography in the Twentieth Century: From Scientific Objectivity to the Postmodern Challenge*. Hanover, NH, and London: University Press of New England, 1997.

Kainz, Howard. *Hegel's Phenomenology*, Parts I and II. Tuscaloosa: University of Alabama Press, 1976.

Kaufmann, Walter. *Hegel: A Reinterpretation*. New York: Doubleday/Anchor 1966.

Kierkegaard, Søren. *Either/Or, Kierkegaard's Writings*. Vol. 3. Ed. and trans. by Howard V. Hong and Edna H. Hong. Princeton: Princeton University Press, 1987.

Kolb, David. *The Critique of Pure Modernity: Hegel, Heidegger and After*. Chicago: University of Chicago Press, 1986.

Kojève, Alexandre. *Introduction à la lecture de Hegel*. Paris: Gallimard, 1967.

Kondylis, P. *Die Enstehung der Dialektik*. Stuttgart: Klett-Cotta, 1979.

Krell, D.F. *Contagion: Sexuality, Disease and Death in German Idealism and Romanticism*. Bloomington: Indianapolis University Press, 1998.

Labarrière, P.-J. *Introduction à une lecture de la Phénoménologie de l'esprit*. Paris: Aubier, 1976.

Lauer, Quentin. *A Reading of Hegel's Phenomenology of Spirit*. New York: Fordham University Press, 1976.

Linden, W. *Solger und Hegel: Bemerken aus Anlass eines Vergleiches ihrer aesthetischen Schriften*. Hamburg: Diss., 1938.

Lipovetsky, Gilles. *L'ère du vide*. Paris: Gallimard, 1983.

Loewenberg, J. *Hegel's Phenomenology: Dialogues on the Life of the Mind*. La Salle: Open Court, 1965.

Lucas, Hans-Christian. 'The Sovereign Ingratitude of Spirit toward Nature.' *Owl of Minerva* 23, 2 (1992): 131–50.

Lyotard, Jean-François. *La Condition Postmoderne*. Paris: Editions de Minuit, 1979.

MacIntyre, Alasdair, ed. *Hegel: A Collection of Critical Essays*, New York: Doubleday/Anchor, 1972.

Marquet, Jean-François. *Leçons sur la Phénoménologie de l'esprit de Hegel*. Paris: Ellipses, 2004.

Marx, Werner. *Hegel's Phenomenology of Spirit: Its Point and Purpose*. Trans. Peter Heath. New York: Harper and Row, 1975.

Matenko, P., ed. *Tieck and Solger: The Complete Correspondence*. New York: B. Westermann, 1932.

Mills, Jon. 'Hegel on the Unconscious Abyss: Implications for Psychoanalysis.' *Owl of Minerva* 28, 1 (1996): 59–75.

– *The Unconscious Abyss: Hegel's Anticipation of Psychoanalysis.* Albany: SUNY Press, 2002.

Moland, Lydia. 'Inheriting, Earning and Owning: The Source of Practical Identity in Hegel's Anthropology.' *Owl of Minerva* 34, 2 (2003): 139–70.

Müller, G. 'Solger's Aesthetics – A Key to Hegel.' In *Corona, Studies in Celebration of the 80th Birthday of Samuel Singer*, ed. by A. Schirokauer and W. Paulsen. Freeport, NY: Books for Libraries Press, 1968; 1st ed. c. 1941.

Navickas, Joseph. *Consciousness and Reality: Hegel's Philosophy of Subjectivity.* The Hague: Martinus Nijhoff, 1976.

O'Brien, George Dennis. *Hegel on Reason and History.* Chicago and London: University of Chicago Press, 1975.

Olsen, Allen. *Hegel and the Spirit.* Princeton: Princeton University Press, 1992.

Philonenko, A. *Lecture de la Phénoménologie de Hegel, Préface – Introduction.* Paris: Vrin, 1993.

Pillow, Kirk. 'Habituating Madness and Phantasying Art in Hegel's Encyclopedia.' *Owl of Minerva* 28, 2 (1997): 183–215.

Pinkard, Terry. *Hegel's Phenomenology: The Sociality of Reason.* Cambridge: Cambridge University Press, 1994.

Pippin, Robert. *Idealism as Modernism.* Cambridge: Cambridge University Press, 1997.

Pöggeler, Otto. *Hegels Kritik der Romantik.* Bonn: Diss., 1956.

– 'Komödie des Lebens – Theorie der Komödie.' In *Hegel in Berlin*, 79–85. Berlin: Staatsbibliothek Preussischer Kulturbesitz in Verbindung mit dem Hegel-Archiv, 1982.

Rapp, Carl. *Fleeing the Universal: The Critique of Post-Rational Criticism.* Albany: SUNY Press, 1998.

Rauch, Leo, and David Sherman. *Hegel's Phenomenology of Self-Consciousness.* Albany: SUNY Press, 1999.

Redding, Paul. 'Absorbed in the Spectacle of the World: Hegel's Criticism of Romantic Historiography.' *Clio* 16, 4 (1987).

Reid, Jeffrey. *Hegel: L'ironie romantique.* Paris: Vrin, 1997.

– 'Hegel et la maladie psychique: Le cas Novalis.' *Science et Esprit* 56, 2 (2004): 189–202.

– 'La jeune fille et la mort: Hegel et le désir érotique.' *Laval Théologique et Philosophique* 61, 2 (2005): 345–53.

– Review of T. Ziowlkowski, *Clio, the Romantic Muse: Historicizing the Faculties* (Ithaca, NY: Cornell University Press, 2004). *Clio* 34, 1–2 (2005): 199–206.

Rockmore, Tom. *Cognition: An Introduction to Hegel's Phenomenology*. Berkeley: University of California Press, 1997.

Rosen, Stanley. *G.W.F. Hegel*. New Haven: Yale University Press, 1974.

Rozenberg, J. 'Physiologie, embryologie et psychopathologie: une mise à l'épreuve de la conceptualité hégélienne.' *Archives de Philosophie* 60, 2 (1997): 243–54.

Russon, John. *Reading Hegel's Phenomenology*. Bloomington: Indiana University Press, 2004.

– *The Self and Its Body in Hegel's Phenomenology of Spirit*. Toronto: University of Toronto Press, 1997.

Schlegel, F. *Kritische Friedrich-Schlegel-Ausgabe*. Ed. E. Behler. Munich: F. Schöningh, 1958–85.

Schleiermacher, Friedrich Daniel Ernst. *Kritische Gesamtausgabe*. Ed. Hans-Joachim Birkner et al. New York, Berlin: de Gruyter, 1980.

Serrano-Marin, Vincente. 'Sobre Hölderlin y los comienzos del Idealismo alemand.' *Anales del Seminario de Historia de la Filosofia* 10 (1993): 173–94.

Shklar, Judith. *Freedom and Independence: A Study of the Political Ideas of Hegel's Phenomenology*. Cambridge: Cambridge University Press, 1976.

Solger, K.W.F. *Erwin: Vier Gespräche über das Schöne und die Kunst*, 2 vol. Berlin: 1815 [Wiegandt und Grieben, 1907].

– *Philosophische Gespräche*. Berlin: 1817 [ed. by Wolfhart Henckmann, Wissenschaftliche Buchgesellschaft, 1972].

– *Solgers nachgelassene Schriften und Briefwechsel*. Ed. Ludwig Tieck and Friedrich von Raumer. Leipzig: 1826 [Verlag Lambert Schneider, 1973].

– *Vorlesungen über Aesthetik*. Leipzig: 1829 [Karl Wilhelm Ludwig Heyse, ed., Wissenschaftliche Buchgesellschaft, 1969].

Solomon, Robert. *In the Spirit of Hegel*. Oxford: Oxford University Press, 1983.

Stewart, Jon. *The Hegel Myths and Legends*. Evanston, IL: Northwestern University Press, 1996.

– ed. *The Phenomenology of Spirit Reader: Critical and Interpretive Essays*. Albany: SUNY Press, 1998.

Taylor, Charles. *Hegel*. Cambridge: Cambridge University Press, 1975.

– *The Malaise of Modernity*. Concord, ON: Anansi Press, 1991.

– *Sources of the Self*. Cambridge, MA: Harvard University Press, 1989.

Verene, Donald Phillip. *Hegel's Recollection: A Study of Images in the Phenomenology of Spirit*. Albany: SUNY Press, 1985.

Von Der Luft, Eric. *Hegel, Hinrichs and Schleiermacher on Feeling and Religion*. Lewiston: Mellen Press, 1987.

Westphal, Merold. *History and Truth in Hegel's Phenomenology*. Atlantic Highlands, NJ: Humanities Press, 1979.

– , ed. *Method and Speculation in Hegel's Phenomenology.* Atlantic Highlands, NJ: Humanities Press, 1982.

Winfield, Richard Dien. 'From Concept to Judgment: Rethinking Hegel's Overcoming of Formal Logic.' *Dialogue* 40, 1 (2001): 53–74.

– 'Hegel, Romanticism and Modernity.' *Owl of Minerva* 27, 1 (1995): 3–18.

Ziowlkowski, T. *Clio, the Romantic Muse: Historicizing the Faculties.* Ithaca, NY: Cornell University Press, 2004.

Index